Politics of Ir

'With impressive analytical clarity and historical depth, this wonderful book illuminates the complex political debates about affirmative action in India. Hasan shows how a necessary and laudable focus on caste has led...to a neglect of other inequalities and, hence, to a very unbalanced and underinclusive set of policies.'

—Martha C. Nussbaum
University of Chicago

'This book deals with one of the most topical issues of Indian politics and society...assess[es] the impact of positive discrimination on the caste system, [and] include[s] religious minorities in the analysis...It is bound to become a reference study.'

—Christophe Jaffrelot
CNRS, France, and Centre d'Études et de Recherches Internationales (CERI-Sciences Po), Paris

'[This book] provides a...critique of the...contemporary failures of the Indian state to address the political under-representation and socioeconomic disadvantages of...minorities. Hasan combines a powerful critique of existing public policies with a clear vision of how the state could address multiple axes of disadvantage.'

—Amrita Basu
Amherst College

'In the midst of what has been called the "second democratic revolution" and the vast literature it has inspired, Hasan has broken new ground[s] in this comparative study...This is a distinctive and commendable work of major importance.'

—Achin Vanaik
University of Delhi

Politics of Inclusion

Castes, Minorities, and Affirmative Action

Zoya Hasan

OXFORD
UNIVERSITY PRESS

Oxford University Press is a department of the University of Oxford. It furthers the University's objective of excellence in research, scholarship, and education by publishing worldwide. Oxford is a registered trademark of Oxford University Press in the UK and in certain other countries

Published in India by
Oxford University Press
YMCA Library Building, 1 Jai Singh Road, New Delhi 110 001, India

First Edition published in 2009
Oxford India Paperbacks 2011

ISBN-13: 978-0-19-807696-4
ISBN-10: 0-19-807696-7

Typeset in AGaramond Pro 11/13.4 by Jojy Philip
Printed in India by Repro Knowledgecast Limited, Thane

For Mushir

Contents

List of Tables and Graphs ix

Acknowledgements xii

1. Introduction 1
2. Reservation, Minority Rights, and the Making of the Constitution 18
3. Policies and Institutional Frameworks for Protecting the Disadvantaged 41
4. Caste, Social Backwardness, and OBC Reservations (Mandal I and II) 78
5. Politics of Representation and Under-representation 126
6. Muslim Backwardness and the Elusive Promise of Affirmative Action 159
7. Social Discrimination and the Reservation Claims of Muslim and Christian Dalits 196
8. Conclusion 227

Appendix 240

Bibliography 272

Index 289

Tables and Graphs

TABLES

3.1 State-Wise Urban Poverty Incidence across Socio-Religious Communities 240

3.2 State-Wise Rural Poverty Incidence across Socio-Religious Communities 241

3.3 Graduates as Proportion of Population by Age Groups 242

3.4 Incidence of Violation of Civil Rights and Atrocities against the Scheduled Castes in India 246

3.5 Representation of Scheduled Castes and Scheduled Tribes in Central Government Services 247

3.6 Vacancies Reserved and Filled in Indian Administrative Service, Indian Foreign Service, and Indian Police Service on the basis of Civil Services Examination 248

3.7 Representation of Scheduled Castes and Scheduled Tribes in Central Public Sector Enterprises 248

3.8 Access to Higher Education by Caste Groups 249

3.9 Representation of Scheduled Castes and Scheduled Tribes in Public Sector Banks and Financial Institutions 250

4.1 Mandal Commission: Caste Groups as a Percentage of India's Population 251

4.2 Percentage Distribution of Postgraduate Enrolment by Course 252

4.3 Inequalities in Higher Education 253

4.4 Graduates and Diploma Holders by Socio-Religious Communities 253

4.5 Over- and Under-Represented Groups 254

4.6 Representation of Social Formations in Different Middle-Class Positions 254

5.1 Caste and Community of the MPs in Uttar Pradesh, Bihar, Madhya Pradesh, and Rajasthan 255

5.2 Evolution of the Other Backward Class MLAs 256

5.3 Muslim MPs Winning in Lok Sabha Elections 257

5.4 Constituencies according to the Percentage of Muslims 257

5.5 Muslim MLAs Winning in Vidhan Sabhas 258

5.6 Constituencies according to the Percentage of Muslims and Number of Seats Won 260

5.7 State Assembly Electoral Constituency/Tahsil Reserved for Scheduled Castes with Relative Share of Muslim Population 261

5.8 State Assembly Electoral Constituency/Tahsil Reserved for Scheduled Castes with Relative Share of Muslim Population 263

6.1 Percentages of Religious Minorities in the Civil Services 264

6.2 Share of Muslims in All-India Civil Services 264

6.3 Muslim Employees in Government Employment 265

6.4 Percentage Share of Muslim Employees in Selected Central Government Departments and Institutions 265

6.5 Share of Muslim Employees in Selected State Governments 266

6.6 Percentage Share of Muslim Employees in Selected State Government Departments 267

7.1 Estimated Class Composition of Dalits by Religion, Rural India 268

7.2 Estimated Class Composition of Dalits by Religion, Urban India 268

7.3 Occupational Structure of Dalit Households by Religion, Rural India 269

7.4 Occupational Structure of Dalit Households by Religion, Urban India 269

7.5 Comparative Educational Profile of Castes among Muslims, Rural India 270

7.6 Comparative Educational Profile of Castes among Muslims, Urban India 270

7.7 Comparative Educational Profile of Castes among Christians, Rural India 271

7.8 Comparative Educational Profile of Castes among Christians, Urban India 271

GRAPHS

3.1 Worker Participation Rates by Socio-Religious Communities 243

3.2 Unemployment Rate by Socio-Religious Communities 244

3.3 Activity Status of Male and Female Workers 245

Acknowledgements

This book has grown out of my engagement with issues of social inequality, disadvantage, and deprivation over the past few years. I have tried to understand how the Indian state's differential approach and policies towards caste-based disadvantage relative to the deprivation of religious minorities affect the welfare, well-being, and representation of these groups. Evidently, deprivation and discrimination in India are widespread and not confined to a single community or group. Yet, official discourse continues to revolve essentially around the issue of caste-based discrimination, leaving unaddressed many other critical areas. While there is no doubt that caste remains the prime source of discrimination, there is a reticence in taking on board the deprivation and disadvantage of religious minorities, even when they suffer from marginalization, as in the case of Muslims who have not adequately benefited from the country's social and economic progress. Nonetheless, policies remain anchored in identifying disadvantage in relation to membership of a particular group. Hence, the large number of programmes and policies targeted at particular groups seen as historically disadvantaged. But it appears we have now reached a stage where we cannot avoid the issues and problems arising out of disadvantage and discrimination in the present day. One way of doing this is to look at the politics of inclusion from a comparative perspective, which can provide insights into the paradoxes of inclusion and exclusion in contemporary India.

This work differs from existing literature on the subject of inclusion in that it compares approaches and experiences with regard to equalizing opportunities and conditions for various disadvantaged groups and is not confined to caste groups alone. The idea of comparison took shape in the context of the Central government's decision to implement 27 per cent reservations for the Other Backward Classes in higher education at the same time as there has been no serious effort to reverse the marginalization of Muslims through affirmative action. The purpose of the comparative assessment is not to critique policies towards the historically disadvantaged groups that have long been discriminated against, but to underline the need for a wider perspective on affirmative action in order to deal with the challenges of the present. There is a need to redress other social inequalities by revisiting and supplementing existing policies of affirmative action and evolve a forward-looking, egalitarian, and just approach of dealing with disadvantage in a democratic society.

A major part of the book was organized and written while I was a visiting professor at the University of Zurich in the winter semester of 2006–7 and during visiting fellowships at the Foundation Maisondes Sciences de'l Homme, Paris. Many of the ideas and arguments expressed in these chapters have been presented at many universities and conferences over the past five years. The discussion with and comments of participants in these conferences have helped to refine the arguments in this book.

During the past few years, as a member of the National Commission for Minorities (NCM) and while chairing the Planning Commission's Working Group on Empowering the Minorities for the Eleventh Five Year Plan, I was able to gain invaluable insights regarding the fundamental and enduring differences in the state's approach towards disadvantaged groups of lower castes and religious minorities. The comparative perspective represented in this book would have been inconceivable without my association with these institutions, especially the NCM. The views articulated in this work, however, do not reflect the position or point of view of any of these institutions, which are in no way responsible for the ideas expressed here.

I am particularly grateful to Amrita Basu, Martha Nussbaum, Suhas Palshikar, and Eswaran Sridharan for reading earlier drafts of this manuscript and making excellent comments and suggestions. There are many colleagues and friends who have helped in various ways, and who have, at one point or another, provided useful advice and ideas. These include Hamid Ansari, Balveer Arora, Sudeep Banerjee, Praful Bidwai, Rajeev Bhargava, Anuradha Chenoy, Satish Deshpande, Francine Frankel, Jayati Ghosh, Christophe Jaffrelot, Ritu Menon, Geetha Nambissan, Saeed Naqvi, Malini Parthasarathy, Prabhat Patnaik, Pamela Philipose, Rajan Prasad, Imrana Qadeer, Abhijit Sen, and Achin Vanaik. I would also like to thank my colleagues at the Centre for Political Studies, Jawaharlal Nehru University, for providing a supportive atmosphere in which this work could be pursued. I wish to acknowledge the help of several of my students who provided research support at various stages of this work, especially Manzur Ali, Adnan Faruqui, Maidul Islam, Poulomi Pal, and Vasundhara Sirnate. I am grateful to the staff of the NCM, the Parliament Library, and the Nehru Memorial Museum and Library for their help. I owe special thanks to Mohammed Saleem and Poonam Singh for their computer support and help in preparing the tables for the book.

My greatest debt, as always, is to Mushirul Hasan for his advice and encouragement over the years. This book, and much else beyond it, would not have been possible without his companionship and support, and his inspiring scholarly example, from which I have tried to learn, albeit unsuccessfully.

1

Introduction

Interest in patterns of political representation and strategies for social inclusion has exploded both in India and around the world. The past few years have witnessed an upsurge of interest in strategies of inclusion ranging from affirmative action to mandatory reservations. The proliferation of democracy in the last decade has led to the emergence of a consensus that within democratic systems one social group should not monopolize political power or governance. This has led to an awareness that creating political systems that address the needs of various groups, especially those that are marginalized on the basis of race, religion, and ethnic background, is necessary for equity, fairness, and political stability.

At an empirical level, political changes around the world have stimulated reflection on questions of exclusion of marginalized groups and ways of redressing this imbalance. Special efforts have been made to include those previously excluded in government and legislatures. In the realm of formal politics the modes of representation are increasingly dominated by descriptive representation and participation in decision making. Overall, it is widely believed that a more balanced representation in governance would lead to better decision making and policy priorities that reflect people's concerns.

At the theoretical level, scholars and activists have questioned the dominant conceptions of liberal democracy, which is typically committed to the politics of ideas, by rethinking the means and ends of the political process.[1] Collective claims made by hitherto excluded groups test the limits of conventional political discourses and power structures in favour of an alternative 'politics of presence'.[2] A great deal of theoretical energy has been expended in figuring out how such demands should be dealt with and how the politics of ideas can be reconciled to the new politics of presence. The new politics of presence responds to a broad sense of ethnic, racial, gender, and minority exclusions by questioning the separation between ideas and identity. These developments have led to a greater emphasis on inclusion and a greater focus on the political process of inclusion. These global trends provide an important context for the discussion on inclusion and representation in India.

Two major reasons for focusing on the politics of inclusion can be advanced: first, the increased presence of historically excluded groups is a sign of inclusiveness of public institutions, and this, in turn, is an important marker of the fairness of democratic regimes; and, second, greater inclusion of excluded groups in decision-making institutions would provide these bodies with the presence of people who can articulate the interests of these sections, which may otherwise be neglected by default. The strongest rationale for representing particular social groups lies in the manner in which public institutions work—which is to say they often do not provide adequate policy concern for groups that are marginalized and deprived. It is this exclusion that provides the strongest justification for what Anne Phillips has described as a 'politics of presence'.

Amartya Sen draws attention to various dimensions of social exclusion. He distinguishes between situations where some people are kept out (unfavourable exclusion) and others where they are included on unfavourable terms (unfavourable inclusion). He further differentiates between active and passive exclusion. The former works by fostering exclusion through deliberate discriminatory policy intervention; the latter works through social processes like the caste system. Exclusion leads to the denial of economic opportunities and consequent powerlessness. Low income, low merit, or low productivity are not the causes but the consequences of such exclusion. While these considerations are valid for India, it must be borne in mind that the challenges we face to ensure equality of opportunity are more severe and complex than anywhere else. There is no other country with such a divergent social plurality—and its consequent institutionalized exclusion—as India.

India is undeniably one of the world's most unequal societies. Social inequality revolves around the axes of class, caste, tribal status, religion, and gender. Inter-group disparities are sharply marked, with major contrasts of social conditions and chances of sharing in society's material and cultural resources—that is, income, employment, education, health, and so on. These inequalities are rooted in the caste system, property, income, wealth, and employment relations. The upper castes are the most advantaged in India and the Scheduled Castes (SCs) and Scheduled Tribes (STs) among the poorest and most disadvantaged. Frequent overlap between social and economic deprivation is a defining feature of India's social structure. With regard to this overlap, Niraja Gopal Jayal observes:

> That there is in India a frequent convergence between cultural and material inequalities is well known. This is an overlap between, on the one hand, the inherited symbolic or cultural disadvantages of caste or religious identity and, on the other, of economic disadvantage. Low caste status is often accompanied by deprivation, and traditional and historical forms of social inequality thus co-exist with, and are reinforced by, inequalities arising out of the sphere of production and economic activity.[3]

There is a frequent convergence between social and material inequalities—which is to say there is an overlap between the inherited symbolic or social disadvantages of caste, on the one hand, and of socio-economic deprivation and disadvantage, on the other. Low caste status is often accompanied by deprivation, and traditional and historical forms of social inequality thus coexist with, and are reinforced by, inequalities arising out of the sphere of production and economic activity. This is true of large sections of the Muslim minority as well, but is not widely recognized and acknowledged owing to a lack of public awareness on the issue.

But India is also one of the few countries in the post-colonial world that took up the challenge of building an inclusive democracy in a highly diverse, multicultural, multilingual, and multi-religious society. The establishment of democracy and universal adult suffrage in a hierarchical society characterized by unprecedented social inequality, deprivation, and oppression was undoubtedly a revolutionary principle, a bold experiment in political affairs, perhaps the most significant in any country.[4] Nearly sixty years after Independence, India remains a major success story in respect of democracy and social inclusion. This is largely due to the primacy given to equality and social justice as the cardinal principles of contemporary political life. It was agreed that procedural democracy and formal equality were not enough to bring about substantive outcomes in terms of empowerment, justice, and equality. The freedom struggle and the social reform movements prepared some ground for social equality, in the sense that they delegitimized the most egregious forms of oppression that characterized Hindu society. Howsoever improbable it might have seemed in 1950, the trend towards greater equalization is unmistakable. The policy of providing benefits to historically disadvantaged peoples, which was established through several provisions in the Constitution, played an important part in advancing this agenda.[5] For the sake of brevity the term 'disadvantaged' refers collectively to all three groups officially designated as backward: the SCs, the STs, and the Other Backward Classes (OBCs) (minorities are not officially included among the disadvantaged). These three groups were targeted for special advantages and protection under Article 46 and the Directive Principles of State Policy.

These programmes permit departure from formal equality for the purpose of eliminating social discrimination.[6] The constitutional understanding of equality is explicitly aimed at securing substantive equality for previously subordinated groups, and is designed to discourage merely formal understandings of equality that have often been used to oppose affirmative action.[7] Substantive equality is not defined, but the Directive Principles give a great deal of attention to its advancement, and the Fundamental Rights are themselves specified in a way that makes room for affirmative action programmes designed to advance the material situation of the disadvantaged groups. Thus, Article 15 states: 'Nothing in this article...shall prevent the state from making any special provision for the advancement of any socially and educationally backward classes of citizens or for the SCs and the STs.' In short, the framers of our Constitution understood the goal of equality in terms of an end to systematic hierarchy and discrimination based on caste. The focus consequently is not on difference but rather on social disadvantage. Substantive equality is directed at eliminating institutional and systemic discrimination against disadvantaged groups, which effectively undermines their full and equal participation in society.

Distinctive and separate strategies were followed for different groups.[8] The Constitution and state made a basic distinction between the cultural rights of minorities and group rights for communities that were discriminated on the basis of caste.[9] While minorities were located in the framework of religion, disadvantaged castes were removed from this realm and located in the framework of social justice. There are several policies aimed at the accommodation of cultural diversity, especially the identity concerns of religious minorities. Minority rights consisted of religious freedom, including the right to worship, propagate, and practise one's religion, the freedom to establish their own educational institutions, ensuring that minority institutions would not be disqualified from receiving state funding, and legal pluralism. There is also a provision for the creation and sustenance of institutions such as the NCM to safeguard the rights and interests of minorities.

However, the idea that India has succeeded in creating public spaces that are equally shared by members of diverse communities, or that various disadvantaged and deprived groups have access to and can actively participate in governance, is a distant one because the trend towards inclusion and empowerment does not embrace all groups equally. Over the years, preferential policies enacted with considerable support have proven controversial. Such policies are contentious because there is disagreement over who should be targeted, why they should be targeted, and because the list of targeted groups is getting bigger and the overall percentage of jobs and seats reserved is very high, and also because the policy is limited to caste groups. There is no consensus on whether reservations should be extended to the backward castes. But despite the philosophical and political controversies surrounding the reservation issue in India, there has been no real opposition to reservations for the SCs and STs. This is largely because there was a consensus that SCs and STs had been subjected to an appalling degree of subordination and exclusion that was too stark to overlook. By contrast, from the beginning, the OBC category has proved to be controversial and there was strong resistance to the extension of reservations to them, leading to the fall of a Central government in October 1990.[10]

Nevertheless, politicians have been eager to extend rather than reduce the remit of reservations and affirmative action programmes.[11] This has raised major debates and controversies over these policies and programmes. The Indian debate centres on both the consequences and distributive effects of these policies and the definition of disadvantage. Few issues stimulate more disagreement among liberals and radicals than positive discrimination policies, especially reservations. Most often these arguments are stated in terms of individual rights versus group rights; equality of opportunity versus equality of results; merit versus efficiency; and affirmative action versus mandatory reservations. An extensive political discourse has emerged on the contradictions between liberal democratic principles and group preferences. Many claim that group rights benefit the privileged and the middle classes among these groups and not the really deserving. Radicals argue that increased reservations cannot change the unequal economic structure of Indian society, reinforced by an uneven distribution of gains under a predominantly capitalist society. Liberals argue that granting rights to identity groups undermines common citizenship and the pursuit of the common good. There is a coexistence of dissimilar and even conflicting strategies of realizing equality: continued assertions of the primacy of liberal principles and continued concessions to collective identities. There is concern that group-specific claims supplant shared concerns and may reduce the likelihood of policies that serve substantive interests. Moreover, with an excessive emphasis on immutable differences, group quotas potentially encourage fragmentation and division. The key issues in this debate, both for the opponents and supporters, centre on the relevance of caste, but these policies are rarely questioned on the conception of disadvantage and rarely locate the debate in the context of the social structure as it has evolved to its present stage.[12]

Finally, it is useful to distinguish between reservations and affirmative action. It is important to note here that affirmative action does not necessarily mean reserving quotas in jobs for the disadvantaged sections like the lower castes or minorities, but taking these identities as a factor for preferential treatment, for example, in college and university admission and employment policies. Starting from different vantage points, both are mechanisms of preferential treatment to facilitate inclusion of disadvantaged groups. Both sets of measures address the recognition that certain patterns of disadvantage and exclusion require measures to promote equality of opportunity.

One of the main issues concerns the approach towards disadvantage and the official definitions and categories used by the state to classify target groups entitled to affirmative action. The question is whether to identify groups on the basis of their historically depressed status with reference to the specific criteria of ritual and social exclusion, or more broadly in terms of deprivation established by a combination of criteria of social, economic, and cultural backwardness. This raises an important question regarding the extent to which backwardness and disadvantage are essentially about inequalities of the Hindu social structure and not discrimination and deprivation as such. In other words, the critical question was, and still is, whether to use class—that is to say, general social and economic criteria which would include individuals outside the caste system—as the basis for classification or to rely principally on caste.[13]

These varied issues and strategies are at the heart of the debate on the uneven treatment of disadvantaged groups and the relevance of affirmative action as a remedy for under-representation and exclusion. On one side, it is argued that reservations are fundamental to equality and this requires that disadvantaged groups be treated differently. On the other side, it is argued that this approach cannot apply to minorities, as it militates against the constitutional project which seeks to make religious identities less salient for participation in the modern economy and politics. It is not clear whether recognizing minorities for policy attention is intrinsically unacceptable, that is, against the rules of a secular democracy, or whether it is unacceptable because of its harmful consequences, that is, it leads to fragmentation and communalization of the polity. The approach towards disadvantaged castes is informed by a substantive approach which seeks to address and redress historical and accumulated inequalities. By contrast the second approach points to culture-related discrimination and disadvantage. The latter is based on a formal conception of equality in which recognition of economic disadvantage is a deviation from the constitutional premises of secularism and equality. The second approach has clearly been a euphemism for identity accommodation and management.

A consequence of these distinct approaches is that policies that aim to promote equality of opportunity and access to public institutions are not applicable to all deprived groups but only to particular social categories. The privileging of certain identities for the purpose of policy making and development is a reflection of the varied positioning of caste and minority groupings in Indian society and politics, which in turn underlines the limitations of the paradigm of social justice. While India remains a success story with regard to the inclusion of excluded caste groups, it has been less effective in the effort to facilitate the inclusion of minorities in public institutions, even though minorities as a whole constitute almost 19 per cent of the population.

Since Independence, some of the most important political debates have related to the rights of minorities and to the question of the state's approach towards them. It is the professed ability of the nation-state to deal with minorities that has often raised serious questions with regard to fairness of these policies. Yet, even with constitutional safeguards for minorities, large sections of them have been feeling a sense of marginalization and alienation from the nation-state. Minority rights were often conceived in the language of respect and protection but social and economic rights were missing from this framework. This approach has been premised on the assumption that the best way of serving the interests of minority groups is not to target them as minorities in policy making and development. We need to see how these policies work in existing conditions, and whether such an approach can serve their substantive interests.

Among minorities, Muslims constitute a significant segment—13.4 per cent—of Indians. They suffer from greater deprivation and disadvantage as compared to other minorities.[14] This has been apparent at least since the Gopal Singh Committee Report in 1983 declared Muslims a socially and educationally backward group requiring special measures to alleviate their backwardness.[15] The prime minister in 2005 constituted a 'High-Level Committee on the Social, Economic and Educational Status of the Muslim Community of India', charged with investigating the socio-economic status of Muslims.[16] The Sachar Committee Report (SCR) found stark under-representation of Muslims and systematic evidence to show that they are in many respects as disadvantaged as the lowest Hindu caste groups. It showed that in the twenty odd years since the submission of the Gopal Singh Committee Report, the Central and state governments had done very little to rectify the backwardness and under-representation of Muslims. This was despite the fact that the 1980s was a period when the government focused specific attention on tackling mass social and economic deprivation. Yet, the policy discourse and public debate have, for the most part, ignored the problems in regard to the exclusion of minorities because of the widespread assumption that the concept of exclusion is applicable primarily to historically oppressed groups and not to minorities.

One reason for this disregard is that caste divisions among Hindus remain central to the definition of disadvantage. Hence, the disadvantages suffered by lower castes in development and access to public services are fairly well documented and addressed through policy intervention. Thus, there is a great deal of policy-driven knowledge and evidence with regard to the SCs, and now increasingly the OBCs. Policies and practices of the state are often judged in terms of how successful they are in promoting the socio-economic development of these groups. For minorities, knowledge and concern are invariably centred on issues of security and identity, and not of equity and justice, whilst the problems of the lower castes are squarely located in the context of justice, equality, and democracy. This lends urgency and primacy to the issue of handling the caste question. The swift decision to extend reservations in Central government jobs to the OBCs underlines this primacy in the policy discourse. There is very little analysis of its implications for those who fall outside this framework. In fact, until the formation of the Sachar Committee, there was no community-disaggregated data generated by the government agencies for policy purposes and hence no official information about the socio-economic conditions of minorities and the disadvantages and deprivation suffered by them. Not surprisingly, many Muslims argue that it is this lack of information and proactive public assistance that is keeping them behind. The result of this is the absence of minorities from public institutions and also from India's policy discourse, intentionally or unintentionally.

Over the last decade or so, questions of inter-group equality and minority participation in the economy and polity have assumed critical relevance within the framework of governance and development, not to speak of the framework of justice and fairness. The critical issue is to level the playing field and give equal opportunity to a range of disadvantaged groups.

Problems and paradoxes of group representation seem particularly stark when we discuss the situation of minorities in India. Minorities as a group have been and continue to be largely excluded from the decision-making institutions, and at the same time, they continue to suffer serious social and economic disadvantages. Thus, it would seem fair that minorities and their interests ought to be represented in public decision making. However, minorities in India, as indeed everywhere, differ so considerably along so many dimensions that it would be difficult to argue for reservation for minorities qua minorities or to claim that those who attain positions as their representatives can truly speak for minorities. The application of an affirmative action policy for minorities will raise a variety of problems and questions as well as social antagonisms that may come with the implementation of such a policy. But then this is true for all groups, including caste groups.

There are two major issues facing democratic practice and the promise of inclusiveness. One is disadvantage or backwardness, which in principle applies to large sections of the population and covers large sections of Muslim community as well; and the second is under-representation, which is more specific to the Muslim community. Under-representation can be an outcome, and disadvantage and discrimination its possible causes, but there can be several other reasons.[17] Under-representation does not by itself imply discrimination, just as over-representation of some groups does not necessarily imply positive discrimination in their favour. For example, if the entry criterion for jobs is education, groups that have initial endowments might get over-represented and groups which lack this requirement might get under-represented, even without discrimination playing any role.

Most studies are concerned with the problems of caste groups, while few have attempted to look simultaneously at the experience of different social groups.[18] This book has chosen to focus on a comparison of the disparate experiences of lower castes and religious minorities and how these have shaped the politics of inclusion, and, most importantly, the differential reactions and responses of the state to the demands for greater representation in public institutions. The experience of groups with comparable and similar histories of deprivation but dissimilar state responses and policies may in fact mask deeper realities not fully explored by the established set of philosophical and political principles of social justice.

The main objective of this book is to examine the politics of inclusion through an analysis of the policies and debates with regard to the strategies of the state in relation to the lower castes and minorities and the implications of the differential approach. It examines the underlying issues that influence state policy towards disadvantaged caste groups and assesses specific strategies to address the contending claims of deprived minority groups. Such a comparison is important if we are to understand the varied policies towards minorities and disadvantaged caste groups. If real development is about widening choices, opportunities, and equality, an analysis of the situation and progress of the most disadvantaged minorities can be a mirror to society; it can be instructive in formulating appropriate strategies of advancement and assessing the successes and failures of existing strategies and policies.

This study is situated at the intersection of policy and political processes. Studies of political processes in India often tend to ignore policy implications or the need to formulate appropriate policy for deprived groups. Likewise, policy analysis often tends to ignore political processes and the constraints they impose on policy making. Attempting an explanation for the paradoxes of inclusion and exclusion, this book combines both, in order to understand the varied trajectories of disadvantaged groups in public institutions and the conceptual framework and inbuilt biases of the policies and institutions that maintain and create power inequalities in India today. It examines the constitutional framework and analyses the institutional structures and the responses and debates surrounding the contrasting strategies of inclusion for lower castes and minorities, especially the strong emphasis on affirmative action for lower castes and the continuing opposition to the inclusion of minorities in this framework. It aims to make a contribution to the study of the politics and strategies of inclusion by comparing the experience of different deprived groups in education, public employment, and legislatures.

An important aim of this book is to examine the prevailing definition of social backwardness and the criteria of affirmative action in the context of evidence of disparity and deprivation of groups beyond caste. It explores both the historical and contemporary context of the strategies of inclusion. What needs to be looked at is whether disadvantage and backwardness should be defined exclusively in terms of cumulative historical disadvantage or by evidence of deprivation and disparities. This provides the point of departure to re-examine the processes of inclusion so as to better meet the needs and requirements of the present. Looking at the broader issue of social inclusion from a comparative perspective can provide insights into the politics of inclusion and exclusion; the analysis of the situation in terms of progress of minorities can be useful in assessing the effectiveness of existing strategies and policies.

Chapter 2 examines the political framework for the protection of disadvantaged groups and the differentiated forms it has taken with regard to lower castes and religious minorities in the historical context of debates in the Constituent Assembly on these issues. It has been noted that the deep commitment of the Indian nation-state to the idea of equal participation of all its constituents was the rationale for enacting substantive and comprehensive social justice measures, and by extension, the recognition of the problem of social and educational backwardness of lower-caste groups by providing reservations for them in these arenas. The chapter highlights the differentiated manner in which the Assembly approached the issue of cultural diversity and historical discrimination in the policy discourse, and the implication of this for the inclusion of both groups.

With this primary concern with regard to the distinct frameworks as the starting point, Chapter 3 explores how the state in post-colonial India has addressed the question of discrimination and exclusion suffered by disadvantaged groups, notably the SCs and religious minorities. In particular, it seeks to understand the policy framework in relation to these groups and the divergences in policy and consequences of this for the protection of the disadvantaged. It attempts to delineate the structure of policies as well as changes in the constellation of policies for these two groups, while arguing that the well-being of minorities has suffered due to a greater lack of attention to issues of institutionalized inequality and deprivation than is commonly supposed. It also examines the institutional framework for protecting the disadvantaged, through a brief comparison of the National Commission for Minorities and the National Commission for Scheduled Castes. The chapter investigates the variation in the functioning of the institutional frameworks of these bodies, which has more to do with policy than the institutional design.

Chapter 4 examines the extension of reservations to the OBCs and the rationale of reservation in relation to the debate over the desirability and feasibility of reservations to them. The first part of the chapter outlines the political context of the emergence of the backward-caste reservation issue in the 1970s and 1980s culminating in the implementation of the Mandal Commission recommendations on OBC reservations from 1994 onwards. The second part discusses the government's decision of 2006 to extend reservations to the OBCs in the field of higher education in the context of economic reforms and the growing importance of technical and professional education in the new economy. It explores the notions of disadvantage and backwardness and unravels the processes whereby caste and class issues have got entangled. It also examines the political, policy, and legal links between caste and class in the designation of backwardness and disadvantage.

Chapter 5 discusses the varied trajectories of political representation for lower castes and religious minorities in the context of reservations for OBCs in the states which has had a positive impact on their political representation. It explores the relationship between reservation policies and political representation, and the political context within which changes in representation have taken place. It is known that the first-past-the-post system disfavours dispersed minorities, but this alone cannot explain the under-representation of Muslims. It argues that a change in the electoral system should be debated; however, the key issue is the political process which can facilitate minority representation in the same way that it has facilitated the representation of backward castes in contrast to the under-representation of minorities. Caste-based affirmative action has given an impetus to identity-driven political mobilization, which explains, at least partly, the willingness of parties to give tickets to lower castes.

Chapters 6 and 7 focus on two categories that are excluded from the reservation regime, in order to understand the implications of the dominantly caste-based policy of disadvantage on the claims of other deprived groups. Chapter 6 examines the specific issue of discrimination against and exclusion of Muslims and the arguments for affirmative action programmes for them in education and government employment to redress this imbalance. More specifically, it focuses on the demands and implications of minority versus backward-caste reservations in the context of differences amongst Muslim groups on the issue and the wider debate on minority quotas versus caste and sub-quotas for Muslim OBCs. In assessing the desirability and feasibility of affirmative action for minorities or Dalits in the Christian and Muslim communities, it is useful to remember that in India, for a variety of reasons, reservations have been the key instrument for social and political inclusion, and they provide voice to the excluded groups in decision-making institutions.

A critical aspect of this exploration, which is a central theme of this book and is one of the main subjects of discussion, is the question of neutrality of reservation policies in India and the claim that they do not favour any religion or that they are not majoritarian as claimed by those who fall outside their purview. This issue is significant because it relates to the primacy of caste inequalities relative to a socially grounded notion of discrimination and deprivation for the purpose of reservations. The claims and counterclaims of Dalits in the Muslim and Christian communities for recognition and inclusion in the SC category are examined in Chapter 7. It also explores the response of various institutions of the state to these contentious claims. Despite a long campaign, these groups have not been able to receive official recognition as SCs. Muslim and Christian efforts to join these categories have led to tensions between Dalits even as they have complicated the whole question of reservations. This conflict raises important questions with regard to the relative importance of ritual aspects of social disabilities as against taking into account the multiple dimensions of disadvantage in the definition of SCs.

It is the endeavour of this book to explore the politics and strategies of dealing with disadvantage and deprivation and to examine whether these need rethinking and reshaping in order to take them forward in India's quest for equality. The evidence suggests that there are unjustifiable disparities prevailing among different groups as a result of discrimination, lack of equal opportunities, and lack of affirmative action for some groups. The varied experience underscores the need to re-examine the political frameworks constructed at the time of Independence in the background of Partition, and judge whether they are appropriate. Affirmative action policies that seek to promote inclusion of marginalized groups must concern themselves with the multiple dimensions of disadvantage so as to be able to address the conspicuous disadvantages and deprivation of a wider range of groups. Some of these issues are taken up in Chapter 8, which argues for re-examining the framework of affirmative action in the context of the demands for substantive equality of minorities.

Notes

1. The most important works on political representation are Hanna Pitkin (1967) and more recently Anne Phillips (1995); Iris Marion Young (2002); Amy Gutman (2003).

2. Anne Phillips (1995).

3. Niraja Gopal Jayal (2006: 31).

4. On India's democracy see Francine Frankel *et al.* (2000); Atul Kohli (2001); Niraja Gopal Jayal (2001).

5. Literature on caste and reservation policy is very large. See, for example, Marc Galanter (1984); V.A. Panandiker (1997); Oliver Mendelsohn and Marika Vicziany (2000); Partha Ghosh (1997); Evan Osborne (2001); B.A.V. Sharma and K. Madhusudan Reddy (1982); Thomas Weisskopf (2004); Sunita Parikh (1997); Myron Weiner and Mary F. Katzenstein (1981).

6. Marc Galanter (1984: 379–80).

7. See Ratna Kapur and Brenda Cossman (1996a). Although the essay deals with the issue of gender equality, it provides an analysis of the difference between formal and substantive equality in the Constitution. Also see the discussion of these questions in Ratna Kapur and Brenda Cossman (1996b: Chapter 3).

8. On this distinction, see also Niraja Gopal Jayal (2007).

9. Susanne Hoeber Rudolph and Lloyd I. Rudolph (2001).

10. For a critique of the Mandal Commission Report and the extension of reservations to the OBCs, see I.P. Desai (1984); André Béteille (1996); P. Radhakrishnan (1997).

11. In India, the term reservation, rather than affirmative action, is commonly used. This book has used the term affirmative action because it has a wider association and refers to various approaches ranging from quotas to targeted intervention to preferential treatment, and because it is more relevant for religious minorities who, for a variety of reasons, fall outside the mandatory reservation regime.

12. The term caste is used in this book as a social group and not as part of the hierarchical order, and mainly in connection with the overall socio-economic and educational condition of the groups concerned. The upper castes are those who have enjoyed dominance over economic resources and the majority of upper-caste people were better educated than members

of other groups and hence dominant in most public institutions. Until recently, the situation of the lower castes was the opposite of this.

13. Galanter (1984).

14. See Report on Socio-Economic Status of the Notified Minority Communities (other than Muslims), National Commission for Minorities (2008b).

15. Government of India (1983), High Power Panel on Minorities, Scheduled Castes, Scheduled Tribes, and Other Weaker Sections, Ministry of Home Affairs. The panel was chaired by Dr Gopal Singh.

16. Government of India (2006a), Prime Minister's High Level Committee, Social, Economic and Educational Status of the Muslim Community of India, Cabinet Secretariat. The Committee chaired by Rajinder Sachar submitted its report to the prime minister in November 2006.

17. It is important to distinguish between under-representation in government employment and legislatures. Under-representation in legislatures can be quite different in terms of its causes from under-representation in government employment. The under-representation in Parliament and state legislatures may be due to a combination of the first-past-the-post electoral system (single-member district, simple plurality, or SMSP, more technically) and the dispersion of Muslims demographically in a way that they are a minority in all but about 11 out of 543 Lok Sabha constituencies and most assembly constituencies; besides the fact that some Lok Sabha and assembly constituencies in which Muslims are concentrated are reserved for SCs. Whereas under-representation in government employment may be due to lack of requisite education required for higher levels of government employment, absence of networks, and discrimination.

18. The exception to this trend is the recent study of ethnic diversity and representation in India by Niraja Gopal Jayal (2006). Jayal examines how ethnic diversity is represented in public institutions.

2

Reservation, Minority Rights, and the Making of the Constitution

At the centre of the post-Independence debates on group preferences is the conflict between those who favour preferential treatment for disadvantaged castes and those who favour the position that the state should provide equal opportunities to all citizens without making distinctions on the basis of identities. A second important aspect of the disagreement is the relative weight given to caste over religious identity and other identities in the conceptualization of backwardness, disadvantage, and deprivation, and in government policies towards these groups. A critical issue in these debates was the way in which the Constituent Assembly approached cultural diversity and historical discrimination and the policy discourse drawn from it. The political discourse of the years immediately after Partition shaped the approach towards social justice and the policies of dealing with backwardness and disadvantage. It sought to strike a balance—at times an awkward balance—accommodating diversity in certain spheres and limiting it in other areas. This awkward balance was marked by inconsistency: India's affirmative action policies take note of caste distinctions but not of religious distinctions, while other policies such as recognition of personal laws accept religious distinctions, and such laws receive full recognition and protection of the state.

There was a near consensus in the Constituent Assembly on reservations for the lower castes. This consensus has shaped the policy of the nation-state on social backwardness and disadvantage and the quest for justice. It marked a turning point in India's political history with regard to the constitutional design and state policies of inclusion and affirmative action for SCs, STs, and backward classes more generally. The underlying argument and justification in support of affirmative action for these groups was primarily reparation-based and therefore focused predominantly on past injustices done to the lower-caste groupings of Indian society.[1] Jawaharlal Nehru and other members like Vallabhbhai Patel, G.B. Pant, K.M. Munshi, K.T. Shah, and N.G. Ranga, notwithstanding their ideological differences, unequivocally endorsed this perspective, which derived strength from the need to compensate for past discrimination.[2] It had little scope for consideration of other types of disadvantage arising out of the present conditions of discrimination. As against this, the religious minorities were given freedom of religion but no safeguards for representation, since they were not seen as having suffered any past injustice.[3] This chapter will examine the political debates over such policies, particularly those concerning the justifications and effectiveness, and societal consequences of the programmes and strategies deployed to represent and frame issues pertaining to disadvantage and deprivation.

Foundations of the Political Discourse

The founding vision of India is intrinsically plural and egalitarian in conception. This vision was a coming together of what constitutional historian Granville Austin has called the 'national' and 'social revolutions' respectively.[4] The national revolution focused on democracy and liberty, whereas the social revolution focused on emancipation, equality, and justice. The Constitution sought to promote national unity and facilitate progressive social change at the same time. The project of the founders of the republic was to create a society whose citizens shared a strong sense of national identity alongside a recognition of cultural diversity, and, at the same time, provide protection to historically disadvantaged and vulnerable groups. The key features of the post-colonial state were therefore the framework of basic civil rights grounded in universal suffrage, safeguards or compensatory justice for backward classes through a balancing of freedom with justice and equality, federalism, and secularism. Equality was to be achieved in part through democratic rules and procedures, and in part through social legislation banning discrimination, and the establishment of a system of reservation for the SCs and STs.

The policy of preferential treatment has a long history. The British put the system of reservations in place over the objections of the Congress and most other political representatives. The early initiatives were deeply influenced by the overall colonial understanding of Indian society. The Indians, the British had decided, represented societies of communities, not individuals, and this was the reason for India's unsuitability for modern political institutions. Therefore, units of representation for elections to provincial legislatures were not defined as territorial constituencies containing individuals with rights; the legislatures of British India represented communities and not individuals. The groups who were accorded representation were identified as 'communities' with absolute rights and collective unchangeable interests. Defined as majorities and minorities they were pigeonholed and categorized into communal electorates whose interests the British had to separate and protect from one another. The reservation of seats in legislatures and other similar political privileges were part of colonial structures since the early decades of the twentieth century. The colonial rulers had, however, come to treat the term minorities in an expansive manner. They were the prime beneficiaries of the colonial state's policies of group preference. Increasingly, minorities came to be recognized as being in need of protection through separate representation in the legislatures and reserved quotas in public services. In fact, some of these arrangements were part of the earlier phases of the discussion on the Constitution.

This understanding was seriously questioned by the upsurge of nationalism that argued for equal rights within the shared bond of nationhood. The nationalist leadership subscribed to the liberal principle of one-man-one-vote, with no representation on communal lines, and opposed tooth and nail the British proposal for separate electorates. The principal aim when framing the

Constitution was to provide the institutional basis for political unity in the country. The proponents of universal citizenship and the Hindu traditionalists were both keen that national unity should be given the greatest importance.[5] The formation of Pakistan had been attributed by most Congress leaders to the introduction of separate electorates. There was thus an inherent conflict between the Congress's emphasis on the principle of majority rule and Muslim representative politics, which insisted that what mattered was not numerical configurations but the ideological differences between Muslims and non-Muslims. The Congress therefore ruled out concessions to the presence of any intermediary bodies, be they castes or religious communities. This was the essence of the Congress rejection of the Muslim League demand for Pakistan, which the Congress criticized as a communal brand of nationalism.[6]

The political discourse in the making of the Constitution was driven by the demands of equality of citizenship and non-discrimination.[7] At the same time, it is important to remember that India's Independence and its Partition were concurrent events. The emphasis on national unity became paramount in the context of deepening Hindu–Muslim tensions. The new framework did involve recognition of plurality of religions, languages, and cultures, and it logically favoured the recognition of minority rights rather than any majoritarian system. However, it needs to be noted that the recognition of minority rights implied a trade-off of these rights with the question of representation of minorities.[8] In one key respect a major break had taken place: minorities and their rights were cut off from the discourse of disadvantage and social justice that dominated the discussion about lower castes, and located in a majority–minority syndrome.

Group Rights and Minority Rights

Minority rights, in a conceptual sense, were not frequently mentioned. The first attempt to do so in terms of principles was by Jawaharlal Nehru in his 'Note on Minorities' published in *Young India* on 15 May 1930. It addressed the question in its totality. These principles were amplified in the resolution adopted by the Congress Working Committee in its meeting at Calcutta on 1

November 1937: 'In all matters affecting the minorities in India, the Congress wishes to proceed by their cooperation and through their goodwill in a common undertaking and for the realization of a common aim which is the freedom and betterment of all the people of India.' Congress President Maulana Abul Kalam Azad summed up the position in two propositions: (i) Whatever constitution is adopted for India, there must be the fullest guarantee in it for the rights and interests of minorities, and (ii) the minorities should judge for themselves what safeguards are necessary for the protection of their rights and interests. The majority should not decide this. Therefore the decision in this respect must depend upon the consent of the minorities and not on a majority vote.[9] A major difficulty in arriving at a constitutional settlement on minority rights stemmed from the conflict between the Muslim demand for community-specific political safeguards and comprehensive guarantees to protect these rights and the Congress party's emphasis on majority rule. Committed to secular and pluralistic politics, the Congress believed that the extension of political safeguards to minorities would lead to the perpetuation of communal differences, which was incompatible with democracy.

Nevertheless, much attention was paid to the recognition of minority rights. A cursory reading of the debates in the Constituent Assembly and the Advisory Committee on Fundamental Rights, Minorities, and Tribal and Excluded Areas suggests that two sets of minority concerns dominated these debates.[10] One related to political and economic rights, and the other to religious, educational, and cultural rights. The discussions in the Sub-Committee on Minority Rights focused on the question of reservations in legislatures, and executive and government services for the minorities, in addition to the right to freedom of religion, which was phrased as 'the freedom of conscience and the right freely to profess, practice and propagate religion'.

Initially, the term minority signified disadvantage suffered by the group in comparison with the rest, which entitled it to special treatment from the state; it did not necessarily denote the numerical or religious status of the group. Thus, constitutional safeguards were considered for three types of groups: religious minorities, backward castes, and the SCs and tribal communities. All three were groups that had suffered disadvantage in various forms and different kinds of safeguards had been put in place for them by the British and the princely states.[11] In fact, each group sought to establish its claim as more deserving of safeguards, some arguing that they were numerically superior, others stressing that they were more socially backward than others, and yet others stating that they were culturally distinct from the majority and therefore deserving of special representation. A lower-caste member argued in the Assembly: 'We are one-fifth of the population of the whole country. It is impossible for a democratic country to ignore one-fifth of its population.'[12] Led by the Congress, nationalist opinion was quick to emphasize that backward classes were not distinct or culturally apart from the Hindu community, while religious minorities were different. In other words, the backward classes were a political minority, not a religious minority, and were therefore entitled to preferential treatment on grounds of backwardness. The problem of social and economic backwardness needed to be addressed by removing social and economic disabilities even as most members justified the grant of cultural rights to minority religious communities but not economic and social rights.

Eventually there were no reservations for minorities in any sphere. However, the Sub-Committee on Minority Rights in its report to the Advisory Committee on Fundamental Rights on 27 July 1947 had recommended reservations for Muslims, Sikhs, and Christians in public employment and legislatures in proportion to their population—but on the basis of joint electorates, not separate ones. The thrust was on (a) representation in legislatures, (b) reservation of seats in the Cabinet, and (c) reservation in government services. It recommended by a majority of 26 to 3 that 'as a general principle, there should be reservation of seats for different recognized minorities in various legislatures for a period of ten years.'[13] With this understanding, the Advisory Committee chaired by Sardar Patel recommended 'as a general rule that seats for different recognized minorities shall be reserved in the various legislatures on the basis of population', in a system of joint electorates. But after Partition this proposal was dropped. A remark by a member of the Constituent Assembly underlined the impulse for the change of approach. 'The birth of Pakistan,' Ajit Prasad Jain said on 22 November 1949, 'smoothened our work of constitution-making,' in particular 'the question of minorities, which had been our headache and which had thwarted all our efforts for the solution of the national problems, has ceased to be a live issue.'[14]

Partition changed the parameters of the constitutional discourse, which was redefined in terms of nationalism versus separatism and secularism versus communalism. Patel summed up the new mood:

> When the House passed the proposals in the August of 1947, the effect of Partition was not felt or known and the vast migrations that took place were at that time in a process of continuation and the position of Sikhs was practically uncertain at the time. So also in Bengal the effect of partition was not fully realized, and both provinces were desirous of postponing the question till conditions were fully settled and the effects were fully realized.[15]

Therefore, in the changed atmosphere, the whole question of minorities was reopened and the Sub-Committee on Minority Rights rejected reservations.[16] The political context was marked by communal violence, mass migration of millions to Pakistan, and unparalleled human suffering, which dominated the debates in the Assembly and formed the subtext of the deliberations. It was an important moment of popular radicalism and anti-imperialism that did at times manage to overcome communal divisions.[17]

Political safeguards were opposed on the ground that these constituted departures from the concept of social justice except for the SCs and STs. The main set of arguments invoked the value of secularism to point out that the continuation of religion-based representation was at odds with the ideal of a secular state and the separation between state and religion.[18] The exclusion of religion from politics was necessary because religion-based divisions had become too dangerous, leading to the Partition of the country. That traumatic event signalled the dangers of religion intruding into party politics. Further continuation of such divisions would encourage the isolation of minorities and sharpen communal differences.[19] A related argument against political safeguards was that it would endanger national unity, as these would reinforce communal divisions and would create a future society in which citizens remain permanently alienated from one another.[20] Finally, rejection of political safeguards was justified on ideological grounds of universalistic values and the principles of equality. The democratic norm of political equality was thought to require equal political rights for all individuals irrespective of religious affiliation.[21] Moving the amendment to the 1949 decision of the Constituent Assembly, Patel said: 'Nothing is better for the minorities than to trust the good sense of and the fairness of the majority, and place confidence in them.'[22] He proposed the abolition of reservations for all categories except the SCs and STs, which he said had the unanimous support of the members including minorities, although some Muslim members contested this.[23] Theodore Wright concludes that 'after the communal carnage following Independence, neither were Hindu representatives willing to continue this concession nor were the remaining Muslim committee members prepared to press for it.'[24]

Both Nehru and Patel justified the abolition of political reservations on the ground that the minorities themselves had changed their attitude and did not want it. It is likely that Partition altered the attitude of most Muslim members who thought it was better to drop this controversial demand, which had the taint of separatism. Many of them recognized that 'the nation's best interests would be served by their self-denial and the creation of an at least politically homogeneous nation.'[25] They came to believe that the result of reservation would be really to reduce Muslims to a statutory minority, which would have a crippling effect on them and end up worsening Hindu–Muslim relations. Nehru described the proposal to abolish reservations as 'a historic turn in our destiny'.[26] He was of the opinion that any demand for minority safeguards betrayed a lack of trust in the majority:

> In our heart of hearts we were not sure about ourselves...but always there was this doubt in our minds, namely, whether we had not shown weakness in dealing with a thing that was wrong. So when this matter came up in

another context, and it was proposed we do away with all reservations except in the case of the SCs, for my part I accepted that with alacrity and with a feeling of great relief, because I had been fighting in my own mind and heart against this business of keeping up some measure of separatism in our political domain.[27]

Nehru called it 'an act of faith above all for the majority community because they will have to show after this that they can behave to others in a generous, fair and just way [by keeping their representation commensurate with their population]. Let us live up to that faith.'[28] All subsequent proposals for political reservations for minorities were opposed on the ground that they were inimical to national unity and incompatible with secularism. As H.C. Mukherjee put it, 'Here we are building a nation and those who choose to divide again and sow the seeds of disruption will have no place, no quarter, here....'[29]

Significantly, there was no effort to balance off the abolition of political safeguards by introducing an electoral system that would facilitate adequate representation of minorities in legislatures as Nehru had hoped. There was no serious consideration of other methods that could facilitate representation of minorities after Independence. Various forms of proportional representation were suggested as a means of giving minority groups greater voice in the election of minority representatives and to enable the representation of minority opinion.[30] At different stages in the career of the Assembly it was argued that proportional representation would make assemblies more representative, but these ideas were jettisoned after Partition as it was commonly associated with separate electorates and the privileges enjoyed by Muslims that were held responsible for Partition. As such, any form of proportional representation was rejected by the Assembly on the grounds that it shared the flaws of separate electorates and was reminiscent of separatism and also because of the fear of fragmentation and governmental instability.[31]

Even though there was an awareness of India's pluralism and diversity, there was no discussion on the electoral system per se to ensure that representation would match the social characteristics of the population. Only four articles of the Constitution expressly pertain to the specifics of the election process. The tendency was to assume the continuation of the first-past-the-post system (FPTP) without taking cognizance of its implications for political representation in relation to India's diversity, especially the presence of large and dispersed minorities.[32] The alternative system of proportional representation, which can provide better representation to minorities, was passed over. The debate focused almost entirely on joint versus separate electorates and later between reservations and proportional representation. The large number of eminent jurists, constitutional experts, and thinkers who laboured for almost three years did not really discuss the pros and cons of which electoral system would be more appropriate. The constitutional advisor, B.N. Rau himself was in favour of the FPTP system, though he conceded that there was 'general agreement even among the critics of the proportional representation system that the application of the system is a necessity in the case of countries with self-conscious racial or communal minorities.'[33] Yet, no systematic discussion took place on an alternative electoral system or on the pros and cons of the simple majority system and its effects on the pattern of representation because of the strong assumption of continuity and the propensity to take for granted this system, which had been introduced by the British, for reasons of sheer familiarity with it.[34] Several members argued for proportional representation but this was never taken seriously. The discussion that did take place was only in the context of amendments moved by Muslim members of the Assembly.

Explicit debate on the intrinsic worth of specific electoral systems was thus largely absent.[35] Some Muslim members favoured proportional representation and criticized the FPTP system for promoting the tyranny of majority rule.[36] Several Sikh members also favoured proportional representation in order to compensate for the abolition of reservations for minorities, on the grounds that it would mitigate the 'tyranny of the majority' of single-member constituencies. Apart from the fear of perpetuation of divisiveness and instability under proportional representation, most members put forward the argument that it was too sophisticated a system for illiterate masses to operate. No one took note of the

Nehru Report of 1928 that considered the system of proportional representation to be 'the only rational and just way of meeting the fears and claims of various communities. We have no doubt that proportional representation will in future be the solution of our problem.' This report did not consider the difficulties in its working as insurmountable. The failure to give serious consideration to alternative voting systems suggests 'a pronounced tendency to assume as somehow natural the familiar Anglo-Saxon FPTP system.'[37] The critics argued that proportional representation would not guarantee adequate representation and, what is more, that the number of minority representatives would be insufficient to alter policies.

The constitutional debate on reservations for minorities in the services was similar to the debates on political representation. The dominant opinion opposed minority reservation in the services as undesirable but felt it necessary to give reservations to the backward classes. The opposition resulted in a critical distinction between cultural rights for minorities and socio-economic rights, which took the form of affirmative action for backward classes. In the event, safeguards for minorities took two forms: first, the inclusion in the Fundamental Rights of the freedom of religion; and, second, special provisions relating to the protection of script and culture and the rights of minorities to maintain their own educational institutions. Once religious freedom had been guaranteed to the minorities, many members felt there was no justification left for specific consideration of any form of preferential or special treatment.

To mitigate the apprehensions of the minorities, the Sub-Committee on Minority Rights supported the provision of these rights in addition to those of citizens. Congress leaders justified this by arguing that in a situation of communal divisions, minority rights had to be guaranteed in order to win their trust.[38] Abul Kalam Azad thought the Congress attached great importance to it. The protection of religious freedom of minorities, especially the large numbers of Muslims who decided to stay back in India, was necessary, even as religiously driven separatism hardened the opposition to special treatment, which had created schisms in society and polity. Furthermore, the Congress's Karachi Resolution of March 1931 had provided for the right to equality and non-discrimination and sought to guarantee the protection of the culture, language, and script of the minorities.[39] It is against this background that the term minority came to be renegotiated and redefined in the process of drafting the Constitution.

Inclusion of Lower Castes/Exclusion of Religious Minorities

Broadly speaking, there was a strong opinion in favour of reservations for the SCs and STs on the ground that they had suffered extreme discrimination and exclusion and that access to power would facilitate their social advancement. Social backwardness was seen as creating the most legitimate ground for reservations, and further that this was seen as attaching to caste groups and tribes, and not to religious minorities. From the beginning the term 'backward' included the untouchables and the tribal peoples, and was later extended to include backward classes. The untouchables were unhappy with the broader definition and the inclusion of backward classes, as it diluted attention from their uniquely unfortunate circumstances.[40] Although members frequently used the term 'backward', it was not defined anywhere; it did not figure in the debates in the Sub-Committee on Minority Rights. Though the word 'minority' was used in Article 296 and the expression 'backward classes' was used in Article 10 (3), H.N. Kunzru argued that 'protection can be granted only to a class, whether you call it minority or backward, only on the ground that it is backward and if left to itself, would be unable to protect its interests.'[41] It was thus felt necessary to separate the two Articles so that there was no confusion that the category of 'backward' referred to the 'educationally and socially backward classes' alone. The case for special treatment of the SCs and STs was distinguished from that of the religious minorities. This tendency was particularly strong in north India, where there existed clear distinctions between Hindus and Muslims and consequently the need to distinguish the backwardness of the former from the cultural distinctness of the latter. In south India the term 'backward classes' was more expansive referring to social or educational backwardness, and the only groups who did not fit into this category were the economically forward sections. But with all this ambiguity in regard to backwardness and backward sections, all the groups called 'backward' came from the Hindu community and from the beginning classes were equated with castes, the basic units of Hindu society.

Not surprisingly, several minority members supported the proposal to delete the word 'backward'. They favoured its deletion on the grounds that the scope of the word was likely to be interpreted by the state in ways that would exclude minorities, thereby adversely affecting their claims to representation in the services. Mohammed Ismail pointed out that in Madras the word 'bore a definite and technical meaning according to which more than 150 communities, all belonging to the majority community came under this label and, with the addition of the SCs, decidedly constituted the majority of the whole population of the province.'[42] Such an understanding would totally exclude minority communities from the purview of backwardness. On the other hand, members belonging to the backward classes, particularly the SCs, welcomed the new definition, as it privileged them as the sole beneficiaries. In fact, their main concern was to contain and limit the expansive scope of the word 'backward', which might include a range of backward groups, whereas they wanted it to be applied only to them. They preferred the term 'Depressed Class' or 'Scheduled Caste' to substitute the word 'backward' to avoid the confusion inherent in the latter.

The Constitution had to reconcile three positions: first, that there shall be equality of opportunity for all; second, that there ought to be no reservations; and, third, that there must be provision for the representation of certain communities which have so far been outside the administration. The introduction of the category 'backward' was to protect the principle of equality of opportunity and satisfy the demand for representation of communities excluded from government jobs. Ambedkar stressed that political reservations can be made consistent with the principle of equality of opportunity only if they are restricted to a minority of legislative seats. Reserving 70 per cent seats and leaving only 30 per cent open to general competition would put at risk the first principle, namely, equality of opportunity. T.T. Krishnamachari, on the other hand, asked what would be the basis for defining backwardness in a country where 80 per cent of the people fell into the category on grounds of illiteracy alone. Replying to these criticisms, Ambedkar acknowledged that they had to reconcile opposing points of view to produce a

> workable proposition, which will be accepted by all. Unless you use some such qualifying phrase as 'backward' the exception made in favour of reservations will ultimately eat up the rule altogether....That I think...is the justification why the Drafting Committee undertook on its own shoulders the responsibility of introducing the word 'backward' which, I admit, did not originally find a place in the fundamental rights in the way in which it was passed by the Assembly.[43]

With reference to the criticism regarding the definition of 'backward community', he believed, 'anyone who reads the language of the draft itself will find that we have left it to be determined by each local government. A backward community is a community which is backward in the opinion of the Government.'[44]

While considerable discussion took place on 'minorities and backward classes', and 'classes including minorities' as alternatives to classes or backward classes, in the end 'minorities' was replaced by 'classes'. K.M. Panikkar, the person responsible for the change, observed that in India 'minorities' had come to denote religious minorities, which would exclude small communities within the majority community who may not have adequate representation in the services. Under this distinction, lower castes were seen as part of the Hindu community and therefore deserving of special consideration on account of the historical wrongs of the caste system. The distinction was specially intended to facilitate the recognition of Dalits, who needed special protections earlier enjoyed by non-Hindu minorities.[45] Congress leader Shiban Lal Saksena argued the point forcefully: As far as we are concerned, we consider the SCs as belonging to Hindus, they are not a minority, they have also always formed part of us. In other words, the SCs were neither a racial minority nor a linguistic minority—and certainly not a religious minority—but disadvantaged Hindus who needed protections earlier enjoyed by non-Hindu minorities. To cut a long story short, when the Assembly dropped protections for minorities it did not do the same for the SCs and STs. This was followed by the decision to drop the concept of 'minority' for the purpose of reservations as out of place in free India. One thing was clear: backwardness as it was defined excluded non-Hindus and this was welcomed by right-wing Hindus.[46] This was the preferred position of the beneficiaries too because it limited the number of claimants.

Cultural distinctiveness from the majority and the need to preserve this distinction was important and it deserved protection, but economic and social backwardness of SCs or backward classes was the only justification for affirmative action. In this perception, the SCs and STs were the two principal groups that deserved the benefits of special treatment as they were the most historically disadvantaged.[47] In the case of the SCs the major concern was to find ways of integrating them in the social and political life of the nation, thus reducing their forced social exclusion. The protection of these two groups was facilitated by the earlier Assembly Resolution that had declared that preferential treatment would be given only to Hindu groups. Hence the discussion was not so much about the desirability of preferential treatment for various groups but about the social criteria for designation of the disadvantaged groups so as to facilitate inclusion of some and justify the exclusion of others. The definition of backwardness was clearly in relation to Hindu society, and did not include social and material deprivation in the broader sense. The key issue was whether to identify groups on the basis of their depressed status, which could be established by their social, economic, and cultural backwardness, or with reference to the specific criteria of ritual and social exclusion, or more broadly in terms of low status in the caste hierarchy.[48] The critical question was whether to use class—that is, general social and economic criteria—or ritual status in the caste system. The former would include groups outside the caste system, while the latter would limit it to the groups at the lowest levels of the caste hierarchy. It is clear the preference was for the latter.

The road to preferential treatment for lower-caste groups was, however, not an easy one.[49] The Congress was initially reluctant to concede SC reservation because of its harmful effect on the

Hindu base of the Congress. In the end it agreed to reservation in legislatures and similar preferences in other public institutions, in part because of its potential for unity, and, moreover, because opposition to it would have proved more detrimental than its acceptance.[50] The tumult within Hindu society has to be seen also in the context of changing Hindu–Muslim relations, and hence a greater stress on accommodation to neutralize further alienation and erosion of social support. The condition of untouchables, which had become a major article of social reform, assumed a new significance in this context. Concern about dwindling of Hindu numbers gained significance when the Census Commissioner suggested that the untouchables should be enumerated separately from Hindus, a suggestion quickly endorsed by the Muslim League. Reform of the caste system then came to occupy a central place in the political programme. This new position reversed the Congress's long-standing policy of excluding social reform from its programme.[51] The non-Brahmin movement and Gandhi's own anti-untouchability campaigns of the 1930s had also helped to legitimate special attention for the lower castes. After the elections of 1937, various Congress governments pushed ahead with preferential treatment for the SCs.

The major credit for the policy of preference put in place by the Constitution makers must go to Ambedkar, who was appointed as law minister in the first independent government formed in 1947. As Oliver Mendelsohn and Marika Vicziani suggest, it is difficult to underestimate the significance of Ambedkar's appointment as law minister, and the fact that he was chosen as the chairman of the Drafting Committee for the Constitution, in terms of the ultimate decision on reservations for the SCs.[52] He strenuously fought for preferential treatment in their favour in education and government employment, and built a new political culture for articulating the socio-political rights of SCs, which culminated in the constitutional provisions for substantive equality for the historically disadvantaged groups, in particular the SCs and STs. The incorporation of group rights was largely because of his insistence that SCs deserved special status and protection and that this was a necessary condition for them to become effective and useful citizens.[53]

There was from the beginning a tension between the goal of an equal, casteless society in which the individual is the unit of public policy and the concept of preference and reservations for groups. Both positions have a place in the Constitution because the nationalist leadership believed that this was a necessary price for the integration of the backward classes: that is to say that the state will in the short run have to recognize differences in order to erase them later. The leadership recognized that although equality of opportunity was important, it was equally important to have provision for the inclusion of groups which had so far been outside the administration.

Even though Nehru had misgivings about reservations, he supported them for the SCs:

> Frankly I would like this proposal to go further and put an end to such reservations as there still remain. But again, speaking frankly, I realize that in the present state of affairs in India that would not be a desirable thing to do, that is to say, in regard to the Scheduled Castes. I try to look upon the problem not in the sense of a religious minority, but rather in the sense of helping backward groups in the country. I do not look at it from the religious point of view or the caste point of view, but from the point of view that a backward group ought to be helped and I am glad that this reservation also will be limited to ten years.[54]

As mentioned earlier, the Congress was not in favour of reservations for any group, whether Muslims or lower castes or women; yet, given the long history of preferential treatment of depressed classes, it was difficult to jettison it after Independence. The experience and approach towards backward classes was different from that towards the SCs. The upper-caste leadership of the Congress was unwilling to give them similar preferences and privileges. This was because they were numerically and politically strong in quite a few regions, and special concessions would encourage them to mobilize opposition to the Congress.[55] The backward classes did not get reservations in government services at the Central level, but the important point is that the Constitution recognized them as a disadvantaged group, which allowed them to get preferential treatment and reservation at the state level. The position of SCs and STs on the other hand was strengthened by the special treatment accorded to them.

The SCs and STs are the only two social groups that are eligible for reservations in legislatures, both at the Central and state levels. Based on the percentage of their population in each state, the Constitution explicitly permits reservations for SCs and STs in Parliament and state assemblies, as also in public employment and educational institutions funded by the state; it also provides for the creation of a body to monitor all these safeguards. The Lok Sabha has 15 per cent of its seats reserved for SCs and 7.5 per cent for the STs. Both the national and state electoral systems use single-member constituencies with FPTP, winner-takes-all majority elections. The proportion of reserved seats is meant to be in proportion to the SC and ST population within each state: that is to say that reserved seats have social characteristics similar to the dominant numbers of the constituency. The allocation of Vidhan Sabha seats closely approximates the proportion of the population of the state. Although there are no clear criteria for the choice of particular constituencies for reservation, the basic idea is that reserved constituencies would have a relatively high proportion of either SCs or STs in order that the MPs or MLAs elected from reserved seats can be seen as representing these groups.[56] In states the percentage of reservation may exceed or fall short of the prescribed levels depending upon the percentage of the targeted group in the state.[57]

Trade-off between Cultural Rights and Affirmative Action

The distinction between the cultural rights of minorities and social discrimination and backwardness of lower castes produced different approaches and policies. Partition applied complete closure on job or educational reservations for minorities, even as it renewed the commitment to the construction of a secular state and to the accommodation of cultural diversity. As mentioned earlier, the framers made a particular point of including a freedom of religion clause in the Constitution. Specific to religious minorities are Articles 14 (equality before law), Article 15 (prohibition of discrimination on grounds of religion, race, caste, sex, or place of birth), Article 16 (equality of opportunity in matters of employment), Article 25 (freedom of conscience and free profession, practice, and propagation of religion), Article 26 (freedom to manage religious affairs, subject to public order, morality, and health), Article 29 (protection of interests in regard to language, script, and culture), Article 30 (right of minorities to establish and administer educational institutions), and Article 32 (right to seek constitutional remedies). In this conceptual framework, the rejection of affirmative action or any form of preferential treatment for minorities was consistent with the acceptance of community-specific social rights. The trade-off between preferential treatment for lower castes and cultural rights for religious minorities proved to be disadvantageous for the latter, as it meant that the real problems of minority citizens in terms of livelihood and access to resources were not tackled.

Broadly speaking, the Indian approach to disadvantage was governed by two defining features of nationalist politics: commitment to social equality and the need to deal with exclusion of the lower castes at the hands of upper-caste Hindus. The twin goals confronting the nation-building project were not only the demands to alleviate the sufferings of the lower castes but also to reduce the power of the privileged elite and redistribute the benefits that they had monopolized. The caste system not only exploited and disadvantaged certain groups, it also concentrated advantage in other groups, namely, the upper castes. Affirmative action policies were above all an acknowledgement of this disparity and a means of bringing these hitherto ostracized sections into the social and political mainstream.[58] This was the moral rationale of Article 16, which creates the right to equal opportunity and preferences in recruitment to government employment. Article 16 (4) covers not only reservations in initial recruitment into government service but also preferences in promotions for under-represented backward classes of citizens. Article 15 (4) extends to all areas of activity such as housing, education, welfare, and government contracts, which are not covered by a more specific provision. Unlike Article 16 (4) this Article does not limit the state to reservations; it enables the government to employ methods such as scholarships, fee concessions, and special facilities which do not involve reservations at all.

Arguably, the Constitution did not provide for reservation for the SCs and STs because they are poor or economically disadvantaged; it did so because they faced an explicit, structured, and systematic exclusion from public life for centuries on grounds of descent.[59] But these measures were also defended for their potential contribution in improving the socio-economic conditions of the disadvantaged. However, for Ambedkar, the chief architect of this programme, 'severe social separation' was the definition of discrimination. Even during the constitutional debates this formulation had led to considerable disagreement, as it excludes other groups which suffered social disabilities simply because they were non-Hindus. Reservations were thought to be one of the most effective ways of helping to break the social exclusiveness of the public sphere. Politically, it came to be seen as evidence that the state cared for the communities that were discriminated and excluded.[60] Above all, this framework provided the basis for distinguishing between different kinds of discrimination/disadvantage and deprivation/poverty. Rather than provide a general standard for selection of beneficiaries, the designation criteria stressed low social and ritual standing as a measure of backwardness, that is, ritual exclusion shared by all untouchables and the incidence of social disabilities as the crucial test with regard to the SCs.[61] Primacy was attached to untouchability, which was intrinsic to Hinduism. This criterion has endured and applies even today. There have been no significant changes and no important policy departures.[62] There has been no further attempt to formulate any new criterion for inclusion, despite the controversy over whether untouchables who had opted out of Hinduism by converting to Christianity or Islam qualified as SCs, since both were initially defined as castes in the Hindu religious framework.

Historical events and debates surrounding the making of the Constitution left a lasting impact on the precedence given to caste, albeit in the guise of backward classes in public policy. It is important to remember that preferential treatment won the day, but not as part of a broader policy of combating economic inequalities and attacking poverty. At the same time, backwardness and disadvantage became the acceptable political language in the public realm for dealing with material deprivation and poverty as well. Important members of the Constituent Assembly used the language of inclusion and integration to address the enormous backlog of deprivation of different kinds. This approach prevailed because it could address the most important problem, which was social exclusion of lower castes from the public domain. The centrality of caste in Indian public life is obvious, as it was not merely seen as a religious institution but one that was inscribed by relations of power, as Nicholas Dirks argues.[63] Hence the removal of disadvantage and exploitation based on caste has been given priority in public policy. One of the important aims of the modern state was to address the unresolved question of caste; a question that had also dominated social reform movements and anti-colonial nationalism. As an institution, its importance lay in structuring and maintaining relations of power among different groups through systematically dispensing various mixes of economic and cultural assets/opportunities and deprivations to different communities, and by endowing religious/ideological sanctification of such dispensations.[64] From the beginning, caste was the benchmark of state policy and an indicator of its commitment to the eradication of social inequalities and discrimination. It thus came to dominate the project of nationalism, democracy, and citizenship, and much of public policy in modern India. Reservations on the basis of caste went on to give a new lease of life to it. Ironically, while the objective of preferential treatment was to weaken and challenge caste, the process of categorization and classification and the endless debates over the rights and wrongs of this policy have contributed to making it all the more significant.

Notes

1. Amarnath Mohanty (2007: 3151–7).
2. *Constituent Assembly Debates* (1989) (henceforth *CAD*). Nehru, K.M. Munshi, *CAD* (30 November 1948: 697); Pant, *CAD* (21 January 1947: 333), K.T. Shah, *CAD* (29 November 1948: 655–6), N.G. Ranga, *CAD* (20 January 1947: 280).
3. Sumit Sarkar (2001).

4. Granville Austin (1986).

5. Christophe Jaffrelot (2004: 126–49).

6. Mushirul Hasan (2001).

7. Rajeev Bhargava (2008).

8. Shefali Jha (2008).

9. Maulana Abul Kalam Azad, Presidential Address, Ramgarh Session of the Congress, December 1940, cited in Mushirul Hasan (2001).

10. The most succinct account of the discussions in the Constituent Assembly is to be found in Shiva Rao (1967).

11. Rochna Bajpai (2008).

12. *CAD* (21 January 1947: 285).

13. *CAD* (26 May 1949: 321).

14. Cited in Mushirul Hasan (1998: 144).

15. *CAD* (25 May 1949: 270).

16. *CAD* (25 May 1949: 271).

17. Sumit Sarkar (2001).

18. *CAD* (27 August 1947: 222).

19. Rajeev Bhargava (2002: 105–33).

20. Ibid., p. 121.

21. Rochna Bajpai (2008: 369).

22. *CAD* (May 1949: 272).

23. *CAD* (25 May 1949: 270).

24. Theodore P. Wright Jr (1997).

25. Ibid., p. 151.

26. *CAD* (26 May 1049: 329).

27. Ibid.

28. Ibid.

29. *CAD* (25 May 1949: 271).

30. Rochna Bajpai (2008: 371).

31. Ibid., p. 376.

32. E. Sridharan (2002).

33. B.N. Rau (1960).

34. E. Sridharan (2002).

35. Ibid.

36. Ibid.

37. Ibid., p. 355.

38. Farzana Sheikh (1993: 81–101) argues that the Congress categorically assumed that the unit of representation had to be the individual.

39. Neera Chandhoke (1999).

40. Bhiku Parekh (2006: 437).

41. *CAD* (29 November 1948: 680–1).

42. Ibid., pp. 692–3.

43. Ibid., p. 701.

44. Ibid., pp. 701–2.

45. Oliver Mendelsohn and Marika Vicziani (2000: 131).

46. Bhiku Parekh (2006: 441–2).

47. Lelah Dushkin notes that probably 'nowhere else in the world was so large a lower class minority granted so much special favourable treatment by a government as the depressed classes in India.' Cited in Marc Galanter (1984).

48. For details of classification scheme, see Marc Galanter (1984: 125).

49. Oliver Mendelsohn and Marika Vicziani (2000).

50. Ibid., pp. 26–7, 130.

51. Ibid., pp. 25–6.

52. Ibid., p. 37.

53. Eleanor Zelliot (1992).

54. Jawaharlal Nehru, *CAD* (Vol. VIII: 331).

55. Oliver Mendelsohn and Marika Vicziani (2000: 133).

56. Alistair McMillan (2005).

57. Niraja Gopal Jayal (2006: 128).

58. Marc Galanter (1984).

59. Ibid., pp. 130–4.

60. Bhiku Parekh (2006: 441).

61. Marc Galanter (1984: 134).

62. Ibid., p. 132.

63. Nicholas B. Dirks (2001: 276–7).

64. Ibid.

3

Policies and Institutional Frameworks for Protecting the Disadvantaged

This chapter deals with how the state in Independent India has addressed the question of discrimination, deprivation, and exclusion suffered by lower castes and religious minorities. It examines how constitutional provisions and public policies have tackled the disadvantages of these groups. In particular, it seeks to understand the policy framework in relation to these groups, and the divergences in policy and consequences of this for the protection of the disadvantaged. It seeks to address the following two questions: (1) how did the state propose to deal with the problems of these two groups and (2) what has been the impact of such provisions and polices in the protection and promotion of the interests of the deprived and disadvantaged? It is an attempt to delineate the structure of policies as well as changes in the constellation of policies for these two groups—that is, lower castes (SCs) and minorities (Muslims)—while arguing that the well-being of minorities has suffered more due to a lack of attention to issues of institutionalized inequality and deprivation than is commonly supposed.

Public policies for these two groups fall into two distinct types: broadly described as empowerment for the lower castes and protection of the religious identity of minorities. It is well known that the government has assumed a wide-ranging responsibility for the welfare of the SCs and STs. The Indian system of positive discrimination is unique, both in terms of the benefits involved and in the magnitude of the groups eligible for them.[1] Policies for the lower castes in turn fall broadly into two types: (1) anti-discriminatory or protective measures and (2) developmental and empowering measures. Anti-discriminatory measures include the provision of legal safeguards against discrimination, and proactive measures in the form of reservation policies for the public sector and state-supported sectors, and measures for economic and political empowerment to overcome the past economic and social handicaps. The policy approach towards minorities consists of measures aimed at recognition and protection of religious identity. Against the background of Partition and Hindu–Muslim violence surrounding it, the state was keen to provide minorities a stake in the new nation, assuage their fears of identity loss, and assure them of their security by ending communal violence.[2] This was a response governed by the urgent need to bridge the Hindu–Muslim divide in the wake of Partition.

Empowering Lower Castes

Historically, SCs are the most oppressed group in Indian society and continue to suffer from discrimination and exclusion even in contemporary times.[3] The category of SCs came into being through the enactment of the Government of India Act, 1935, whereby a conglomerate of castes whose defining feature was untouchability were identified and placed in a schedule in order to render them eligible for certain safeguards and benefits. Caste was the primary basis for the designation of SCs. They constituted 16.2 per cent of the country's population in 2001. More than half the SC population is concentrated in five states: Uttar Pradesh, West Bengal, Tamil Nadu, Andhra Pradesh, and Bihar. Punjab has the highest proportion of SCs at 25 per cent. The Indian nation-state's commitment to the idea of equal participation of all its citizens found its greatest manifestation in the substantive conception of social justice measures for the SCs and STs and the establishment of an elaborate regulatory framework for the implementation of reservations in legislatures, education, and government employment for the SCs and STs. This dimension was virtually absent from the approach towards minorities. The state was not concerned with the social and material disadvantages that minorities suffer from; rather, it constructed its response solely in relation to the question of religio-cultural identity and its protection. No doubt, equality of opportunity has been provided in the Constitution for all citizens irrespective of religious background, but the required equality of conditions to translate this into reality does not exist for the minorities.

It is in the context of differing conceptions of public policy that one factor needs to be noted. This pertains to the existence of a national consensus among political parties, leaders, and intellectuals with regard to affirmative action for the promotion of substantive equality for the disadvantaged castes. There is a strong agreement that SCs deserve affirmative action because they carry a burden of historical injustice and oppression. By contrast, there is no political support for special treatment of minorities except with regard to protection of cultural identity which too is questioned by sections of civil and political society. The state, by earmarking religious minorities for special attention in the cultural sphere, and denying them crucial state support in the area of social welfare, placed them at a relative disadvantage.[4] It is within the contending claims of identity and equity that the relationship between citizenship and minority rights had to be negotiated.[5] The problems arise from the failure to reconcile the demands of identity and well-being resulting in the institutional deficit that minorities have suffered. Cultural rights are not enough for the protection of minority interests, particularly for those that are also socially and economically disadvantaged. The relationship between well-being and protection of cultural identity of minorities is complementary, and minority rights must exist alongside a broader regime of rights.[6]

In regard to the SCs, the strategy of the government focused both on removing past disadvantage and also on providing protection from continuing discrimination and exclusion in the present through the introduction of public policies of empowerment. The Constitution envisaged a three-pronged strategy to remove the social disabilities suffered by the SCs, provide for punitive action against violence inflicted on them, and protect their economic interests through legal and legislative measures. These policies aimed at promoting equality, stamping out caste, and secularizing society. The basic understanding was that disabilities derived from caste were the consequence of traditional restrictions and denial of economic and social rights in the past. This strategy was designed to ensure proportional participation in various public spheres, which may otherwise not be realized due to the practice of exclusion and discrimination.[7] The Constitution contains explicit provisions spelling out state obligations towards protecting and promoting the rights and welfare of SCs and STs; it provided a good number of social, educational, economic, and political safeguards, and also a set of social policies and measures for the amelioration of their conditions.[8] The state also undertook development initiatives to bridge the gulf between the SCs and the rest of society with respect to economic conditions and social status. Over the years the scope of these policies has been expanded to cover a wide array of governmental schemes and programmes to safeguard against discrimination.

Government policy in relation to the lower castes has evolved over time; it has expanded both in terms of spheres of intervention and strategies and methods of implementation. To begin with, the focus was on tackling social injustice by enforcement of legislation to prevent atrocities against SCs. Simultaneously, the approach focused on specific programmes that were a supplement to the general development schemes to benefit the SCs as well. The latter approach assumed that caste-based exclusion could be tackled by overall development programmes adopted at the local level to suit the needs of deprived groups. However, it did not produce the desired results because development expenditure did not focus specifically on these groups. Thus, until the end of the Fourth Five Year Plan (1979–80), the funds available for the development of SCs and STs were under the general head of Backward Class sectors, although all Five Year Plans emphasized that SCs must get their due share from the general sectors of development. The 1980s marked a shift in approach with greater focus on special schemes and targeted programmes for the disadvantaged groups. This period witnessed the introduction of a new strategy for the development of SCs and

STs. It took the form of special plans such as the Special Component Plan (SCP) for the STs and later the same for the SCs.[9]

The government introduced the SCP for the SCs in 1979 (Sixth Five Year Plan) as a principal instrument for the rapid development of SCs. The Planning Commission recognized that the 'Area Development' approach it had followed until then was not relevant in the case of SCs because they were dispersed and in most parts of the country, unlike the tribal people who were concentrated in certain areas. The Commission formulated the SCP as an alternative programme in the Sixth Plan and it is being implemented since then. All states which have a sizeable SC population prepare an SCP for the development of the SCs; they have to identify schemes and programmes already under implementation or which can be implemented to benefit the SCs. The SCP is meant to be an umbrella programme under which all schemes implemented by the Central and state governments are dovetailed for addressing different needs of the SCs. In addition to special schemes for the SCs, there is reservation for SCs under major centrally sponsored schemes, and also several development schemes specifically for SCs in the states.

The SCP's prime objective was to ensure allocation of adequate funds to implement schemes that would benefit SCs, reduce the gap between them and the rest of the society, and speed up the process of integrating them with the mainstream. The key idea was to promote overall development through education, capacity building, employment- and income-generating devices, asset building, and so on. Although the SCP was clearly a landmark provision for SCs, it has not been implemented effectively. 'Proper implementation of the SCP would have brought about a sea-change in the condition of Dalits', notes the Sixth Report of the NCSC/ST.[10] Combined with the Scheduled Castes and Scheduled Tribes (Prevention of Atrocities) Act, the SCP had the potential to make a signal contribution to the reduction, if not removal, of poverty and untouchability.

The Planning Commission renamed the SCP as the Scheduled Castes Sub-Plan (SCSP) in 1979, which was itself a special device to compensate for the failure of the government and its agencies to see that the benefits of planned development reached people who had been victims of social exclusion for centuries. While introducing the scheme, the government said that the allotment of funds must be more than proportionate to the percentage of SCs in the population. Out of the twenty-seven states which have formulated SCSPs, a large number have not made financial provisions for them in proportion to the SC population in the state. Only a few states such as Tamil Nadu, Uttar Pradesh, West Bengal, and Gujarat have adhered to the prescribed norms in allocation of funds. For example, Punjab has generally failed to implement the SCP despite having the highest concentration of SC population in the country. In Punjab the outlay provided for the SCP for 1999–2000 was less than half the ratio of the state's SC population.[11] At least eighteen states had not reported the flow of funds from their annual State Plan Outlays to the SCSP in 2007–8.

The fundamental problem is the manner of formulation and allocation of funds for the programme. Many states apportion outlays under State Plan and classify them as SCSP without taking into consideration whether implementation of such programmes has any bearing on the development of the SCs or not. Such classifications of outlays are often made without in-depth study of the problems or the handicaps faced by the SCs. In addition, many states did not allocate funds in proportion to SCs' share in the population as the bulk of the allotments went to 'non-divisible' sectors such as roads, power, communication, and irrigation, leaving little for the 'divisible' sectors from which funds for the SCSP were to be drawn.

There are also major complaints of diversion of funds to other sectors. Besides inadequate allocation of funds for the development of the SCs, the funds under the SCSP are usually notional, and these are either underutilized or diverted to other sectors. The Eleventh Plan Working Group for Empowerment of the Scheduled Castes observed:

> Many of the states are not formulating and implementing SCSP as per the guidelines issued in this regard. The allocation under SCSP has not been commensurate with the percentage of SC population of the states. The gap between the percentage of SC population and the percentage of

allocation under SCSP has been particularly wide in states such as Andhra Pradesh, Assam, Gujarat, Himachal Pradesh, Karnataka, Madhya Pradesh, Maharashtra, Orissa, Punjab, Rajasthan, Tripura, West Bengal and Union Territories of Chandigarh and Pondicherry.[12]

Dalit leaders and activists blame social discrimination and the prejudices of bureaucrats for the unsatisfactory implementation of special plans because they disapprove of these plans or are unenthusiastic about them. Thus, owing to the reluctance of the political leadership and bureaucratic apathy, funds allocated for socio-economic development of SCs went unspent or got diverted to other sectors. Overall, it would appear that a 'lack of political will, the lethargy of the bureaucracy and the deep-rooted prejudice against Dalits among large sections of civil society, which gets reflected in the attitude of those in the administration, are among the reasons cited for the failure of many a development initiative,' concludes the NHRC Report.[13]

Protecting Minorities

India was also among the first democracies to provide social policies for the protection of religious minorities. However, these policies were very different from those for disadvantaged castes. In the case of minorities, there was a tendency to overemphasize identity, which resulted in a situation where inequalities and deprivation were not adequately recognized and hence not frontally addressed. This approach is quite different from that towards the disadvantaged castes, who were perceived as development subjects with economic deprivation and social exclusion as the defining characteristics that required the state to address the problem through a wide range of preferential policies. The point is not whether special treatment for the lower castes has been adequate or not; what is important is that it embodies a political will and a readiness to enhance the social welfare and rights of these groups. On the other hand, there was a clear reluctance to be similarly proactive with regard to minorities, despite mounting evidence of their deprivation and disadvantage.

After Partition, India remained a home for Hindus, Muslims, Christians, and others, and though Pakistan was a Muslim state, there were more Muslims in India than in Pakistan. One way of facilitating the integration of these Muslim communities was to recognize them as members of religious minorities.[14] The Constitution envisages that minorities would have the right to freedom of religion, to conserve their language, script, and culture, and to establish and administer educational institutions. These rights offered them an alternative identity as citizens without the political or socio-economic rights that frequently go with citizenship. While this framework focused specifically on cultural rights, the general public policies and provisions applicable to all citizens were expected to address issues of equity and representation in governance. Undoubtedly, the great bulk of state policy is framed in a universalist language which is indifferent to religion, but its implementation is far from universal, as local and political interests shape regulation on the ground. The practices of the state have not always conformed to the principle of equal participation due to which state policies have benefited some groups and not others. Over six decades after Independence, it is evident these policies, both general public policies and provisions for minorities, have proved insufficient in overcoming the problems of minorities. All in all, the policy-making process and the operation and practice of state structures were largely responsible for the deprivation of social opportunity, lack of access to education, health care, other public services, and to employment opportunities.

The prime minister's High-Level Committee constituted under the chairmanship of Justice Rajinder Sachar, which submitted its report in November 2006, demonstrates that the educational, social, and economic development of Muslims has fallen far behind that of other groups in our society and that the Muslim community is barely distinguishable from the SCs on most indices of social, economic, and educational deprivation.[15] But in terms of access to political representation and governance they are worse off than the SCs. The SCs can, on account of affirmative action, get access to schools, colleges, and government jobs, and get elected to legislatures on the reserved quota. This is not a new assessment for those who have investigated the socio-economic status of Muslims in India.[16] However, the significance of the SCR lies in the fact that it carries an official stamp, and, more importantly, the report uses data from state institutions, which are the most important sources of social statistics all over the world. It confirms that Muslims face economic deprivation, social exclusion, and political under-representation.[17] It is hardly surprising that they emerged as India's principal underclass. Thirty-eight per cent of them in urban areas and 27 per cent in rural areas are poor (see Tables 3.1 and 3.2).

When it comes to education and employment, the average Muslim is at the bottom of the heap and trailing behind SCs and OBCs on many indicators of social development. The SCR shows that while there is considerable variation in the conditions of Muslims across states (and among the Muslims, those who identified themselves as OBCs and others), Muslims as a group exhibit deficits and deprivation in practically all dimensions of development. In fact, Muslims rank somewhat above the SCs/STs but below Hindu OBCs, other minorities, and Hindus (general category) (mostly upper castes) in almost all indicators considered. Among the states that have large Muslim populations, the situation is particularly dismal in the states of West Bengal, Bihar, Uttar Pradesh, and Assam.

There is a significant disparity in the educational status of Muslims and that of other socio-religious communities; Muslims across the country have less access than other groups to educational facilities, particularly in higher education.[18] The number of Muslims with graduate degrees (for 21–30 year-olds) of any type is roughly 4.5 per cent compared to 18.6 per cent for the Hindus (general category) (Table 3.3). The economic participation rates of Muslims are low and unemployment rates are high (Graphs 3.1 and 3.2). The probabilities of Muslims being in self-employment and of being casual wage labourers are high, and the probability of being in regular salaried or wage employment very low. Indeed, the most striking feature of the Muslim community is the high share of workers engaged in self-employment activity (Graph 3.3). This is particularly true in urban areas. Their participation in regular salaried jobs, especially in government or large public and private sector enterprises, is much less than that of workers of other communities. Only 18 per cent are in regular employment as against 25 per cent Hindus. They tend to be relatively more vulnerable in terms of conditions of work as their concentration in informal sector employment is higher, and their job conditions (contract length, social security, etc.), even among regular workers, are worse as compared to other socio-religious communities. The SCR notes that disproportionate numbers of Muslims have responded to their exclusion from formal employment by going into business for themselves. Self-employment was not a preferred choice but perhaps the last option; it is by no means a symbol of empowerment of minorities.[19]

Hindus and Christians are more likely to be in formal employment because they have a higher educational status and history of regular salaried work compared to Muslims (Graph 3.3). The SCs, STs, and OBCs have obtained government jobs, which helps in bringing them on par with the non-SC, non-ST groups. This avenue does not exist for minorities despite their under-representation in the government sector. The latter types of jobs are principally teachers, clerks, security personnel, and office attendants, which are not necessarily of a high status but ensure regular income and other benefits that come with government jobs such as security and prestige.

The Gopal Singh Committee Report in 1983 had noted the backwardness of Muslims and found virtually the same gap between Muslims and other groups, and the lack of voice and presence in decision-making institutions. In the words of Rafiq Zakaria, its member secretary: 'Its findings sent shock waves through the corridors of South Block. Indira Gandhi thought it best to shelve its findings. She told me that a post-mortem never helped; it would be prudent to forget the past and plan for the future.'[20] With respect to economic development of minorities, the Committee made the following observation:

> Some attempts have also been made to take some special measures relating to national integration but the economic aspects of the problems of the minorities have hardly received any attention either at the central or at the state level. Departments at the central and state levels, no doubt have implemented to some extent different programmes for the economic

development of all sections of society, which include minorities, but no specific programme has been chalked out for them and no concerted effort made to tackle their problems imaginatively and boldly.[21]

Despite this, there was no serious policy intervention, leave alone affirmative action, to mitigate the deprivation of minorities. Twenty-three years later, the SCR underlined that the 'non-implementation of recommendations of several earlier commissions and committees has made the Muslim community wary of any new initiative.'[22] The development deficit has been compounded by the inadequate presence of minorities in the governance structures. Not surprisingly, Parliament and public institutions have rarely discussed issues concerning deprivation of minorities.

This differential treatment of disadvantaged castes and minorities has had an overwhelming influence on public policies and outcomes for these groups. For a long time the state avoided the subject of development of minorities and this was one factor responsible for keeping them backward. There was very little serious public or policy debate with regard to minority development, no agreed thinking over precisely what constituted the interests of minorities and the policies needed to alleviate their problems. In these circumstances, it is hardly surprising that the actual status of minorities did not figure in the formulation of public policies until the submission of the SCR in 2006. Ironically, this hands-off approach resulted in the separation, rather than integration, of Muslims from the development discourse.

Although there are a large number of centrally sponsored schemes and Central plan schemes available for the welfare of deprived groups, such schemes specifically for the welfare of minorities are rare. The progress and implementation of the government welfare schemes that do exist have been slow and tardy. The access to beneficiary-oriented schemes such as Integrated Child Development Programmes and Mid-Day Meal Schemes is unsatisfactory. Most notably, the outlays for welfare of minorities are usually minuscule. The two flagship schemes of the government are the National Minority Finance and Development Corporation (NMFDC) and the Maulana Azad Educational Foundation.[23] But the corpus fund for these institutions is quite modest despite the fact that the NMFDC is the only exclusive institutional support for the economic development of minorities.

After more than five decades of neglect, there was an awareness that India can no longer afford to ignore the deprivation of Muslims. There was recognition that the educational and economic backwardness of minorities, especially of large sections of the Muslim population, requires focused attention. In this regard, the Tenth Plan Report had noted 'the point that economic marginality is certainly one of the roots and, consequently, one of the major explanations for minority alienation and frustration.'[24] Prime Minister Manmohan Singh also acknowledged that government programmes have not had their desired effect in providing the basic needs of minorities. He made this clear at the Congress chief ministers' conclave held in September 2006: 'Our problem, which I must mention, is that our understanding of minorities needs to improve. For example, their enrolment in schools, their educational levels, and their participation in employment is much lower than the state averages. We need to pay special attention to this issue.'[25] In a similar vein, Sonia Gandhi, president of the Congress party and chairperson of the United Progressive Alliance (UPA) had earlier accepted that

> The levels of development of considerable sections of the Muslim population ought to be a matter of concern in terms of equity and social justice, under-representation in public life and public employment. Differentiations of this kind are unacceptable in a modern society. They retard the overall progress of India itself. This despite their enjoying the same right to equality, equal protection of the law and all other fundamental rights as any other citizen.[26]

Sonia Gandhi spoke about the need 'to move the debate from the general to the specific and direct effort at producing results in a specified time frame' in an effort to make the minorities 'stakeholders in the new India that is emerging'.

Conscious of this ground reality, the UPA government took a number of steps and established new institutions and policies to address the concerns of minorities. These included the setting up of the Ministry of Minority Affairs, the National Commission for Religious and Linguistic Minorities, and the National Commission for Minority Educational Institutions. The Prime Minister's New 15-Point Programme for the welfare of minorities was recast to focus action sharply on issues linked with the social, educational, and economic uplift of minorities and provide for earmarking of outlays in certain schemes so that the progress can be monitored.[27] In 2006, the Union Cabinet directed that wherever possible, 15 per cent of targets and funds be earmarked for the minorities in the schemes included in the [Prime Minister's 15-Point] Programme. The new initiatives mark a conceptual shift in favour of socio-economic development as against the past preoccupation with identity politics and the secular–communal divide to the exclusion of equity issues. It represented a long overdue recognition that the concept of minority rights needed to go beyond formal equality. The basic issue is the educational and economic backwardness of minority groups and the need to devise and implement policies for the protection of their basic needs. The Eleventh Five Year Plan offered an important opportunity to correct the deficits in empowering of minorities bearing in mind the acknowledgment that although the previous five year plans have attempted to focus on weaker sections, they have failed to include many groups, especially Muslims, in the development process.[28]

The Eleventh Plan laid greater stress on 'enhancing opportunities for education, equitable share in economic activities and employment and improving the condition of living of minorities'.[29] The Plan sought to accord the highest priority to the development of innovative programmes, expansion of existing schemes, implementation, and monitoring of all initiatives for minorities by making budgetary allocations at every level of governance. However, the 'Minorities' chapter was a mere nine pages in three volumes running into 950 pages. Even though there is greater concern for the socio-economic development of minorities, there are hardly any substantive measures to achieve this. This was most apparent from the reluctance to introduce a special plan for minorities on the lines of the tribal sub-plan or the SCCP. Notwithstanding all the deficiencies in the SCCP, a well-directed and visible thrust such as a special plan for minorities can go a long way in making a dent in the widespread economic and social backwardness of Muslims. Most of all, this could have a beneficial impact on the self-perception of minorities that they too have equal access to resource allocation. Furthermore, it is an idea that could go some distance in facilitating the realization of the goal of inclusive development through appropriate allocation of funds and resources for the promotion of fair and just development of all sections of society, especially the marginalized sections.

The proposal for a minority sub-plan formed part of the recommendations of the Eleventh Plan Working Group on Empowering the Minorities.[30] The Group recommended an allocation of divisible funds under different heads broadly based on the minority share in the population. Such a need arises from the specific needs of minority communities in the areas of education, livelihoods in certain sectors, and infrastructure. A special plan would set concrete physical and financial targets and allocations for improving the socio-economic conditions of minorities. However, this proposal faced stiff opposition within the Group itself. A social activist and member of the Eleventh Plan Working Group on Empowering the Minorities pointed out:

> The Eleventh Five-Year Plan provided a historic opportunity to turn things around. The only way forward is to stop this coyness. Call Muslims, Muslims. Shift lenses, change paradigms. For once, see them not as a 'religious community' (of veils and fatwas), but as development subjects, suffering from undeserved want. Accordingly, design interventions, schemes and programmes with 'Muslim' targets that will be monitored and met.[31]

Senior bureaucrats in the Group rebutted:

> It is not constitutional to have schemes just for Muslims. We cannot design schemes for Muslims, or have budgetary allocations for Muslims, or call Muslims, Muslims. It is simply not constitutional. The Constitution makes special mention of SCs and STs for affirmative intervention, not of Muslims. We can only have intervention for all minorities.[32]

The Eleventh Plan does not include a minority sub-plan. At the annual conference of State Minorities Commissions (2008), the NCM chairman expressed his disappointment with 'the absence of a minority sub-plan in the Eleventh Plan document'.[33] Disagreeing with the need for a minority sub-plan, Planning

Commission member Bhalchandra Mungekar remarked that 'if the Prime Minister's 15-Point Programme was implemented, there would be no need for such a sub-plan as the PM's plan covered all those points which were sought to be included in that sub-plan.'[34] The absence of minority sub-plan was justified on the ground that the SCCP was ineffective and it would therefore be unwise to replicate a programme which has not produced the desired results. However, though the 15-Point Programme (1983) has also been ineffective, this did not deter the government from reissuing it in 2006. The New 15-Point Programme was highlighted as an alternative to the sub-plan even though it had not been a success in its earlier incarnation and did very little to provide security or welfare to minorities.

The Planning Commission did not approve a minority sub-plan because of the fear that it would be charged with communalizing the planning process. It did not question the concept of a minority sub-plan per se, but there was a great deal of scepticism that had more to do with fears of the political fallout than conceptual doubts with regard to the efficacy of special plans. Besides the Planning Commission had approved large sub-plans for the SCs and STs for the Eleventh Plan, which means the SCCP scheme itself was not flawed. The reluctance stemmed from a sense of unease that a minority sub-plan was sure to fuel the communal propoganda of minority appeasement. This assessment was not unreasonable because there was a very real possibility of a backlash given the constant attack whenever an issue of affirmative action for minorities came to the fore. Indicating the importance of the idea of 'Muslim appeasement' in its thinking, the BJP had earlier assailed the prime minister's call for 'a fair share in jobs for minorities', 'fiscal priority for minorities', and the 15-Point Programme.[35] The Cabinet had adopted the 15-Point Programme on 22 June 2006. Moreover, this was not the first time that a programme of this kind was under implementation. In May 1983, Indira Gandhi had addressed a letter to all the chief ministers containing, again, fifteen points. Rajiv Gandhi reiterated these in August 1985. Yet, the BJP criticized the second instalment as though this was the first time such a programme was unveiled.

Countering the BJP charge, the prime minister stated in the National Development Council (NDC), 'The plan does not attempt to divide people on the basis of caste, creed, gender, but there are certain social groups who are relatively badly placed on all the developmental indicators. The plan does pay special attention to the needs of these marginalized groups and targets them in a precise manner. This is, after all, the true meaning of inclusiveness.'[36] Regardless of this forthright statement, the BJP leaders continued their criticism against the 15-Point Programme and 15 per cent outlays under various schemes for minorities in the NDC meeting (2006) and outside it.[37] At the same time, the BJP declared that it had no problem with special allocation for disadvantaged groups based on caste or gender, as that kind of affirmative action was rooted in the Constitution. However, there was no place for positive state action for Muslims or other minorities. The sharp attack on the prime minister's statement on fiscal priority prompted a guarded response on the part of the government with regard to such initiatives. As it turned out, the government's preference was in favour of prudence over a special plan that could substantively advance minority welfare. Even the Prime Minister's New 15-Point Programme for the welfare of minorities found no mention in the budgetary documents or the budget speech of the finance minister in the budgets since its announcement. In fact, one way of institutionalizing 15 per cent budgetary allocations for socially and educationally backward minorities would have been to follow the practice initiated for the SCs and STs in the 2005–6 budget which included a statement on schemes exclusively for SCs and STs and schemes where 20 per cent of the benefits would be earmarked for SCs and STs.

The UPA's cautious response has much to do with the politics of polarization practised by communal parties and organizations, which has targeted minority groups, Muslims and Christians, charging them with extraterritorial loyalties, with the intention of diluting their national credentials and thereby questioning their entitlement to special measures and benefits given by the state. This has increased the contestation over minority policies, more so in the context of Congress's belated attempt in the past few years to shift towards issues of social welfare and well-being of minorities through the Prime Minister's New 15-Point Programme or the initiative to focus development and infrastructure projects in minority concentration districts. Accusing the UPA of 'communalizing the development processes', the BJP said that 'it will go to any extent to stop these efforts and discontinue schemes that allocate more funds to minority dominated districts.'[38] As in the past, the party objected to the incorporation of any special measures or budgetary allocations for minorities and disparaged the latter as 'communal budgeting' and minority appeasement. The rise of communal politics since the mid-1980s has no doubt given a strong boost to the misleading notion of minority appeasement. Even a mention of special treatment provokes cries of minority appeasement, due to the active presence in the public arena of political agents and parties whose sole objective, indeed the very rationale of their existence, is to gain power by encouraging polarization based on the alleged historical division between Hindus and Muslims.[39]

Any notion that India's Muslims are privileged and have enjoyed veto power over the Central and state governments' actions is completely at odds with facts of their actual socio-economic status. As noted earlier, the SCR provides overwhelming evidence of the under-representation of Muslims in the governance of the country. It comprehensively nailed the fallacy of minority appeasement and has shown that the earlier direction of a universalist approach, which is expected to benefit everyone including minorities as against a targeted approach, has not produced the desired results. The SCR observed that Muslims 'carry a double burden of being labeled "anti-national" and as being appeased at the same time.... While Muslims need to prove on a daily basis that they are not anti-national and terrorists, it is not recognized that the alleged appeasement has not resulted in the desired level of socio-economic development of the community.'[40]

For its part, the Congress rejected the argument that it was following a minority appeasement policy. But it appears that these accusations cast a shadow on the UPA government; indeed the reluctance to introduce a minority sub-plan or substantial development programmes towards minorities was largely due to this.

Institutional Framework: NCSC

In each case to monitor the progress of public policies for disadvantaged groups and to provide an institutional forum where communities could present their demands, the Constitution and subsequent legislations created specific institutions. These institutions, designed to monitor constitutional safeguards for different groups, were arguably a major institutional innovation. Among the most significant institutions are the National Human Rights Commission (NHRC), National Commission for Scheduled Castes and Scheduled Tribes (NCSC/ST), the National Commission for Minorities (NCM), and the National Commission for Women (NCW).

Established by Acts of Parliament, both the NCSC/ST and NCM are institutions dedicated to the protection of the interests of disadvantaged groups, and were accorded statutory status roughly at the same time.[41] There are differences with regard to the constitutional mandate, but the internal design, membership, and process of appointment of members of NCSC/ST and NCM is very similar. Over the past fifteen years or so, the two commissions, as statutory bodies, have had varied trajectories and impacts on the patterns of discrimination and exclusion in our society. Apart from the policy approach and institutional context, it is important to note that political processes have the greatest influence on the performance of institutions, and impact on the nature and effectiveness of implementation of pluralism.

The establishment of the NCSC/ST is one of the principal features of the constitutional provisions for this group. In 1978, a multi-member Commission for SCs and STs was established through an executive order of the Ministry of Home Affairs. In 1992, the erstwhile unit of the commissioner for SCs and STs was placed under the multi-member Commission which was given constitutional status. The Commission had the powers of inquiry, and so on, but as a non-statutory body such powers were ineffective. Its basic purpose was to protect and promote the welfare of the SCs and STs. Embedded in an elaborate constellation of laws, policies, and institutions, the NCSC/ST was only one constituent of a set of institutions, policies, and laws designed for protecting the SCs/STs against a variety of injustices and historical discrimination, and monitoring the provisions for access to public institutions.

A separate National Commission for Scheduled Castes came into existence in 2004 when the government took the decision to bifurcate and create two separate commissions for the SCs and the STs. This Commission investigates and monitors the implementation of safeguards provided to the SCs—it covers a wide range of activities which include implementation of laws, provisions relating to reservations in recruitment, promotion, and admission to educational institutions, and economic development, including educational development. The reports of the commission are supposed to be placed before Parliament. However, the First Report of the NCSC (2004–5) was not placed in Parliament until 2008. It is important to note that the responsibility for promoting the welfare of the SCs does not vest exclusively in the NCSC. Besides the Commission, there is the Standing Committee of Parliament on Social Justice and Empowerment, in addition to a parliamentary forum exclusively of SC MPs.[42]

Overall, the NCSC monitors the working and implementation of safeguards on the one hand, and redresses violations of safeguards on the other.[43] It investigates and monitors all matters relating to social, economic, educational and cultural, political, and service safeguards provided for the SCs in the Constitution; evaluates the working of such safeguards; inquires into specific complaints pertaining to the deprivation of rights and safeguards to these sections; advises in the planning process and evaluates the development of these communities; and submits reports annually on the working of the safeguards with appropriate and specific recommendations. It has taken an active interest in investigating complaints of violations of reserved quotas or the abolition of reserved posts or discrimination in promotion. As a result of its concerted efforts, significant gains have been registered in the implementation of reservations and in giving representation to the SCs in public employment. But the attention paid to ensuring the participation of the SCs in public employment is sometimes at the expense of more substantive concerns such as the implementation of social welfare schemes for SCs. The second major area of intervention is monitoring the progress of SCs in education at all levels. The third issue concerns atrocities and here the main focus is on the monitoring of the legal provisions with regard to such incidents. It is least effective in dealing with atrocities largely because the Commission refers the complaints to the very institutions that are either complicit or implicated in the perpetuation of violence.[44] Besides, the Commission has chosen to focus on the implementation of reservations and on monitoring service-related safeguards and has continually monitored recruitment patterns and promotion procedures adopted by the government as well as those in public sector enterprises, nationalized banks, scientific and technical organizations, and universities. Thus, in this context it has taken an active interest in investigating complaints of violations of service safeguards.[45]

There is an elaborate framework of laws and regulatory arrangements which are intended to enforce the constitutional provisions and administer social justice to the SCs. There are at least two major laws to address the problem of anti-Dalit prejudice: the Protection of Civil Rights Act, 1955, and the SC and ST (Prevention of Atrocities) Act, 1989. Under the Protection of Civil Rights Act, 1955, 'enforcing religious disabilities' on the SCs, including preventing their entry into temples, is a punishable crime. Under the same Act, 'enforcing social disabilities', including preventing SCs access to a sanitary convenience, is a punishable crime. The SC/ST (POA) Act, 1989, broadens the definition of atrocity, envisaged as a bold step in Dalit emancipation.[46] Both these Acts aim to eradicate discrimination against SCs and seek to empower them.

Social discrimination persists and so does the stigma attached to persons belonging to lower castes.[47] Numerous studies show the continuation of the practices of untouchability and discrimination.[48] Reports of the NCSC/ST reveal the continuance of social discrimination and that too without penalty.[49] Nowhere in the country has the SC/ST (POA) Act been vigorously enforced and hence it has had a negligible impact on the level of atrocities against SCs. The NHRC Report on Prevention of Atrocities against Scheduled Castes (2004) blamed the 'lopsided enforcement' of the SC/ST (POA) Act, 1989, in several parts of the country for the continuing discrimination against Dalits.[50] Most of the complaints are directed against the conduct of police personnel and security agencies. Both police and civil authorities often collude with dominant castes to deny political rights to the SCs. This report indicts successive governments for their lukewarm attitude to the oppression of Dalits: 'The frequency and intensity of violence,' the report observes, 'is an offshoot of desperate attempts by the upper-caste groups to protect their entrenched status against the process of disengagement and upward mobility among lower castes resulting from affirmative action of State Policy [enshrined in the Constitution of India].'[51]

Official statistics show that on an average 28,016 cases were registered under the Protection of Civil Rights Act (1955) and Prevention of Atrocities Act (1989) (Table 3.4). The highest incidence of crimes against SCs are in Rajasthan (73 cases per one lakh population) followed by Gujarat (62 cases) and Madhya Pradesh (42 cases).[52] While there is a decline in the reported number of cases under the Protection of Civil Rights Act, this does not necessarily represent a marked reduction in the practice of untouchability. Rather it is a reflection of the ineffectiveness of law—a conclusion which tallies with the view expressed by NCSC/ST in its Sixth Report, which observes that a large number of deserving cases are not registered under the SC/ST Prevention of Atrocities Act.[53] State governments have shown no seriousness in identifying untouchability-prone areas and even where this has been done there is no concerted plan to eliminate this practice.[54] The ideology of the caste system has considerably weakened, but it has sometimes assumed newer forms, particularly in the wake of the implementation of the Mandal Commission Report in the 1990s. While caste discrimination is still widespread and untouchability is prevalent in several states, numerous accounts do show that things are changing as a result of new avenues of social mobility. The most radical change has come through admission of SCs in schools and colleges.

Thanks to reservations in the civil services, large numbers of SCs and STs have gained jobs. Most of the progress has come in government employment, where the reservation system offers some protection at all levels from peons to secretaries. Representation of SCs in 1999–2000 was 11.29 per cent in Group A services, 12.68 per cent in Group B, 15.78 per cent in Group C, and 19.99 in Group D posts under the Central government (Table 3.5).[55] Reports of the UPSC and the Ministry of Personnel indicate some improvements in the implementation of reservations, and consequently significant changes in the social background of the bureaucracy.[56] While there still is a shortfall in filling up reserved vacancies, the Ministry of Personnel reported that all vacancies for SCs in the three premier Central services have been filled in 2004–5 and 2005–6.[57] In 2005–6, there was a shortfall of 14.6 per cent of reserved posts, but this was significantly lower than the shortfall of 19.0 per cent in 2004–5. However, the upper castes continue to disproportionately occupy the more prestigious Class I services, while SCs/STs have been relegated to jobs lower in the hierarchy. The total representation of SCs in public sector enterprises was 18 per cent in 2000, but here too they were under-represented in Groups A and B and overrepresented in Group D (Table 3.7).[58]

The noteworthy aspect is the concentration of SCs in Group C and D posts, particularly in the post of sweepers.[59] This shows the persistence of the old caste-based occupational distribution, which affirmative action was supposed to alter. While reservations have surely provided public employment to this traditionally excluded group it has yet to make a dent at the top administrative levels of decision making, which remain predominantly in the hands of the upper castes.[60] This pattern of distribution perpetuated the relation between low-pay/low-status jobs and low castes. Even after nearly sixty years of SC/ST quotas, upper castes control key secretary-level positions in both Central and state governments. A newspaper reported that Brahmins alone occupied 33 of the 78 secretary-level appointments in 2003.[61]

On balance, reservations have worked more effectively than critics would have expected. Every series of data shows steady progress towards higher proportions in government jobs specially and in the public sector generally. Recent data published in the UPSC and the Ministry of Personnel reports mentioned earlier show improvement in the implementation of reservations in the past few years.[62] Similarly, the Planning Commission's Eleventh Plan Report on Empowering the Scheduled Castes commends the implementation of reservation during the last 55 years, especially in the last three decades. The report observes, 'The implementation of reservation policy in public employment and education has succeeded to a greater extent in getting SCs and STs in government services, educational institutions and in legislative assemblies and other bodies.'[63]

Yet, after six decades of reservations, SCs remain worse-off compared to almost all other social groups in terms of social and economic conditions. On most human development indices, the SCs fall below the national average. But they would have been in an even worse situation without mandatory reservation and affirmative action for them. As a consequence of affirmative action, there has been some improvement in the status of SCs. The success lies in a discernible improvement in literacy, school and higher education enrolment, and placement in government jobs. Student enrolment has increased substantially. Although percentages of SCs are still low, they have been able to get access to the fields of engineering, medicine, teaching, law, and the civil services (Table 3.8).[64] Even though it is difficult to estimate the direct benefits gained from reservations in higher education, the presence of about a third of SC and ST students enrolled in significant programmes in universities is attributable to quotas.[65]

Despite all the limitations of reservations, it has enabled the emergence of a middle class among SCs, whose members have been able to join mainstream society and enter new professions and occupations. This is confirmed by D.L. Sheth's empirical study of disadvantaged groups which underlines the point that regardless of historical inequality that characterizes the social condition of SCs, they have begun to enter the middle class.[66] Once one member of the family became a graduate, it was almost certain that his/her children would be graduates as well and would join government service. While the proportion of SCs in the middle class is still small and lower than that of other backward castes, this study shows that significant numbers have been able to acquire education, white-collar jobs, and assets—about 12 per cent have received higher education, almost 10 per cent have white-collar jobs, and almost 21 per cent own houses and other assets.[67] This positive feature was also acknowledged by the NHRC report which was otherwise critical of the inadequate efforts of both government and civil society to radically change the situation of SCs:

> There is no denying that these beneficiaries of affirmative action do encounter some biases in the behaviour of their higher caste colleagues, bosses and even subordinates within institutions/offices they are employed which generate considerable agony and stress. But the economic emancipation affected as a result of a secure job with opportunities for upward mobility and a non-oppressive environment at least ensures a future delinked from their centuries old caste background.[68]

Much of this change has come through political awareness, organization, movements for self-upliftment, and the ability of SCs to take advantage of the state policy of affirmative action in education and employment. This expansion of a middle class among lower castes was vital in providing, from the 1970s onwards (especially in north India), a new layer of activists who took the lead in creating and strengthening cultural and political 'self-respect' movements. Most importantly, low ritual status does not stand in the way of entering the middle class and acquiring middle-class identification. In short, even though the middle class still remains dominated by the upper castes, the possibility for acquiring new means of upward mobility has clearly opened up for the lower castes.

Of all the policies, the provisions for political representation for the SCs have been the most important because it has given considerable power to the disadvantaged groups, but this success has much to do with the political mobilization of the SCs.[69] The best effect of electoral reservation has been to provide a guaranteed minimum number of legislators from the SCs; this provides political presence for a group that would not otherwise get adequate representation. They have the opportunity to influence decisions concerning their group, and through that the restructuring of society as a whole. As a number of commentators have noted, their presence has helped to promote the implementation of preferential treatment programmes even at a time when the economically powerful groups make demands for greater resources. Barbara Joshi points out that 'legislators from reserved constituencies are some of the most consistent supporters of a wide range of policies designed to reduce general social and economic disparities.'[70] Affirmative action policies not only directly benefit lower castes through welfare schemes but also have a larger impact on public policies when individuals from lower castes are given a voice in the decision-making process.[71]

The significant increase in the presence of the SCs in public institutions has been the most important achievement of these policies. The increased representation helps to advance the overall welfare and development of SCs. Recent studies show that welfare policies in conjunction with political reservation have increased redistribution of resources in favour of these groups.[72] The improvement in human development indicators such as income levels, employment, health, and education, with some alleviation of poverty levels, is to some extent due to affirmative action.[73] However, the rate of improvement is slow and it is not enough to bridge the gap and to bring the SCs and STs on par with non-SCs/STs, which has indeed been the declared objective of government policy towards these groups. Even at an improved level of human development, the disparities between the socially marginalized SCs and STs and the non-SCs/STs persist to a significant degree. This is because the improvements in case of SCs/STs are comparatively less than in case of other groups (excluding the minorities). The unsympathetic attitude of the bureaucracy is among the main reasons for the failure of many a development initiative. Thus, a number of schemes meant for SCs have been ineffective for want of funds, or because much of the funds allotted for special projects remain unspent. Schemes such as the SCP have also not done enough to bring relief to SCs, owing to the lack of political will to implement it.

India embarked on a programme of affirmative action, which is perhaps without parallel in scale and dimension in human history. However, much remains to be done to bring to an end the discrimination and inequality perpetuated on SCs over the centuries. Affirmative action has brought them into central roles considered unimaginable a few decades ago. It has made Dalits conscious of their rights and they have learnt that in a democratic environment these rights and claims will come through social movements and electoral mobilization.[74] But the redistributive effects have not been spread evenly throughout the beneficiary groups or different regions. The single-minded focus on reservation as the sole instrument of social equality has allowed political regimes to recognize the claims of subordinate groups without having to bring in structural changes or concede to them an important share of economic power.

National Commission for Minorities

Initially set up as a non-statutory body through a home ministry resolution in January 1978, the creation of the NCM was a response to the frequent appeals from Muslim organizations that the government set up a Minority Commission to check the increasing incidents of violence and discrimination against minorities. With the enactment of the National Commission of Minorities Act, 1992, it became a statutory body. The first statutory commission was set up in 1993. Since 1992, fifteen states have set up state-level minorities commissions.

The NCM was established as an institutional mechanism to monitor the working of constitutional safeguards provided for minorities in the Constitution and in laws enacted by Parliament and state legislatures. It performs a number of functions for the implementation and protection of safeguards provided under the law and makes recommendations in this regard to Central as well as state governments. The mandate of the NCM was to (1) evaluate the progress of the development of minorities under the Union and states, (2) monitor the working of the safeguards provided in the Constitution and in laws enacted by Parliament and the state legislatures, (3) look into specific complaints regarding deprivation of rights and safeguards of the minorities and take up such matters with the appropriate authorities, (4) study problems arising out of any discrimination against minorities and recommend measures for their removal, (5) conduct studies, research, and analysis on the issues relating to socio-economic and educational development of minorities, (6) suggest appropriate measures in respect of any minority to be undertaken by the Central government or the state governments, and (7) make periodical or special reports to the Central government on any matter pertaining to minorities and in particular the difficulties confronted by them. For the past few years a system of holding meetings in state capitals to review pending cases with respective state governments was introduced; as a result of the review pending cases could be settled.

The listing of responsibilities of the NCM is more or less on the same lines as the other statutory commissions for the disadvantaged communities or the NCSC. However, the NCSC (or NCST) monitors very specific and substantial safeguards which include the abolition of untouchability, child labour, traffic in human beings, and restrictions on temple entry; educational safeguards (reservations in educational institutions); political safeguards (reservations in legislatures); and service safeguards (reservations in public employment and for purposes of promotion). While the NCM's mandate is to monitor progress of minorities, which provides the commission a wide-ranging remit, it is the implementation of constitutional safeguards that has been its central concern.

The NCM works under the Ministry of Minority Affairs. Before the formation of this ministry it came under the Ministry of Social Justice and Empowerment. Theoretically, all the commissions are autonomous, but practically they lack effective autonomy from the government. This is most evident in the operations of state minority commissions, which function roughly like government departments and are dependent on the state government. Besides the lack of autonomy, both state commissions and the NCM do not have the powers for proper investigation of complaints. Its functioning is contingent on the goodwill of state governments which are often unwilling to heed the advice of the Commission if it is politically inconvenient for them.

The NCM receives complaints from individuals as well as organizations. During 2002–6, the Commission received approximately 15,644 complaints.[75] These relate to three areas. The first pertains to security concerns of minorities, the second concerns complaints of discrimination faced by minorities, and the third concerns the educational and economic backwardness of minorities.

However, there are very few complaints on economic matters because there are no constitutional safeguards on service matters for minorities. It is also supposed to monitor the representation of minorities in public employment and has routinely documented the under-representation of Muslims in government jobs, but in the absence of affirmative action, this exercise has not had much impact in increasing their representation in government jobs. From the vantage point of institutional efficacy, it is obvious that the NCM has been least effective with regard to socio-economic and job-related grievances of minorities.

In the absence of a clear definition or law on discrimination in relation to religious minorities, it is difficult to establish that an individual complaint or grievance arises from discrimination and not general unresponsiveness, lack of interest, or sympathy on the part of the officer concerned as against discrimination against minorities. Because discrimination against minorities is not legalized, government departments are reluctant to recognize or concede the existence of discrimination. Hence, complaints and grievances of discrimination are routinely processed without much chance of redressal.[76]

The NCM submits to Parliament annual reports on the implementation of safeguards provided for minorities along with the action taken by the Union government on the recommendations relating to and the reasons for the non-acceptance, if any, of such recommendations. However, in practice, despite the statutory directive to have the reports placed in Parliament, these reports do not regularly come to Parliament. The Commission recommended 'a time bound system for laying the Annual Reports of the NCM in both Houses of Parliament so that the Members of Parliament may know what the Commission has done for the minority communities.'[77] In this regard the Standing Committee of the Ministry of Social Justice and Empowerment observed that the tabling of reports 'would inspire a sense of confidence amongst minorities and would portray the commitment on the part of the government to work for the welfare of the minorities.'[78] The NCM calls for an Action Taken Report (ATR) from the government on its recommendation. When ATRs get placed in Parliament, they indicate that the government has not taken much action. For example, the NCM recommended the need to establish a Joint Parliamentary Committee (JPC) for minorities on the pattern of the JPC for SCs/STs. Such a Committee can examine the NCM Annual Reports, irrespective of whether such reports have been tabled in Parliament or not. However, despite repeated suggestions and recommendations of the Commission[79] and of the Ministry of Minority Affairs for a separate Parliamentary Standing Committee, it did not materialize even two years after the creation of the ministry in early 2006. The minister for parliamentary affairs could not establish it as the requisite number of MPs did not convey their willingness to be members of the Committee. Hence, the Standing Committee of Parliament on Social Justice and Empowerment continues to have the jurisdiction to look after the interests of minorities as well. But this is not enough. In the absence of a parliamentary forum exclusively for minorities, there is a lack of voice and articulation of the needs and concerns of minorities.

Some differences in the functioning of the two commissions are worth noting however. These differences relate to their powers and, more significantly, to the very different conception of safeguards for caste and minority groupings. Envisaged as a proactive organization, the NCSC has power to investigate any matter relating to safeguards for the SCs, inquire into specific complaints regarding deprivation of rights and safeguards, and participate in the planning for socio-economic development of the SCs.[80] There is a substantial government apparatus (replicated in the states) to cater to the needs and concerns of the SCs.

Although the NCM has the powers of a civil court to summon any person, receive evidence on affidavit, or examine any witness, it does not have the machinery to investigate complaints of discrimination and deprivation of rights and safeguards of minorities. In view of this limitation, the UPA government promised to upgrade the status of the NCM to a constitutional body. The Constitution (103rd Amendment) Bill, 2004, seeks to confer constitutional status on the NCM. This has been approved by the Parliamentary Standing Committee on Social Justice and

Empowerment, which noted that 'in the absence of vocal powers of inquiring and investigation the NCM would be a toothless tiger and hampered a great deal in carrying out its mandate.'[81] The power to investigate and to advise in the policy process of socio-economic development of minorities would put the NCM on par with other commissions. It would also enhance its watchdog role as also its efficacy. The proposed legislation granting constitutional status was introduced in December 2006 but had not been passed by Parliament till 2008.

The NCM does not participate and advise in the process of socio-economic development of minorities as there is very little by way of planning for minority development. In comparison, a crucial advantage that the NCSC has over the NCM in this regard is that it works within an established policy framework backed by reservations and encouraged by the constitutional provisions of social equality in favour of disadvantaged caste groups. The NCSC is part of an ambitious structure of policies and institutions for the social uplift of the SCs/STs. Consultations and interface with the Planning Commission and various ministries on matters relating to SCs can therefore take place on a regular basis.

The lack of national consensus on policies towards minorities stems from the pervasive belief that the focus, post-Partition, of state policy towards minorities has to be on religious and cultural dimensions rather than on social and economic aspects of minority rights, since the latter is prohibited by the Constitution. Some of this reluctance was obviously due to continuing resentment against the colonial policy of special rights and separate electorates that created and reinforced a space for hardening of religious identities and laid the seeds for the emergence of majoritarianism in India. Afraid of wading into politically contentious waters, secular politicians have been reluctant to take stand in this regard. This hands-off approach left socio-economic issues largely unaddressed.

However, in the light of the SCR's conclusions with regard to the deprivation and marginalization of Muslims, there exists a strong case for state intervention to ensure that the dismal picture in this respect changes, whether in educational or socio-economic terms. Affirmative action in the form of minority welfare programmes or allocations of funds for minority development are as constitutional as any other programme meant for the protection and advancement of other disadvantaged and deprived groups. This is because all plans and schemes for affirmative action, whether for the deprived minorities or disadvantaged castes, are decisions regarding allocation of funds and distribution of resources which depend on the discretion of the government. This does not involve issues of constitutionality or otherwise as these are choices that governments are called upon to make in relation to their social priorities. The basic issue, therefore, is not with regard to constitutionality but with regard to political processes because of which the category of minority remains contentious and is always seen as perpetrating vote-bank politics. The Constitution provides enough space to give social equality overriding priority. Such an approach is entirely consistent with the unique constitutional compact between the Indian state and disadvantaged groups, and the exceptional constitutional stress on non-discrimination and equal rights for all. As Irfan Habib has observed, 'The state needs to undertake measures to remove such backwardness; it is immaterial whether class, caste, region, or religion defines such a section of the people.'[82] Nevertheless, the constitutional issue has cropped up repeatedly to frustrate any policy of affirmative action. A major forward movement has been blocked by the argument that minority development schemes militate against constitutional principles, which seek to make identities less salient for participation in the modern economy and politics.

Such neglect is gratuitous, especially since the politics of Muslim communities in the last two decades has been quite similar to that of other disadvantaged groups who are struggling for a greater share in power and governance. The centre of gravity has moved away from Muslim elites, who had traditionally provided leadership and focused on identity concerns, to the more underprivileged sections and their leaders, who are relatively more concerned with the welfare and well-being of their constituents. In this respect, the politics of the newly active groups among Muslims is very similar to the politics of groups adjacent to them in socio-economic status. The demolition of the Babri mosque brought about a radical change in the orientation and disposition of Muslims towards the nation and the state.[83] Since then there is no dearth of social/political mobilization in defence of secularism and around development issues. Much like the assertion of lower castes, which has taken an organized form since the late 1980s, Muslims have invariably rallied around positive demands for economic and political empowerment. Across India, the winds of democratic politics and the influx of the underprivileged into the field of democratic participation reinforced the importance of these groupings in policy making and the public domain. This has produced a new political discourse, which is clearly in favour of empowerment and more willing to demand their rights as citizens and due share in governance. The discussions and mobilization around the SCR have reinforced the trend of democratization of Muslim communities, described by Javeed Alam as 'citizen politics'.[84] Thus, issues of equality, equal rights, jobs, education, health, and housing have come to the forefront of Muslim politics.

Overall, it is important to note that minorities are not the only targets of neglect. In fact, SCs have been the main victims of neglect, discrimination, and violence. However, special treatment and constitutional safeguards for SCs have begun to change this to some extent. Over six decades after Independence, the project of empowering SCs remains a matter of substantial national consensus, although there have been some questions as regards its continuation, and concerns that its benefits are cornered by a few elites, not the really deserving. This consensus has much to do with the ideology of India's freedom struggle, the social contract it stood for, and the kind of nation it sought to build. Keen to eliminate caste inequality, the framers of our Constitution took an unequivocal view of the nature of the state and public intervention required to reduce social inequities and discrimination, ranging from the abolition of untouchability to giving representation in public services and legislatures. The state in turn devised numerous policy schemes for the social welfare and advancement of the SCs. The improvement in the performance of the SCs in certain sectors illustrates the importance of these policies of affirmative action in bringing about change.

With respect to both groups, there remains a gap between policy and practice, however. The laws and safeguards promoting social equality are on the statute books but most disadvantaged groups remained poor and marginalized. The functioning of these two Commissions—each intended to address a particular facet of disadvantage and marginalization in a society and under a state committed to democracy, equality, and pluralism—illustrates that real empowerment of the disadvantaged groups would come only from the state and society unveiling concrete strategies geared to a larger vision of achieving substantive equality.

However, policies towards minorities have been further constrained by the absence of a substantive conception of equality to promote the principle of equality of opportunity for minorities. The key issue is the contested nature of minority rights and the attempt to ground it in a minimalist conception of minority rights.[85] Even after all these years it has not been possible to achieve a political consensus on substantive state support and special provisions for minorities. The lack of a national consensus on public policies towards minorities tends to undermine the institutional efficacy of the NCM. However, from the standpoint of minority protection the sheer existence of the NCM has helped to signal the importance of minority rights and protection of these rights. Today there is much greater focus on social sector programmes that include access to education (scholarship schemes for students from minority backgrounds), enhanced access to credit through priority lending, and infrastructure development in minority-concentration districts. Some of these are aimed at poverty alleviation and provision of physical infrastructure such as housing, civic amenities, and health infrastructure.

The trajectory of government's minority policy suggests that it can work effectively only when there is a strongly articulated political and policy consensus on minorities. The foot-dragging on the part of political leadership in coming to grips with the facts and actual details of the deprivation of minority groups, especially Muslims, would indicate that the prevailing international and national political context has an inhibiting effect on the willingness of politicians to chart any new course of action for minority empowerment. Sure enough, empowerment and advancement of minorities is an uphill task because the deeper notion of minorities entails the inclusion of minorities in the development process and the sharing of shrinking jobs and scarce resources for social development among various disadvantaged groups, which can engender conflict and competition.

Notes

1. Lelah Dushkin (1967: 626–36).
2. David Stuligross and Ashutosh Varshney (2002: 440–2).
3. S.K. Thorat (2002).
4. Rajeev Dhavan (1987).
5. Bhiku Parekh (1999).
6. Bishnu Mohapatra (2002: 172–3).
7. S.K. Thorat (2002).
8. For an overview of policies, see S.R. Sankaran (2000: 507–33); B.N. Srivastava (2000: 573–602).
9. On central initiatives such as the SCP, see Chapter III on Economic Development of the Scheduled Castes, Sixth Report 1999–2000 and 2000–01, NCSC/ST (2001: 28–32).
10. Ibid.
11. Ibid., pp. 29–31.
12. Report of the Working Group on the Empowerment of Scheduled Castes, Eleventh Five Year Plan (2007–2012).
13. NHRC Report on Prevention of Atrocities Against Scheduled Castes (2004).
14. On minority rights, see Rajeev Bhargava (2000); Gurpreet Mahajan (1998 [a] and 1998 [b]); Akeel Bilgrami (1996); Myron Weiner (1997); Bishnu Mohapatra (2002).
15. The SCR used data from the Census of India, National Sample Surveys, and data from banking and financial institutions, government commissions, ministries, public sector undertakings, universities, etc. For details see *SCR* (2006: 5–6).
16. Zoya Hasan and Ritu Menon (2004), see especially Chapter 2 on socio-economic status of households.
17. *SCR* (2006: 2).
18. Ibid., p. 65.
19. Ibid., pp. 89–93.
20. Rafiq Zakaria (2004).

21. Gopal Singh Committee Report (1983).

22. *SCR* (2006: 10). See also, the symposium on the Sachar Committee in *Economic and Political Weekly*, Vol. 43, No. 30.

23. The corpus fund for the Maulana Azad Educational Foundation which shoulders the responsibility for the promotion of education was a modest Rs 70 crore in the Tenth Plan. Report of the Working Group on Empowering the Minorities, Tenth Five Year Plan, Planning Commission (2001:19).

24. Ibid., p. 14.

25. *The Asian Age*, 25 September 2006.

26. Speech of Sonia Gandhi, at the inauguration of India Islamic Cultural Centre, New Delhi, 12 June 2006. Reported in *The Hindu*, 13 June 2006.

27. The Prime Minister's New 15-Point Programme covers, among other things: (1) Enhancing opportunities for education, (2) Equitable share in economic activities and employment, (3) Improving the conditions of living of minorities, and (4) Prevention and control of communal riots. It was also decided that 15 per cent of the funds may be earmarked wherever possible in relevant schemes/programmes for the nationally declared minorities.

28. Report of the Working Group on Empowering the Minorities, Eleventh Five Year Plan, Planning Commission (2007a).

29. Eleventh Five Year Plan, Chapter on Minorities, Planning Commission.

30. Report of the Working Group on Empowering the Minorities, Eleventh Five Year Plan, Planning Commission (2007a).

31. Farah Naqvi (2006).

32. Ibid.

33. NCM chairman's speech at the Annual Conference of State Minorities Commissions held in Delhi on 16 January 2008. Reported in *The Tribune*, 17 January 2008.

34. Bhalchandra Mungekar's comments made at the Annual Conference of State Minorities Commissions. Reported in *The Tribune*, 17 January 2008.

35. *The Economic Times*, 12 December 2006.

36. Prime minister's speech reported in *The Indian Express*, 19 December 2007.

37. *The Indian Express*, 20 December 2007.

38. *The Indian Express*, 29 January 2008.

39. Gyanendra Pandey (1993: 2338–72).

40. *SCR* (2006: 10–11).

41. Bishnu Mohapatra and Niraja Gopal Jayal (2004); Niraja Gopal Jayal (2006); and Tahir Mahmood (2001).

42. The nodal ministry for SCs is the Ministry of Social Justice and Empowerment, while for the minorities it is the newly created Ministry of Minority Affairs. Before the formation of the Ministry of Minority Affairs, the Ministry of Social Justice and Empowerment was dealing with minorities as well.

43. Sixth Report 1999–2000 and 2000–2001, NCSC/ST (2001).

44. Ibid.

45. See discussion of NCSC in Niraja Gopal Jayal (2006: 76–7).

46. Ibid. This Act defines atrocity as an offence punishable under Sections 3 (1) and (2), and lists twenty-two offences relating to various patterns of behaviour inflicting criminal offences for shattering the self-respect and esteem of the persons belonging to the SCs/STs, denial of economic, democratic, and social rights, discrimination, exploitation, and abuse of the legal process, etc.

47. Report on Prevention of Atrocities Against Scheduled Castes, NHRC (2004). The report indicts successive governments for their lukewarm attitude to the oppression of Dalits. 'The frequency and intensity of violence,' the report observes, 'is an offshoot of desperate attempts by the upper-caste groups to protect their entrenched status against the process of disengagement and upward mobility among lower castes resulting from affirmative action of State Policy [enshrined in the Constitution of India].'

48. See articles on different aspects of the continuing impact of caste on discrimination in *Economic and Political Weekly*, Vol. XLII, No. 41, especially Sukhdeo Thorat and Katherine S. Newman. This paper highlights the ways in which caste persists as a system of inequality and its continuing influence on the economy and allocation of labour and other critical resources.

49. NCSC/ST, Sixth Report 1999–2000 and 2000–2001 (2001).

50. NHRC (2004), Report on Prevention of Atrocities Against Scheduled Castes.

51. Ibid., p. 102.

52. NCSC/ST Sixth Report 1999–2000 and 2000–2001 (2001).

53. Ibid., pp. 207–19.

54. Report on Prevention of Atrocities against Scheduled Castes, NHRC (2004: 25).

55. NCSC/ST Sixth Report 1999–2000 and 2000–2001 (2001).

56. Annual Report, Union Public Service Commission (2004: 29).

57. Annual Report, Union Public Service Commission (2005).

58. Sixth Report 1999–2000 and 2000–2001, NCSC/ST (2001: 181–2).

59. Report of the Working Group on the Empowerment of Scheduled Castes, Eleventh Five Year Plan (2007: 79).

60. Sixth Report 1999–2000 & 2000–01.

61. *The Indian Express*, 23 June 2003 cited in Niraja Gopal Jayal (2006).

62. Ministry of Personnel, Public Grievances and Pensions (2005).

63. Report of the Working Group on the Empowerment of Scheduled Castes, Eleventh Five Year Plan (2007b: 81).

64. Ibid., p. 25.

65. Thomas Weisskopf (2004).

66. D.L. Sheth (2002: 227).

67. Ibid., p. 228.

68. Report on Prevention of Atrocities against Scheduled Castes, NHRC (2004: 142).

69. For an assessment, see Oliver Mendelsohn and Marika Vicziani (2000:145–6).

70. Barbara Joshi (1982).

71. Rohini Pande (2003).

72. Ibid., pp. 1132–51.

73. Sukhdeo Thorat, M. Mahamallik, and S.Venkateshan (2007: 51–2).

74. Partha Ghosh (1997: 143).

75. Information on complaints on the NCM Website: URL CMS http://110.21.151.69/cms/welcome.htm.

76. Niraja Gopal Jayal (2006: 78).

77. Annual Report, National Commission for Minorities (2006: 45).

78. Report of the Standing Committee of the Ministry of Social Justice and Empowerment (2005).

79. Annual Report, National Commission for Minorities (2006).

80. Report of the Standing Committee on Social Justice and Empowerment (2006).

81. Ibid.

82. Irfan Habib (2006).

83. Javeed Alam (2008: 45–54).

84. Ibid., p. 49.

85. Bishnu Mohapatra (2002: 187).

4

Caste, Social Backwardness, and OBC Reservations (Mandal I and II)

In the last few decades, the expansion of group-based preferential policies has dominated public debates in India. Even as affirmative action programmes worldwide have come under fire from people advocating group-blind policies, India has persisted with and even gone ahead to expand mandatory reservations and affirmative action, which are by any standards unprecedented in their scope and extent and radical in their content. Both Central and state governments have implemented, in varying degrees, policies for reservations that aim to increase opportunities for backward classes/castes in government employment and education.[1] The access of these castes to public institutions was traditionally low. Though the government's position in 1950 was that only two groups—the SCs and the STs—are entitled to reservations, it had been extended to OBCs in public employment in 1994, but not to the legislatures. Earlier in August 1990, Prime Minister V.P. Singh of the Janata Dal-led National Front government had announced the implementation of reservations in government jobs for the OBCs in the Central government (we shall call this 'Mandal I'). More than fifteen years later, in April 2006, the UPA government made moves to introduce reservations for the OBCs in institutions of higher and professional education ('Mandal II'). The Mandal Commission, which submitted its report in 1980, had recommended 27 per cent reservations in both the government and the education sector, but V.P. Singh did not extend it to educational institutions because he was apprehensive that it was likely to fuel even stronger protests, and could thus dissipate the political gains from reservations in public services. Both decisions have been a major source of conflict. For any understanding of why this is so, it is important to separate Mandal I and Mandal II. Mandal I essentially acted as a catalyst to open up the political and bureaucratic system for sections of the OBCs. Mandal II seeks to increase educational access and opportunities for disadvantaged groups at the point when the post-Independence consensus on the Nehruvian mixed economy model has broken down and been replaced by a market-driven model; hence, reservations for the OBCs in the new context have proved to be more controversial.

The first section of this chapter outlines the political context of the emergence of the backward-caste reservation issue in the 1970s and 1980s. The second section discusses Mandal I and the third focuses on the controversy generated by the UPA government's decision to extend reservations for OBCs in higher education. The last two sections seek to explore the OBC reservation controversy by drawing from the public debate over the decisions of the governments of the Janata Dal and the UPA to introduce reservations in government employment and higher education. They also look at the processes whereby the caste and class issues got entangled, and also the questions of how to classify traditionally disadvantaged and under-represented groups and where to draw the line in terms of caste versus class.

Two issues have dominated policy debates regarding reservations for OBCs. The first issue is whether caste is presently an indicator of disadvantage at all, especially in the case of OBCs. The key issue is whether OBCs should be identified on the basis of caste or on the basis of economic and occupational criteria. The second issue pertains to the conception of backwardness itself. Backwardness, as it was widely defined, excluded non-Hindus. Both issues assume a new importance in the context of the vast social and economic changes that have taken place in the country in the past two decades which affect social relations and also raise further questions with regard to the fairness and relevance of reservation policies and their implications for excluded groups.

Who are the Backward Classes?

Unlike the SCs and STs, the groups identified under the OBC category are not enumerated in the decennial censuses. The National Commission for Backward Classes (NCBC) only lists *jatis* without any demographic data about these jatis. Their population is estimated to range from 25 per cent to 52 per cent (Table 4.1). Viewed from the national or the state level, the OBCs constitute a more heterogeneous category than the SCs and STs. However, the category of OBCs has become extremely influential in the public policies and democratic politics of the post-Independence period. Marc Galanter identifies two main types of usage of backward classes that emerged after the listing of SCs in 1935: (1) an inclusive usage to designate all those who need special treatment including the SCs and STs, and (2) the stratum above the SCs, that is, the OBCs of present-day reservation policy.[2] Most of the OBCs belong to peasant and agrarian communities; they are not untouchable but are considered backward owing to their lowly peasant status and because they lack education and access to public institutions.

The Constitution provided clear policies of reservations for SCs but it did not do so in the same unambiguous terms for the backward castes, even though the OBCs as an official category gained currency during the Constituent Assembly debates. There was no clarity regarding the definition and criterion of social backwardness in relation to the OBCs; the 'backward classes retained a multiplicity of meanings.'[3] Some would confine this category to the lowly and those that are comparable to the SCs and STs; others use it to describe a wide middle stratum of society. There is further disagreement over whether the term refers to the less well-off or whether it encompasses only those communities that suffer historical discrimination or 'backwardness' as a group.[4]

There was considerable debate going back to the colonial period over whether reservations should be extended to the backward castes that have not suffered the stigma of untouchability. The idea that the OBCs do not suffer from the historic wrongs of the caste system was quite strong among members of the Constituent Assembly and the

Congress, which did not accept the reasoning that remedies similar to those for the SCs should be extended to them. The discussion revolved around the question of whether to identify groups on the basis of social and economic criteria of backwardness, or with reference to the specific criteria of ritual and social exclusion, or more broadly in terms of low status in the caste system.[5] Despite these disagreements, the OBCs have been the beneficiaries of reservations from the colonial period. But there is a difference in the purpose of reservations for these two categories. In the case of SCs and STs, reservations aimed to enhance equality of opportunity for these groups, while the intention of reservations for the OBCs was to increase representation and power sharing.[6] The former aimed to achieve greater equality while the latter sought to change the balance of power.[7] It is important to note that reservations for the SCs and STs never came under serious challenge because their identity exists outside the reservations regime. There was a strong consensus that SCs/STs had been subjected to such extreme subordination that their case for reservations was self-evident.

After Independence, the number of groups entitled to reservation was expanded to include the OBCs. The expression 'backward classes' had appeared for the first time in 1870 in Madras Presidency. From the beginning it varied from region to region and it was left to each state/region to define the term 'backward' and the category of 'backward communities'. Despite the ambiguity, one thing was clear: the point of reference was the Hindu social structure and not classes in the broader social sense. Also, despite ambiguities, the provinces of Bombay, Madras, and Mysore had instituted reservations of jobs and seats for them in education. When India became independent, Nehru gave them a new name—'other backward classes'[8]—implying classes other than the untouchables and tribes. The Constitution refers to 'backward classes' in Articles 15 (4) and 16 (4), under which the state is empowered to make special provision for any socially and educationally backward classes of citizens.[9] But in its usage it was an all-encompassing category that would include the underprivileged and the marginalized castes: 'it was not a class category and it has been understood to mean certain castes.'[10]

Article 340 empowers the state to appoint a commission 'to investigate the condition of socially and educationally backward classes'. At the all-India level two such commissions have so far been appointed. In 1953, Kaka Kalelkar, an erstwhile disciple of Gandhi, was asked to head the first Backward Classes Commission to investigate the possibility of giving reservations to OBCs. The Commission comprising eleven members submitted its report to the Central government in 1955. It drew up a list of 2,329 castes representing about 32 per cent of the population as forming the bulk of the 'socially and educationally backward classes'. The majority of members selected four criteria for defining backwardness: (1) low social position in the caste hierarchy of Hindu society, (2) lack of general educational advancement among a major section of the caste or community, (3) inadequate or no representation in government service, and (4) inadequate representation in trade, commerce, and industry.[11] The caste criterion was accorded the key role in the identification of beneficiaries. Five of the members, including Kalelkar, voiced their dissent on various grounds. In his dissenting note, the chairman argued that 'backwardness could be tackled on a number of bases other than caste.'[12] For him the establishment of casteless and classless society was important and this demands identification of backward classes based on economic criteria and not on the basis of caste. In an important sense, Kalelkar's disapproval of the use of caste as the most important criterion for identifying backward classes and his argument that it may serve to perpetuate distinctions represented the agreed view of the time.

The report was tabled in Parliament but its recommendations were not implemented by the Central government, which was lukewarm about it as it was in favour of the economic criteria. The government was worried that the report had given too much importance to caste compared to other socio-economic indicators and this could deepen social divisions. The Ministry of Home Affairs in 1956 argued that the use of caste category may serve to maintain and even perpetuate the existing distinctions on the basis of caste.[13] Home Minister Govind Ballabh Pant added another argument in 1961 when he informed the chief ministers of Nehru's decision not to adopt the specific policy in favour of OBC at the federal level:

reservation measures would have the drawback of penalizing the most capable (and deserving) people, and would therefore hinder efficiency in the administration and business.[14] The Congress government decided not to act on the report's recommendations with regard to Central government jobs, but invited the state governments to go ahead and 'draw up their own lists of backward classes and fix their own quotas for reservations'. Its negative attitude has been attributed by some scholars to the 'the modernist attitude which permeated Nehru's government'.[15] Arguably, this attitude also explains why Pant rejected the Commission's report.

It is true that the Kalelkar report was rejected by the Central government because of uneasiness with the divisiveness associated with caste categories in policy making. It obviously indicated the Congress's reluctance to recognize caste as the sole criterion for affirmative action. Caste and caste-based reservation were disregarded in favour of economic criteria, but the latter was not used as the basis for devising an economically driven reservation programme. The rejection of the report made no material difference to the primacy of caste, which dominated both political and policy discourse. Several states set up Backward Classes Commissions and instituted reservations for castes.

The Congress leadership as a whole was not so immersed in class-oriented politics as to leave no space for the accommodation of caste identities. If backward castes found the Congress less accommodating, this was because of the strong influence of upper castes over the Congress rather than any high-minded concerns for economic deprivation. Even in the high noon of modernist politics and economic planning and development under state auspices in the 1950s, caste had not been relegated to the background. During this period, public policy debates and party strategies continued to be organized around the categories of caste and region, and not class, with the sole exception of the communist parties, which focused on class politics. In the decades immediately after Independence, the Constitution, parliamentary legislation, and the Congress party made symbolic commitments to provide for educational, social, and economic advance of the poorest sections under the rhetoric of socialist pattern of society. But economic interests and class issues did not become the basis of mobilization, while caste categories and issues did. This was even though liberal modernist intellectuals and left-radical parties, who believed that caste had lost its significance, dominated the political discourse on caste. The fact remains that reservation policies, with caste as the main units classified as backward, were the most concrete and well defined of all government policies.[16]

Even though the Congress was reluctant to recognize caste as a justifiable criterion for reservations for backward classes, there can be little doubt that 'backwardness' was defined mainly in caste terms and this was privileged over all other social axes of differentiation. Rejection of the report set in motion a process of mobilization by the backward castes for recognition of the primacy of caste over the economic criterion.[17] The rejection of reservations in the Central government was only a partial setback for the OBCs, as several states had already granted them extensive reservations in government employment and educational institutions. States in south India were the first to implement the affirmative action programmes for low castes, and these policies were gradually applied to other parts of India. In most southern states, which have had some form of reservations since at least the 1920s, governments have been responsive to the demands of the backward castes for job quotas and upper castes have had to accept it, albeit reluctantly. The appointment of Backward Classes Commissions in the 1960s led to an increase in reservations in all the southern states, although their representation in the Central services was inadequate.[18] Reservation quotas vary from state to state, ranging from 73 per cent in Karnataka and 60 per cent in Tamil Nadu to 5 per cent in Himachal Pradesh.

Consequently, when attention is shifted from the national to the state level and to broader historical dynamics, it becomes apparent that the political mobilization of backward castes was quite strong and long-standing in certain regions where they constituted a large proportion of the population, and it would have been difficult to disregard their claim for too long even at the national level. It is thus important to distinguish between Central and state policies and to note that several states had not only provided reservations for the OBCs but had gone much beyond the 50 per cent limit. (This limit was later prescribed by the Supreme Court in 1994 as the upper limit for reservations.) Besides, it is useful to bear in mind that opposition to reservations at the Central level did not rule out sharing power with lower castes and political formations supported by them in other parts of the country. In the context of the emergence of a federal polity and the enormous clout exercised by states and regions, one cannot overstate the critical part played by backward-caste politics and the success of political formations in Tamil Nadu, Karnataka, Kerala, and Maharashtra in shaping the debate on affirmative action policies and backward-caste-led power-sharing arrangements. An emphasis on the Central level and Congress opposition to reservation for OBCs at this level tends to obscure the broader dynamics of growing backward caste influence in the states which was bound to affect the Centre.

The presence of a relatively larger proportion of upper castes in some key northern states such as Uttar Pradesh and Bihar acted as a constraint on the advance of backward castes in north India. It was the influence commanded by upper castes over the Congress party in Uttar Pradesh—the heartland of the Congress—that led to a corresponding refusal to accommodate backward-caste interests. This paved the way for non-Congress parties to take up the backward-caste issue in a major way from the late 1960s, and more forcefully after the defeat of the Congress in the post-Emergency 1977 elections. The backward-caste mobilization had already called into question the upper-caste dominance in national public institutions, which had been taken for granted in the early decades of Independent India, particularly as this dominance remained unaffected by the centrally administered reservations for SCs and STs. However, there was recognition of the need for the accommodation of backward castes in the political system. The social demographics and the larger proportion of upper castes in some of the northern states, and not differences over the primacy of caste as against class, delayed this process of accommodation and the evolution of a consistent national policy.

It was only a matter of time before the state officially acknowledged caste as the principal criterion for defining backwardness. Besides, the states had the option to choose their own criterion to define backwardness and many commissions appointed by the state governments between the mid-1960s and 1980s chose to define it on the basis of caste for the purpose of preferential treatment in education and employment under Articles 15 and 16. Initially, courts favoured the use of economic criteria for the implementation of quotas. In *Balaji* v. *The State of Mysore* the court clearly stated that 'the classification of backwardness cannot be made on the basis of caste.'[19] The All India Backward Classes Federation (AIBCF) had since the early 1960s been pressing for the implementation of reservations on the basis of caste. The Backward Class Commissions in the states identified backwardness on the basis of caste, and government policies that emanated from their reports granted reservations on this basis. By the time the Mandal Commission came up for implementation, economic criteria had been all but given up. The courts intervened to resolve the issue of eligibility invariably in favour of an acceptance of the caste basis.

Mandal I: Reservations in Public Employment

It was left to the Second Backward Classes Commission, constituted on 20 December 1978, during the Janata Party regime at the Centre, to examine the desirability or otherwise of making a provision for the reservation for backward classes that were not adequately represented in public services.[20] The Commission fully embraced caste as the defining criteria for backwardness. Its report marked a watershed in redefining the official discourse, which had from the time of Kalelkar's dissenting note sought to emphasize economic backwardness as an important factor for decisions with regard to social and educational backwardness. Disregarding the approach of the Kalelkar Commission, the Mandal Commission charted its approach on the lines adopted by State Commissions which had defined backwardness in caste terms rather than socio-economic terms. The Mandal Commission Report argued: '... It may be possible to make out a very plausible case for not accepting caste as a criterion for defining "social and educational backwardness". But the substitution of caste by economic tests will amount to ignoring the genesis of social backwardness in Indian society.'[21] The point to note is that it drew on a Supreme Court judgment which states that 'class means a homogeneous section of people grouped together because of likenesses or common traits, and who are identifiable by some common attributes such as status, rank, occupation, residence, race, religion and the like.'[22] The Commission, headed by Bindeshwari Prasad Mandal, former chief minister of Bihar, estimated the population of OBCs to be around 52 per cent. It recommended a reservation of 27 per cent for OBCs; this would be in addition to the 22.5 per cent posts for SCs and STs already reserved in all services and public sector undertakings.

When the Commission submitted its report in 1980, the Congress party was in power and it was unwilling to act on the report. Indira Gandhi did not do anything on the Mandal report. Neither did Rajiv Gandhi. He told his aides, 'It's a can of worms; I won't touch it.'[23] Thus it was only in 1990 when a non-Congress coalition government came to power that it proposed the implementation of the Mandal Commission recommendations. In this context, V.P. Singh's decision to implement reservations of government jobs had far-reaching implications in changing the balance of power between castes. It signified a major victory for the backward castes and the non-Congress parties advocating 'Mandalization' (a term coined to convey the upward mobility of the backward classes) of opportunity structures and politics.

The historic decision prompted widespread disturbances and violence in several parts of the country. Although the number of jobs involved was only 15,000 a year, the decision produced a violent upper-caste backlash, especially in Delhi, Orissa, Bihar, and Uttar Pradesh, including instances of self-immolation by upper-caste students.[24] The uproar was not about caste hierarchies or pollution and purity; rather, the high-pitched campaign was directed against the changing power equations and the undermining of the dominant status of upper castes. Upper-caste students feared they would lose job opportunities to the upwardly mobile backward castes. Employment opportunities are highly inadequate, particularly in north India, and conflicts are greater than before because of rising levels of education and expectations. Until the introduction of economic reforms in the early 1990s, government jobs were much sought after as they provided security, good salaries, and the only path for upward mobility.

Despite the violent protests the government went ahead and implemented the decision on 27 per cent reservation for OBCs in Central government jobs. This was not done through legislation (as in the case of Mandal II in 2006) but through an executive order following a decision in the Cabinet. As Arjun Singh was to say much later in April 2008 after the Supreme Court upholding 27 per cent reservations for OBCs in higher education, 'V.P. Singh's was a knee-jerk reaction.'[25] There was no build-up to it, there was no discussion with other political parties, and several of them criticized the government for acting hastily without consulting them. However, all of them extended support to reservations because none of them could afford to alienate the huge lower-caste constituency.

Social justice was the 'key legitimating concept in the political arguments over reservations in the Mandal debate.'[26] V.P. Singh described his decision to implement the recommendations of the Mandal Commission as 'a momentous decision of social justice'.[27] For its proponents, social justice connoted a set of measures to rectify social inequalities in status and power, and not economic inequalities in the distribution of wealth and income.[28] For them reservations were not a means for economic well-being and improvement in material needs; they were a means to facilitate inclusion of OBCs in arenas of education and state power where they had been under-represented. The principal rationale of OBC reservations was therefore to break the upper-caste monopoly over government jobs and professions that remained unchanged after nearly half a century of democracy. The motivation of the project was quintessentially political—the point was that it would help to weaken the hold of upper castes on public employment and thus open opportunities for participation of backward castes in running the affairs of the country.

Social Backwardness

For identifying backwardness and OBCs among Hindus, the Mandal Commission formulated eleven indicators: four indicators for social backwardness (that is, caste-based backwardness), three points for educational indicators, and four for economic indicators. In its conception, 'caste based social backwardness was the crucial element, educational backwardness as linked indicators and economic backwardness as the derived element.'[29] The main principles put forward were: (1) caste membership rather than individual class should determine beneficiaries; (2) low social ranking in the caste hierarchy of Hindu society rather than individual per capita income or other economic criteria should be the principal consideration for inclusion in the OBC list; (3) inadequate representation in government services and in the fields of trade, commerce, and industry; and (4) religious and linguistic groups, no matter what their economic condition, should not qualify for inclusion in the backward class category.

Disparities in education and government employment provided the main evidence of social inequalities that reservations would seek to rectify. Most importantly, the conception of social justice connoted groups and not individuals as the beneficiaries of special treatment—that is, disadvantage is on account of group membership, and the latter must be taken into account in rectifying disadvantages. The main difference between this framework and the one that was set out during the debates in the Constituent Assembly was that disadvantage then was conceived mainly in terms of reduction of socio-economic disparities between groups, whereas now the emphasis was on reducing inequalities in status and power of groups. In other words, it had been assumed by nationalist opinion that reservations would contribute to the reduction of inequalities through an improvement in the socio-economic conditions of beneficiaries. By contrast, the Mandal debate held political power for the disadvantaged to be the principal engine of social transformation. Hence, group preferences defined in caste terms came to dominate policy making and this has remained so in subsequent political processes. The Mandal position held empowerment and participation of the backward castes in public institutions as critical for the creation of a more just society.

For the critics the key issue was that individuals and not groups should be the unit for assessment of backwardness and disadvantage.

Even more importantly, the disadvantages that reservations sought to rectify concerned primarily economic inequalities and their consequences for opportunities for individuals, and not inequalities in distribution of power. The basic issue was with regard to the importance attached to historical discrimination as against current inequalities. The use of caste groups as the units of assessment for social justice as well as the notion that a caste's position in the ritual hierarchy provided a fair indication of the socio-economic conditions of its members was thought to be problematic for the critics of this scheme.[30]

Between Caste and Class

The usage of classes instead of castes in the constitutional reference to OBCs in Articles 15 (4), 16 (4), and 340 (1) has led to many legal disputes on the primacy of class versus caste, and whether caste stands for class. The main question of whether class or caste should be the criterion for defining backwardness was in large measure decided by State Commissions, the Mandal Commission, policy makers, and the judiciary in favour of caste as the crucial factor in designation of backward classes.[31] Yet, the lack of clear guidelines on the definition of backward castes—their exact composition, precise identification and scheduling—had an important role in triggering discontent over these policies and these differences have intensified as the regime of reservations has steadily grown.[32]

Although the Congress was not opposed to caste-based reservations per se, it was nevertheless in favour of exclusion of the economically privileged sections of OBCs. It favoured a means test to exclude the privileged among OBCs and to accommodate the underprivileged amongst the upper castes. In pursuance of this position, the Congress government of Prime Minister P.V. Narasimha Rao, which came to power after the general elections of May–June 1991, added a notification for reservation of 10 per cent for 'other economically backward sections of people' who were not covered by existing schemes of reservations. The constitutional validity of this notification was challenged in the Supreme Court. A special bench of nine judges heard the matter in view of its importance and the unprecedented controversy over

OBC reservations. There are two aspects to this issue. The first was that the OBCs are not a homogeneous group, and policy must therefore take into account the ground reality of backwardness and not go by group criteria alone. Second, OBCs were basically caste groupings but are nevertheless treated as a class grouping.

Given the political momentum behind OBC reservations, a shift to an economic criterion was unlikely; yet, the controversy placed the economic criteria in the political centre stage. The final word on this controversy came in the form of the Supreme Court judgment in the *Indra Sawhney* v. *Union of India* (Mandal case) on the challenges to both the Singh and Rao government decisions.[33] In a majority decision the apex court upheld the 27 per cent reservation for socially and educationally backward classes but struck down the 10 per cent reservation for economically backward people. The main opinion, authored by Justice Jeevan Reddy, supported the argument that in the context of contemporary Indian society, economic criteria alone cannot be the basis of backwardness, although this may be a consideration along with or in addition to social backwardness. In deciding the constitutionality of reservations for the OBCs, however, the court mandated that the government must make use of economic considerations in helping the truly backward, by which it meant that government must find ways to disqualify the more advantaged individuals in these classes. At the same time, in the same decision the court also forbade reservations for economically disadvantaged upper castes. In other words, the court ruling suggested that to be a member of an OBC, it was not enough to be in a lower caste if one's father was a government minister or bureaucrat in the government, just as it was also not enough to simply be poor if one was of a high caste. It is worth quoting the court's judgment in the *Sawhney* case (paragraph 83):

> Any authority entrusted with the task of identifying backward classes may well start with the castes. Since caste represents an existing, identifiable, social group spread over an overwhelming majority of the country's population, we say one may well begin with castes, if one so chooses, and then go to other groups, sections and classes. If the real object is to discover and locate backwardness, and if such backwardness is found in

a caste, it can be treated as backward; if it is found in any other group, section or class, they too can be treated as backward.[34]

The court upheld caste as a criterion for identifying OBCs, declaring: 'A caste can be and quite often is a social class in India.'[35] In rejecting the economic criterion as the test of backwardness and in giving importance to the caste factor for purposes of Article 16 (4), the court was guided by social realities revealed by the Mandal report and the need to compensate for handicaps from which certain sections of society suffered in the past. The reparation argument, though subdued and weak, did find a place in the court's opinion. Similarly, the social justice argument of empowerment found favour with the court, as it was felt that the backward classes are entitled to a fair share in the administration. Articles 15 (4) and 16 (4) are intended more for ameliorating caste disabilities rather than for distributive justice. The latter object can be achieved by invoking Article 14 itself. Reservation was limited to 27 per cent. By validating caste as a criterion by which to identify OBCs, the court verdict in *Sawhney* case put an end to thirty years of jurisprudence founded on the *Balaji* decision. Silencing critics who said that caste could not be the basis for reservation, the majority judgment pronounced that social backwardness was complex and could include caste.

Importantly, the court also put a stop to the attempts of the Congress government to implement a 10 per cent quota for 'economically backward' people on the ground that the economic criteria could not be a sufficient basis for reservation and extending the benefit of reservation on this basis would therefore be unconstitutional. The court imposed a means test for individual eligibility and exclusion of the creamy layer; it directed the government to develop criteria and mechanisms to skim off the creamy layer of the OBCs, which means that the government must find ways to disqualify the more advantaged individuals in these groups. This addresses two different but related concerns: (1) the benefits of reservations are not distributed evenly throughout the backward group but are instead cornered by persons at the top of the group; (2) reservations are going to persons who do not in fact need them because they have the economic and political clout to overcome discrimination, and hence it is important to exclude them. Such rules have created numerous administrative challenges, especially getting authentic caste and income certificates. Both criteria are difficult to apply because of India's large informal economy and the obfuscation of the economic criteria through corruption in issue of caste certificates, etc. However, the exclusion of the creamy layer provides a way of bringing in the socio-economic criteria instead of going by purely group-based categories of reservation. It is one important way of meeting the demands of social justice by giving benefits to the most deserving.

The Supreme Court verdict in the *Sawhney* case recommended the need to review quotas once in ten years. But this exercise has never been undertaken. The courts also directed the Central government to set up a permanent body at the Central and state levels to look into complaints of over-inclusion or under-inclusion in the OBC lists. This was necessary because a caste group can enter the OBC category only on the recommendation of the National Commission for Backward Classes (NCBC). The NCBC, formed in 1993, has issued a set of guidelines, based on social, economic, and educational indicators, for castes/communities to be included in the Central list of OBCs. Under Section 9 of the NCBC Act, the Commission 'shall examine requests for inclusion of any class of citizens as a backward class in the lists and hear complaints of over-inclusion or under-inclusion of any backward class to such lists and tender such advice to the Central government as it deems appropriate.'[36] Under Section 9 (2) of the Act, the advice of the Commission shall be binding on the Central government. From time to time there has been pressure to bring about changes in official categories to recognize economic and social mobility, but backward-caste politicians and backward-caste organizations make it difficult if not impossible to take hard decisions 'to put out of the benefit system' communities with political and economic clout.[37] Justice T.K. Thommen remarked: 'Identification of backwardness is an ever continuing process of inclusion and exclusion. To allow the undeserving to benefit by reservation is to deny protection to those who are meant to be protected.'[38] Until 2007, the NCBC had recommended 297 claims for inclusion. At the same time, it rejected 288 claims for inclusion of main castes and 243 requests for inclusion of sub-castes/communities in the Central List of Backward Classes.[39] Overall, the more influential OBCs corner the benefits of reservations at the expense of the more backward sections among them.

The *Sawhney* judgment spawned a large number of constitutional amendments. There have been five amendments to get around the ban on reservations in promotions and the stipulation that reservations cannot exceed 50 per cent of the seats. Three of five amendments were designed to undo the court's decision to end the practice of providing reservations in promotions for the SCs and STs. Parliament amended the Constitution by the 77th Amendment (1995), the 81st Amendment (2000), and the 85th Amendment (2001) to strengthen the SC and the ST reservation in promotions at all levels. The other two amendments sought to circumvent the 50 per cent limit on reservations.[40] These five amendments have restored to the backward classes much of what was taken away from them by the 1993 judgment. All the five amendments had cross-party support, which makes it that much harder for the courts to interfere with these amendments.

Over the years caste has become synonymous with class for the purpose of reservations. Government policy has relied on courts, which have given their imprimatur of approval to the conflation and substitution of caste and class. The deliberate use of the term classes rather than castes in the constitutional text has been interpreted by the court to mean general social groupings rather than economic classes. Clearly, the judiciary has played an active role in imposing procedures for programme design and in striking a balance among the competing interests articulated in the constitutional blueprint and group interests in society.[41] The Mandal I decision led to widespread protest and unrest but once the court approved the proposed changes, there was widespread public acceptance.[42]

The changing face of the Indian bureaucracy is in a large measure attributable to this elaborate regime of reservations. Even though the full impact of the Mandal initiative will be known only after twenty years, the recent data on social profiles of the 400-odd individuals who annually clear the civil service examination to join the IAS, IFS,

IPS, and other services reported by a newsmagazine show that 'people who had no access to the civil services are coming in. The city-born and city-bred are busy chasing a plethora of new economy options while those born and schooled in district and small towns, often from the lower castes, are flocking to the IAS.'[43] The OBCs had a negligible presence of about 2 per cent in government employment in 1990 when the Mandal recommendations were accepted. Even this small representation in employment was restricted to the lower rungs of government jobs. Upper castes constituted 37.6 per cent of the civil services.[44] The radical change began after the implementation of OBCs reservations in government jobs. The significant increase registered by the OBCs has been made possible entirely by the 27 per cent reservations for them. Their representation in the civil services has been boosted as many have made it to the general category also. By 2000, the SCs, STs, and OBCs together accounted for more than 55 per cent of the total recruitment in the Union civil services. This marked a dramatic shift from the pattern that was prevailing until the early 1990s when 60 per cent of all Hindu officers belonged to the upper castes.[45]

Political Consequences of Preference

In assessing the logic and consequences of Mandal I and the complex regime of reservations, three points need to be noted. One, despite the constitutional commitment and other legislative and social measures to root out the evil of the caste system, castes and caste-based discrimination constitute a reality. Second, the basic approach of policy makers has been that reservations do not violate the basic constitutional scheme of equality; rather they are one of the major tools used to promote it. Third, reservations should be granted to all backward communities irrespective of religion and should not be limited to Hindus.

However, reservations in India are open to the objection that they only focus on groups which were excluded from the Hindu caste system and do not cover other backward groups. The OBC category seeks to meet this objection and in principle includes non-Hindu backward sections of Muslims and Christian populations. But overall reservations remain confined to three groups of Hindus: SCs, STs, and OBCs, the last of these also being primarily a Hindu caste category. Even in the case of non-Hindus, caste considerations remain primary, which makes their application difficult to these groups. Some state-level backward classes commissions had cautioned that using purely caste-based criteria would result in the exclusion of educationally and socially backward sections among non-Hindus.[46] But this cautionary note has been largely ignored.[47]

An additional point of note is that the policies of the Central government with regard to the backward classes were the products of changing electoral dynamics rather than social movements and mobilization by the groups themselves. In fact, more agitations and campaigns have resulted from upper-caste opposition to reservations than in its favour. The decision to reserve seats for the OBCs was driven by political considerations. Electoral pressures plus the rising political representation of backward castes in state legislatures from the early 1970s were mainly responsible for the policy decision in favour of them. Whether or not political parties backing it were committed to the promotion of social justice is besides the point: caste politics went on to be used as basis for organizing electoral constituencies and waging major political battles against upper-caste domination. At the same time, it was obvious that the Mandal I decision would push groups to demand more inclusions in the OBC lists. More importantly, in the absence of a proper system of exclusion, dominant groups or castes have monopolized benefits.

Mandal II: Reservations in Higher Education

In April 2006, Human Resource Development Minister Arjun Singh made an announcement that the Central government was planning to extend reservations to OBCs in Central educational institutions. It stirred a huge public debate even though it was not for the first time that the Central government was considering reservation for backward castes. Supporters called the proposal a belated move to promote social justice and inclusion in upper-caste-dominated higher education, even as opponents warned that India's edge in the knowledge economy would dwindle, competitiveness erode, and multinational companies move away.

For the UPA government, OBC quotas in higher and professional education were a logical corollary to the 27 per cent reservations in public employment in operation since 1994: the objective of both was to promote empowerment and enhance opportunities.

The preceding discussion indicates that OBCs have been the subjects of preferential treatment previously because of under-representation in governmental structures. But this group, unlike the SCs or Muslims, is not a statistical minority; in fact the OBCs are a statistical majority as they constitute roughly 40–50 per cent of the population. Neither are they a statistical minority in the sociological sense of lacking political and bureaucratic power as noted earlier. But they are under-represented in significant levels in higher and professional education.

Higher education has grown enormously since Independence—from twenty-five to 348 universities and 700 to 17,625 colleges. About eight million students in India join undergraduate studies each year. Only 8–9 per cent of the relevant age group between twenty and twenty-four years are presently enrolled in these institutions, as against 50–85 per cent of this age group of the population availing of the benefits of higher education in developed countries. With the changes in India over the past twenty-five years, especially the phenomenal economic growth of recent years, there has been an escalating demand for higher education, particularly professional and technical education, in engineering and medical colleges and management institutes (Table 4.2). Elite institutions like the Indian Institutes of Technology (IITs), Indian Institutes of Management (IIMs), and medical colleges are in great demand from various sections, most notably the upwardly mobile middle classes, because these institutions provide heavily subsidized high-quality education which can fetch a good job anywhere in the world. These institutions are under enormous social and political pressure from all sides because they are the principal avenues of upward mobility for everyone. The emergence of knowledge-based empowerment as a major source of income and privilege has further enhanced their significance as professional courses have become an even more important means for upward mobility.[48] In India, the imperative of providing education to all, especially from educationally deprived groups, has been recognized by the government as being crucial for the development of the country and the creation of a more inclusive and democratic society. Additionally, the entry of marginalized groups in higher education would enhance the diversity and plurality of the educational system and enrich education overall. However, six decades after Independence the opportunities for admission to these institutions are largely monopolized by a small privileged section of society.

Despite decades of preferential treatment in different forms, public life in India outside of politics is disproportionately dominated by upper castes. They continue to dominate public institutions, skilled professions, and the media, while the SCs, STs, OBCs, and Muslims are way behind the upper castes in all spheres of public life, and in higher and professional education specifically. The spread of higher education among deprived groups is generally low; the gaps across categories remain very large. It is these large differences in educational attainment and access that state intervention in the form of reservations seeks to address.

OBC Quota Demand in Higher Education

The forerunner to the 2006 political controversy was the decision of the Supreme Court in August 2005 which made it clear that it was impermissible to introduce reservations in private educational institutions which do not receive financial support from the state. This meant that educational opportunities in the private institutions would remain outside the purview of affirmative action policies of the state for disadvantaged groups. The 93rd Amendment was thus necessitated by the Supreme Court's judgment in the *Inamdar* case in 2005.[49] The seven-member bench went into all these issues and noted that though the issue of reservation was not a central one in the *Pai Foundation* and *Islamic Academy* cases, it had to be taken into account, especially where minority institutions were involved.[50] The judges observed: '...neither the policy of reservation can be enforced by the state nor any quota of percentage of admissions can be carved out to be appropriated by the state.' One of the key issues considered by the court in these judgments was the right of minority institutions to run their colleges the way they want to.

The issue of access to higher education has always been an emotive one, especially in India where the barriers to entry in higher education are still very high. This was the subject of the first constitutional amendment; it was frontally addressed through the Constitution (1st Amendment) Act, 1951, with the insertion of clause (4) in Article 15. This provision has been implemented for admissions in regard to the SCs and STs and not for the backward classes. The national-level data from the 55th Round of the NSSO (1999–2000) showed in stark terms the inequalities in access to higher education (Table 4.3). Students from the middle classes and upper castes traditionally associated with more education—comprising roughly 20 per cent of the population—dominate higher education, compared to 9 per cent or less for all other categories.[51] The Hindu upper castes formed a little more than a third of the total urban population, but they accounted for two-thirds of professional and higher education—in other words, their share in higher education is twice their share in the population.[52] The obvious consequence of the upper-caste over-representation is the under-representation of other groups (Table 4.5). Although the Hindu lower castes (SCs, STs, OBCs) plus Muslims constitute 57 per cent of the population, they are hugely under-represented in higher education. Muslims are educationally disadvantaged relative to all other groups except the SCs—at the graduate level, only one in twenty students is a Muslim. Their share among graduates is roughly 5 per cent while their share in population aged twenty years and above is about double that, at over 11 per cent (Table 4.4). They constitute only 1.3 per cent and 1.7 per cent, respectively, of the student body of the elite IIMs and IITs. Hindu upper-caste dominance in higher education is undeniable while the lower castes and Muslims are significantly under-represented. Yet, the critics of reservations contend that higher education itself cannot be viewed as a right in the same way as primary education, and that the upper-caste dominance is justified in view of the inevitable element of selectiveness that inheres in higher education.

The UPA government amended the Constitution in 2005 to permit reservations in aided and unaided educational institutions in favour of SCs, STs, and OBCs, except in institutions run by minorities.[53] This was in response to the *Inamdar* judgment which had limited affirmative action to aided institutions, following which almost all state governments and political parties made a strong plea to the Central government to introduce a legislation that would cover both aided and unaided institutions while excluding minority institutions. The only dissent came from the BJP, which demanded that minority-run institutions should not be excluded from the proposed law. The backward-caste MPs demanded that the words 'any socially or educationally backward classes of citizens' appearing in the new clause (5) of Article 15 be replaced with the words 'Other Backward Classes' to ensure that its provisions would apply specifically to the backward castes. The deadlock was resolved only after it was categorically assured by the prime minister that the amendment of the Constitution would definitely benefit the OBCs.

After the passage of the 93rd Constitutional Amendment Act, which was essentially an enabling provision, the supporters of OBC quotas argued that it necessitated a legislation to ensure the implementation of affirmative action in publicly funded institutions of higher education. Once the demand for reservations gathered momentum, the Central government had to implement the provisions of Article 15 (5) in respect of all institutions and universities under its purview. Moreover, several states had either already made laws or were going to make laws to implement this provision. Treating this as an enabling legislation, the UPA government decided to introduce reservations for OBCs in publicly funded educational institutions, premier technology institutes, medical colleges, and Central universities. The government was under considerable pressure from coalition partners and political parties which unanimously favoured an expeditious introduction of reservations in higher education for the OBCs.

The official argument in favour of reservations offered two principal justifications: first, extending quotas in higher education was the continuation of preferential treatment in public employment to the OBCs since 1994; and, second, it came up in 2006 mainly in the context of the legislation on private unaided institutions. The government's position was that it had already amended the Constitution; a new clause (5) had been added to Article 15 (which is a fundamental right); the constitutional amendment has been carried out with near unanimity by Parliament; and there was an all-party consensus on the issue. Moreover, unlike the Mandal I decision, which was rushed through without adequate consultations, this legislation was the result of wide-ranging consultations with MPs and political parties, and it had been routed through the Cabinet and various government departments.

Many factors play a role in the desire for higher education. The perception of improved employment prospects is the most important. Acute dissatisfactions arising out of unequal representation in prestigious educational institutions and the historical disadvantage in education of certain groups are among the primary reasons for the institution of reservations in higher education. Therefore, the principal justification was cast in terms of the need to enhance equality of opportunity for the weaker sections of society, especially under the new economy. Government reasoning regarded equality as a positive right which requires the state to minimize existing inequalities and to treat the underprivileged with special care as envisaged in the Constitution. Promotion of equality and elimination of inequality formed an essential part of the basic structure of the Constitution, and not providing reservations to SCs, STs, and OBCs would be a violation of this basic structure. For the first time, the government put forward the basic structure doctrine in its affidavit to the Supreme Court: reservation is part of the basic structure of the Constitution and therefore the government had no option but to introduce reservations for the OBCs. Further, clause (5) of Article 15 was inserted to enable the state to implement it.

SCs and STs are the beneficiaries of reservations because they have suffered endemic discrimination and disadvantage.[54] Preferential treatment for backward classes derives its support largely from the argument for greater representation. But a dominant view does not accept these reasons and places emphasis on the intrinsic value of merit in higher education.[55] This view sees reservations as benefits being handed out to particular caste groups. Finance Minister P. Chidambaram, a member of the Group of Ministers (GoM) appointed to decide on reservations for OBCs in Central institutions, summed up the official position on reservations:

> As I understand...there is no ground to review whether there should be reservation or not. There is no ground at all. If a review means questioning the justification of reservation, I say no. Amongst all the instruments available to us for affirmative action the one that has proved most effective is reservation. Experience tells us that reservation has helped many, many, many members of the OBCs to rise in the southern states. I am totally convinced about that.[56]

Controversies and Protests

The UPA government decided to introduce the Central Educational Institutions (Reservation in Admission) Bill, 2006, to cover Central universities, institutions of national importance set up by Parliament, and institutions directly or indirectly aided by the Central government or linked to Central universities or centrally created institutions. It excluded private unaided institutions and it excluded minority educational institutions. The Bill provoked a major agitation by doctors. The countrywide agitation was organized by a group which calls itself Youth for Equality (YFE). It started from the All India Institute of Medical Sciences (AIIMS) and included students from premier medical colleges and from the IITs and IIMs. Protestors demanded that the quota proposal be scrapped, and a non-political commission formed to review the policy, including for the SCs and STs. Spearheaded by the doctors of AIIMS—the agitation originated in this institute—which remained its 'nodal point' throughout.[57] It was planned by a group of people who had strong views against the reservation bill.[58] A government-appointed committee headed by the University Grants Commission Chairman S.K. Thorat (to look into complaints from MPs and media reports on allegations of harassment of SC and ST students at AIIMS) noted that the 'AIIMS became the venue of the protest primarily to paralyze healthcare for thousands of people and attract public attention against reservation. Paralyzing of the healthcare services including emergency services would put pressure on the government.'[59] The administration of AIIMS went to the extent of penalizing and punishing students and staff that did not support the agitation.

For nineteen days, doctors and medical students were on strike, bringing essential health services to a standstill. The main support came from the corporate sector, traders associations, chambers of commerce, industry lobbies, the Indian Medical Association, executives of information technology companies, residents welfare associations in many cities, business executives, and, above all, owners of private professional colleges.[60] As in the anti-Mandal agitation of 1990–1, the students engaged in mockery of lower castes by enacting casteist forms of protest such as the symbolic sweeping of streets, shoe-shining, and shouting slogans that lower castes are indeed fit only for menial jobs, while others are 'naturally' suited to respectable professions such as engineering and medicine.[61] The doctors called off their agitation after the court's directive that they resume work or face contempt. Declared the *Hindustan Times* in an editorial: 'The striking medical students have played a heroic role in resisting the irrational government policy of enforcing quotas for the OBCs in institutions of higher learning. The Supreme Court's decision to look into all the aspects of the issue is a victory, and the students should see it as such.'[62]

The National Knowledge Commission opposed OBC reservations and publicized its opposition through its majority (6:2) report in the media.[63] Two members of the NKC decided to quit in protest against OBC reservations. Despite the protests and media support for the agitation against OBC reservations, public sympathy was largely in favour of OBC quotas, except among the elites and the upper middle classes, who were clearly unhappy with the decision. The media coverage may have succeeded in making it a national and emotive issue but it does not seem to have made much difference to the established pro-reservation position on this subject. Asked if they were in favour of reservations, 63 per cent of the respondents in the *Indian Express*–CNN-IBN poll expressed support for reservations and only 34 per cent were against them.[64] But it is important to note that a larger majority of respondents—67 per cent—expressed a preference for economic criteria, irrespective of caste, for identification of beneficiaries.

Shifts in Public Debate

In the years since Mandal I, the political and economic landscape has changed almost completely. Market reforms have contributed to the breakdown of the Nehruvian consensus on a mixed economy and the Congress social coalition of upper castes, minorities, and SCs. India's GDP has grown steadily over the past two decades, and between 2004 and 2007 it has exceeded 8 per cent. The economy has moved into a new orbit of high growth and high consumption, driven by the services and knowledge economy. It has witnessed an explosion of high finance, stock market, information technology, software exports, media, entertainment, and real-estate speculation. But the bulk of people have not gained significantly from the paradigm shift in economic policy. Economic boom and high growth have brought benefits to the top 20 per cent of the population, which has seen an unprecedented rise in income and job opportunities. [65] Most of the middle classes have not known so much prosperity and affluence, which is coming from private sector employment or a career abroad after receiving highly subsidized education in elite institutions. This sector formed a closed social circuit that was almost entirely under the domination of upper castes.

According to the Economic Survey (2006), economic disparities have increased sharply between 1993–4 and 2003–4; for more than half of the country's total population, per capita consumption has actually declined during a decade when national incomes were growing rapidly.[66] The basic feature of the process of economic development has been exclusion—from control over assets, from benefits of growth, from education, and from income-generating opportunities. The imbalances and exclusions have led to the creation of two economies across the social and regional landscape of India. Government jobs were drying up, even as salaries in government continue to be modest in comparison to the astronomical pay packets in the private sector and the media.[67] Consequently, the upper castes and middle classes have flocked to the booming managerial and executive jobs in the corporate sector, but they want subsidized high-quality education which provides them the credentials for access to such jobs. Graduates from these institutions find immediate placement in the private sector; hence the increased stakes in elite institutions, which open up opportunities for high-salaried jobs as opposed to the civil service, which has lost its sheen for the upwardly mobile middle classes. These are the groups that took an active part in the anti-quota agitation. The agitators in 1990 were primarily from the lower middle classes interested in government jobs, whereas in 2006 the protestors were principally interested in private sector employment.

The euphoria over the high growth rates of the economy in the past few years has led to the belief that market reforms have levelled out social distinctions and disadvantages. There is hence a strong reluctance to see, let alone acknowledge, social inequalities. The middle class dominates the new economy and perceives itself as a global class. Its entitlement to privilege comes from open competition and monopoly over admissions to state-funded premier educational institutions such as the IITs, the IIMs, and the AIIMS.[68] But these institutions are in great demand from everyone from the elite downwards because they offer good affordable education. Mandal II was playing into these conflicts and tensions between competing interests, as lower castes began to challenge the long-standing monopoly of upper castes over these premier institutions.

For the past two decades or so the politics around reservations for OBCs has centred on two dimensions. At one level, it has been characterized by clashes between social and political forces that support and oppose reservations for OBCs in education and employment. Those who support quotas perceive reservation-based affirmative action as an instrument to uplift sections that have been oppressed for centuries and to lessen the dominance of upper castes. Those who oppose reservation look at the issue of upper-caste dominance differently. They claim that their dominance is solely due to merit, and that any attempt to undermine merit will result in the erosion of progress. This will hurt India's rise as an economic power and therefore the government would be well advised to allow market forces and merit to produce a twenty-first-century economy. The crux of the argument is that reservations militate against merit and allow degrees or qualifications to be awarded to people with less than deserving performance and aptitude. Such a system is inefficient as compared with openly competitive systems. These measures are unfair benefits given to particular caste groupings undeserving of such protection and hence pandering to vote banks of politicians. A study by Satish Deshpande has noted however that: 'Merit in the Indian context refers to certification of competence, aptitude or knowledge acquired through examination of some kind.... What matters is not how well one does in the exam but how much better one does than others taking the same exam.'[69] Supporters of reservations argue that higher education inherently involved exclusion and 'merit' legitimizes such exclusions. Unlocking the gates of higher education was therefore necessary to dilute the upper-caste monopoly.[70]

At another level, in the past fifteen years, the Mandal initiative has helped to change the face of the polity; the grammar of entitlement has become part of the new language of politics, and all parties now accept the logic of quotas. The political class, including the BJP which brought down the V.P. Singh government for implementing the Mandal report and whose political base lies among upper-caste Hindus, seems to realize that a reversal of reservation policy is no longer possible. However, outside the political domain, the opposition to reservations amongst the intelligentsia, media, and civil society largely continues to be strong. The arguments in civil society were broadly of two types: arguments about institutions and arguments about caste disadvantage. The institutional argument mainly focused on the importance of merit for maintenance of institutional efficacy in the field of higher education. Merit and inclusion were interpreted as irreconcilable in the new post-economic reforms discourse.[71] On the issue of caste disadvantage, two sets of arguments came up. One argument recognized that caste is associated with inequalities and discrimination, and it is the responsibility of public policy to address these. But there were differences among those espousing this argument with regard to the efficacy of reservations for achieving these outcomes or whether alternative strategies could be devised for this. A second set of arguments highlighted the difference between SCs, who are poor and exploited, and the OBCs, who are powerful and do not deserve reservations—a point that had been emphasized by Rajiv Gandhi in his Lok Sabha speech. There is also the argument that the regime of reservations does not actually help the weaker sections among the deprived since the benefits are cornered by the affluent among them (this too was highlighted by Rajiv Gandhi). The OBCs were economically empowered through the democratic system in the 1960s and 1970s; they have economic and political power and are administratively empowered by reservations in government service and therefore do not require reservations in higher education as well. This line of reasoning was particularly strong among the upper-middle-class opponents of Mandal II and in regions which have had no tangible exposure to reservations in the education sector. Not surprisingly, in the four south Indian states as well as in Maharashtra and Gujarat, which have had a long experience with quotas, the opposition to OBC reservation was muted.

A third important feature of the civil society debate in Mandal II was its disengagement from the political process, as there was a pervasive feeling among the protestors that they were above the political process. The disdain towards the political class and Parliament encouraged the protestors to concentrate on the judiciary and the media, which they perceived as friendly towards their cause. This was evident from the tendency to arrogate powers to decide on public policy of affirmative action rather than leave it to the state to decide. It also derives sustenance from the belief that excluded groups do not possess the intelligence or aptitude for higher education. This was palpable from the condescending attitude of the student leaders to the very policy of quotas: the state could address the problem of discrimination and disadvantage as long as state intervention through affirmative action did not reduce opportunities for them.

Mandal II sought to cut through the conceptual tangles that have besieged the issue of OBC reservations. The UPA government relied on previous court rulings which had clearly given their approval for the substitution of caste for class to privilege caste over other identities. It was repeatedly argued that often caste is social class and if a group was backward socially it would be a backward class for the purposes of Article 16 (4). While caste cannot be the sole criterion to determine the class of persons for whom reservation must be sought, caste can indeed be one of the factors (or even the primary factor) relevant in determining which cross sections of society in India require reservation in employment or in the reservation of seats in institutions of higher education. In other words, it is constitutionally justified to take caste as the social unit or class to be examined and tested for backwardness or its absence in terms of the criteria of social and educational backwardness devised by the government.

Political Response

The UPA government's decision in favour of OBC reservations in higher education was part of a plan to demonstrate the backward-caste and social justice credentials of the Congress party. This party had traditionally supported the reservation principle, starting with Nehru, who pushed the constitutional amendment in 1951.[72] However, the Congress leadership was ambivalent on the issue since Rajiv Gandhi questioned the scientific basis of OBC quotas in his Lok Sabha speech in September 1990 and argued for a comprehensive action plan for the disadvantaged groups. He had criticized the V.P. Singh government for thinking only 'around caste' and 'vested interests in particular castes'.[73] The 2006 move was an attempt to counterbalance the long-standing distrust of the backward castes towards the party, which was seen as generally an upper-caste-friendly party. Against this perception, the reservation gamble was a crucial element in the new strategy to wean away the OBCs from regional and state-based parties which have been the preferred choice of the backward-caste voters. Even though there was disagreement within the Congress with regard to the timing of the reservation proposal (and more so with Arjun Singh for trying to take credit for it), the party leadership could hardly afford to vacillate or disown the issue. On the other hand, open support would alienate the upper castes. If, however, the Congress stuck firmly to its pro-reservation stand, it could hope to win some OBC support and offset the lower-caste advantage enjoyed by regional parties like the Samajwadi Party and the BSP who claimed to be the champions of the disadvantaged in north India. The Congress general secretary stated: 'The issue isn't politics alone. At its core is social justice. We will not, I repeat, we will not recant on the quota issue. That is settled and the perceived silence of the prime minister and the Congress president must not be mistaken for ambivalence or confusion. Both are supportive of this policy.'[74]

Propelled by the pressures and counter-pressures, the UPA government was keen to strike a fair balance between competing claims of the disadvantaged and the advantaged. The UPA chairperson Sonia Gandhi underscored the point that extension of OBC reservations to Central educational institutions would go hand in hand with an increase in seats for general category students. This approach found approval in the Cabinet. One newspaper reported that the Union Cabinet meeting that cleared the bill on reservation for the OBCs 'witnessed the most serious and purposeful discussion so far in the life of the UPA Government.'[75] The advocates of quotas made a strong case for a total and complete changeover to the new reservation regime for the OBCs. A senior minister cited 'centuries of injustice' that had been the OBCs' lot and argued that the Backward Classes were not asking for a 'backlog' compensation but were merely demanding correction of the injustice. In other words, the OBCs are demanding today their legitimate, long-delayed share in social privileges like centrally funded higher education. Some ministers drew the attention of the Cabinet to the Supreme Court pronouncements on the concept of creamy layer and on the need to gradually phase out these strata from the reservation regime. However, the opinion was firmly in favour of retaining the creamy layer. The prime minister urged his colleagues 'not do anything that would destroy the country's "knowledge strength".' The final decision reflected his three main concerns: (a) there should be no dilution in the existing seats and opportunities available in the 'non-reserved' categories; (b) the extension of the 27 per cent reservation for the OBCs should be staggered to ensure that the requisite infrastructure was in place; and (c) certain institutions of 'national/strategic' importance should be kept out of the reservation regime.[76]

The UPA government decided to increase the number of seats in the general category so that seats filled by 'open competition' do not shrink. Under this formula the number of unreserved seats would be increased in proportion to the 27 per cent to be reserved for the OBCs. However, the government's plan of accommodation through expansion rather than cutting into general category seats failed to halt the protest. The opponents remained unconvinced, indeed sceptical about the government move, which according to one critic 'exemplified the way government thinks of admissions: goodies be distributed to whoever they want, a mechanism for buying out different groups.'[77]

The Lok Sabha unanimously approved the legislation for reservations for OBCs in Central educational institutions by a voice vote in December 2006. Cross-party support marked the Lok Sabha debate on the bill as virtually every speaker lauded the UPA government's initiative to introduce reservations for OBCs in higher education, which they argued was long overdue. The support for the legislation cut across parties, barring the BJP's opposition to the provision on the exclusion of minority educational institutions. Inspired by key provisions in the Constitution, namely, Articles 46 and Article 15 (5), the new legislation was a significant measure, as it was the first time that Parliament has through laws recognized reservation of seats in educational institutions for OBCs as a necessary measure to give effect to the constitutional provisions.

The most striking feature of the political response was the wide-ranging political support for Arjun Singh's proposal, in contrast to the more limited support for V.P. Singh's attempt to provide reservations for OBCs in government jobs: reservations in higher education garnered the support of all parties and MPs. As Arjun Singh put it: 'In the present case there was a gradual build-up, and therefore, when all parties in Parliament came on board, it was that much stronger.'[78] In the first round, the Congress, which initiated Mandal II, had opposed Mandal I. The second noteworthy difference is that prior to this Act, reservations at the Central level were the result of an executive decision implemented usually through an office memorandum; there was no statutory backing for these polices. This led to several court rulings interpreting constitutional provisions in a manner perceived to be against the interests of backward classes.[79] As executive actions, the court found it easy to stay the operation of such memorandum in 1990. Mandal II went through a much wider consultative and legislative process. Yet, the court stayed the operation of the Act. Thus, an active role of the judiciary is a strong feature of both episodes. In both cases the judiciary questioned procedures and methodologies for design and assumed the role of policy making.

Judicial Intervention

The court intervened in the middle of the Mandal II agitation, staying the law and declaring that the OBC reservation issue 'requires judicial review'. This put paid to Congress–UPA quota plans of rolling out OBC reservations in 2007. As *The Hindu* editorial remarked: 'It halted in its tracks what all political parties together had crafted as a major social justice measure that struck a fair balance between the interests of different sections.'[80] But significantly, the court had not overturned reservations for OBCs. The petitioners in *Ashoka Thakur* v. *Union of India* claimed that the Act and the Amendment violated their fundamental right to equality. The court's two-judge bench had issued an interim order on 29 March 2007 partly staying the law based on two principal contentions. First, it held that the 1931 census could not be the 'determinative factor' in fixing the quantum of reservations under the new law, because the 1931 census does not take into account the demographic and socio-economic changes that have taken place over the past eighty years.[81] Second, the court was dissatisfied with the government's defence of the non-exclusion of the creamy layer, which went against the basic structure of the Constitution, and also the factual basis of the 27 per cent reservation for the OBCs in educational institutions. The UPA government had defended the non-exclusion of the creamy layer on the ground that there is a basic difference between job quotas and educational reservations. It maintained that exclusion of the creamy layer as evolved in the Mandal case was applicable for jobs and not for education. The government reasoned that a successful candidate in the former begins to earn immediately; in the case of the latter, selection for admission through reservation is the beginning of heavy expenditure for the family. Even before selection, the family has to incur heavy expenditure for coaching.[82]

As it involved substantial constitutional issues, the government sought the reference of the case to a Constitution bench. This included Chief Justice K.G. Balakrishnan and Justices Arijit Pasayat, C.K. Thakker, R.V. Raveendran, and Dalveer Bhandari. The five-judge bench heard marathon arguments for twenty-five days spread over three months from 7 August 2007 to November 2007. The basic issue was whether the 93rd Amendment was unconstitutional and violative of the basic structure of the Constitution and whether it confers on the state unbridled power to make special provision for the OBCs. The five-judge Constitution bench on 10 April 2008 upheld the Constitution (93rd Amendment) Act, 2005, under which the state had been empowered to make special provisions for socially and educationally backward classes in admission to educational institutions providing for 27 per cent quota for OBCs in IITs, IIMs, and other Central educational institutions. The bench, while declaring that creamy layer should be excluded from the quota, held that the Act does not violate the basic structure of the Constitution. It also said that reservations should not be in perpetuity but should be revised at periodic intervals.

The judgment was in keeping with the Supreme Court's long-standing interpretation of the constitutional provisions on equality, which is that the fundamental right to equality is compatible with schemes like reservations that confer benefits on disadvantaged groups. The near-unanimous verdict came about in the wake of elaborate arguments advanced by the government counsel stating that reservation is one of the many tools that are used by the government to promote equality so that disadvantaged groups can be brought into the mainstream of public life.[83] The Chief Justice agreed that affirmative action, though 'apparently discriminatory, is calculated to produce equality on a broader basis.' He reasoned that a constitutional amendment which 'moderately abridges or alters the equality principle' but does not abrogate it would not violate the basic structure of the Constitution.[84] The government counsel justified the 'identification of socially and educationally backward classes on the basis of caste in view of the societal structure of the country' while making submissions on the 27 per cent quotas in higher education for the OBCs.[85] As in Mandal I, the government counsel argued that caste should be construed as a unit leading to reservation. However, the Chief Justice, referring to the arguments made against the application of creamy layer to educational institutions, stated that: 'They are excluded because unless this segment of caste is excluded from that caste group, there cannot be proper identification of the backward class. If the creamy layer principle is not applied, it could easily be said that all the castes that have been included among the SEBCs (Socially and Educationally Backward Classes) have been included exclusively on the basis of caste.'[86] Overall, the judgment was a balancing act taking into account larger interests in society.

The Die is Cast(e)

Several important issues and concerns emerge from these controversies. From the beginning, reservations for backward castes have been haunted by questions regarding definition and identification, role of caste in the selection, relationship between caste and deprivation, its implications for the core commitment to SCs/STs, and the exclusion of minorities. A striking point with regard to the political and legislative history of affirmative action for backward classes is that caste remains the most important unit of identification in reservation policy which has intensified competition among the disadvantaged groups and caused resentment among those excluded from preferential treatment.

One issue that has been far from settled is the question of the relationship between caste and class and whether OBCs constitute a caste or class. By the time of Mandal II, caste and class had become almost inseparable—in fact, caste stands for class. The 2006 OBC quota law said that 'caste is the starting point for identification of socially and educationally backward classes.' Legal jurisprudence has accepted caste as a basis of classification, as is evident from the Mandal II judgment. Several court verdicts in favour of the equivalence of caste and class held that class included persons grouped on the basis of their castes.[87] The court ruling in

Thakur case reiterates that caste itself can be used as a criterion for identification.

The internal differentiation and social heterogeneity among the OBCs suggest that the creamy layer or the privileged within the OBCs must be excluded. However, governments have been wary of excluding the influencial castes from the ambit of reservations for fear of political repercussions. In fact, the most contentious aspect of government policy was its silence on the exclusion of the creamy layer of OBCs from the beneficiaries of the 2006 Act. The *Thakur* judgment unanimously directed the government to issue a notification excluding the creamy layer from the OBC beneficiaries. It reiterated the creamy layer formula established in the *Sawhney* ruling. This could have been addressed in the 93rd Amendment itself, but the UPA government was under tremendous pressure from the powerful OBC lobby of MPs not to exclude the creamy layer, even though they were aware that not doing this would violate the constitutional provisions.[88] The OBC-dominated parties like Rashtriya Janata Dal, Dravida Munnetra Kazhagam (DMK), and the Pattali Makkal Katchi (PMK), which dominate the UPA, were opposed to it. The NCBC has periodically conducted social audits to determine the status of various castes, but has not excluded them.[89] The dominant castes such as Nadars and Yadavs, for example, continue to remain on the list. As a result, caste groups that benefited from past systems of quotas or which have disproportionate political/economic power continue to enjoy the benefits of reservations and keep the majority still deprived.

The principle behind the creamy layer exclusion is that if the starting points in most respects for various groups are equal, there is little justification for giving them the benefits of reservation. To put it differently, when it comes to the OBCs, caste alone cannot be a justification for treating them differently. The court, recognizing the multiple disadvantages that characterize Indian society, was demanding that government should provide justification for policies and balance different considerations. It felt that the exclusion of creamy layer would imply that reservation was not based on caste alone but on other factors such as social and economic backwardness. Without excluding the creamy layer, the affluent among these castes would stand to benefit more from reservations in higher education and in effect get more benefits than the poor.[90]

The supporters of OBC reservation, on the other hand, argue that the move to exclude the creamy layer is 'misplaced' and would negate the very purpose of reservation which is not removing poverty but changing the social composition of higher education. Since the opportunities for higher education are generally availed by the privileged in every social group, only the creamy layer in every group is able to access higher education. 'By disqualifying those most likely to succeed in elite institutions, creamy layer exclusion undermines the very purpose of the proposed law.'[91] Consequently, most of the seats reserved for the OBCs would remain unfilled. But the fact remains that group rights do not entitle all individuals in the group, which means there has to be a criteria for admitting specific members of the OBCs to educational institutions. Creamy-layer norms could be used to ensure that the more privileged are given last preference.

The third important issue pertains to the attitude towards affirmative action for minorities. If there was one group that needed preferential treatment in view of its educational backwardness and under-representation in government employment, it was Muslims. Affirmative action was above all needed to tackle their educational backwardness. The chairman of the NCM made a strong plea for greater access for Muslims in the available higher educational institutions. He suggested the need to evolve 'a suitable mechanism' to ensure equitable share of minorities in higher education.[92] But there was no serious consideration of 'suitable mechanisms' for ensuring access for educationally backward Muslims to modern higher education. This was because backwardness is only recognized in relation to castes despite the fact that there are glaring disparities between Muslims and other groups in higher education. College completion among the 20–24 age population is 5 per cent for Muslims and 12 per cent for others. Likewise, compared to other groups their access to universities and professional colleges is low. Overall, the participation of Muslims in higher education is lower than the national average despite considerable improvement in the educational participation of all groups in the past few decades;

in fact, the improvements of Muslims have been much slower compared to other groups. There is neither affirmative action nor adequate provisioning of schools and colleges in minority-concentration areas. Moreover, disadvantage is so defined as to exclude non-Hindus, although theoretically the OBC category includes backward classes from all groups. Given this definitional bias, it would be natural for such groups to see themselves as objects of structural discrimination.[93] Yet, there was no agreement on a suitable mechanism for doing this, despite a recommendation of the Parliamentary Standing Committee that a suitable mechanism to ensure access of minorities should be created.

The exclusion of religious minorities in affirmative action was Rajiv Gandhi's major complaint against the V.P. Singh government's quota policy in 1990 and he asked the government to explain this omission.[94] But the Congress-led UPA government has followed the same strategy. Much before Rajiv Gandhi, one of the important reasons motivating Kaka Kalelkar to discount the use of caste criteria for determining backwardness was the ramifications it might have for religious minorities and their rights:

> My eyes however opened to the danger of suggesting remedies on caste basis when I discovered that it is going to have a most unhealthy effect on the Muslim and Christian sections of the nation....The Government of India recognized certain castes among the Hindus as backward and offered...privileges to these communities. This led Muslims and Christians also to assert that although their religion was fundamentally different and that theoretically it is opposed to caste, in practice their society was more or less caste-ridden.[95]

These issues highlight the unresolved tensions in regard to reservations for OBCs as through the evolution of this policy there has been little philosophical or constitutional consensus on preferential treatment for the OBCs. It also echoes the contradictions between social and economic equality arguments in accommodating claims of competing groups of the disadvantaged. As long as the beneficiary group continues to experience overall economic and educational disadvantage, as is clearly the case in regard to SCs, special or preferential treatment can be easily justified by reference to past injustice or the commitment to provide equality of opportunity. But if the group in question is not so badly off—the OBCs, for example—or has attained a measure of economic progress, the opposition is enormous. Some of these concerns have been highlighted in the critique of OBC reservations by contrasting the original SC/ST reservations with OBC reservations and the problematic aspects of the concept of backwardness which privileged 'social' (effectively caste) criteria over economic and educational.

Official attempts to categorize and expand the list of the disadvantaged castes have spurred many other groups left out into political action. There is a growing disquiet that reservations have become excessive under political pressure and that the pursuit of equality has been hijacked by politics to become the pursuit of votes. Rajeev Dhavan argues that 'India's reservation policy was designed to make "unequals" equal—not to open the door to every demand for preference by all or any community....Today's politics of reservations follows a quest for electoral victory, not social justice.'[96] These numerous controversies suggest that the social consensus underlying these policies is not as watertight as it may seem. But most political parties do not oppose reservations, which testifies to the clout of the lower castes in the polity. Mandal I effectively changed the polity through the politics of recognition of backward castes and the democratic assertion of the disadvantaged. While there is continuing conflict on the system of reservation or on issues of caste versus class, all parties are agreed on the need for it and accept the logic of caste quotas. As a result, there is an acceptance among many upper castes of the inevitability (if not the desirability) of efforts to increase the access of the hitherto excluded groups to social opportunities, if necessary through reservations. On the other hand, these very parties and governments led by them—enthusiastic champions of reservations—have done very little to promote foundational changes required to take us from the politics of reservations to a politics of redistribution. In that respect the politics of recognition has not led to, or promoted, or even seriously joined, a politics of redistribution. The critical issue is to level the playing field so as to give genuinely equal opportunity to the disadvantaged.

When reservations were introduced by the new state, the idea was to tear down the barriers to social exclusion and promote the participation of historically excluded and disadvantaged groups. Policies of affirmative action were viewed as instruments through which to offset the advantage enjoyed by some and to equalize opportunities for others. The Constituent Assembly debates indicate that these were meant only as a temporary measure and that the backwardness contemplated was extreme backwardness and not the one contemplated now. Moreover, they were seen as complementary to the commitment to an active welfare state that would ameliorate the conditions of the masses by providing an additional boost to the hitherto excluded and poor. It must be remembered that the liberalization of the economy has resulted in widening inequalities and disparities between the rich and the poor and social conflicts have become more acute during the past decade of growth. In the context of the rising economic divide, reservations address only the most exclusionary aspects of one axis of inequality and that too only caste-driven exclusions.

There is doubt that reservation policy has benefited its intended beneficiaries. A sizeable section of India's middle classes consists of OBCs, SCs, and STs.[97] Reservation policy had created a small but significant middle class among the lower-caste groups, which have acquired modern education and entered the bureaucracy and other non-traditional occupations (Table 4.6). If one were to look at reservations narrowly as a policy instrument designed to break down group disparities, it has certainly helped in the advance of disadvantaged groups through the last decades. They have placed their representatives in important positions of power and ensured that their voice is heard and schemes for their welfare introduced and implemented. Even with these gains we have not achieved a level of progress where we can afford to jettison affirmative action as an instrument of integration and inclusion.

The policy of reservations, however, has its limitations, some of which we have noted in the preceding paragraphs. Basically, social justice has come to be defined exclusively in terms of reservations and the criteria for identification in terms of caste. There is a need to revisit the framework of affirmative action, not with a view to discarding it but to improve and increase its reach and to include other groups within its ambit. The notion of review—on a decennial basis—was written into the Constitution. The need for regular review cannot be overstated. Furthermore, reservations, though politically necessary and practically helpful, are not the main instrument for the construction of a more egalitarian society. For that far more foundational changes are required, such as a major redistribution of income and wealth, generating assets like land, better schooling and colleges, special training and skill development programmes, preferential treatment in the allocation of government licences and contracts, employment-generating policies, and so on. Once the need for foundational changes is recognized and taken forward, there is certainly a strong case to be made for alternative, more sophisticated forms of affirmative action than reservations. It is now time to think about how to use different and new means to bridge disparities and deepen social equality so that the pursuit of equality and justice does not remain anchored in caste and caste alone.

Notes

1. See for example, Rochna Bajpai (2006); Frank De Zwart (2000); Clark Cunningham and N.R. Madhav Menon (1999); Krishna Thummala (1995); D.L. Sheth (2004a); Surinder Jodhka (2005); P. Radhakrishnan (2006).
2. Marc Galanter (1978: 1812–28).
3. Marc Galanter (1984).
4. Ibid., p. 185.
5. Ibid., p. 125.
6. Dipankar Gupta (2005: 400–27).
7. Marc Galanter (1978: 166).
8. Nehru's inaugural speech in the Constituent Assembly on 13 December 1946. *CAD* (Vol. I: 59).
9. Clark Cunningham and N.R. Madhava Menon (1999).
10. Marc Galanter (1984: 166).
11. *Report of the Backward Classes Commission*, Volume III (1955: vi).
12. Ibid.
13. Christophe Jaffrelot (2003: 227–9).

14. Ibid., p. 226.

15. Ibid.

16. D.L. Sheth (2000).

17. Christophe Jaffrelot (2003: 233).

18. K.C. Suri (1995).

19. *Balaji* v. *State of Mysore*, AIR 1963 SC 649.

20. *Report of the Backward Classes Commission*, Volume I (1980).

21. Ibid., p. 4.

22. *Triloki Nath* v. *The State of Jammu and Kashmir*, AIR 1969 SC 1.

23. Quoted in *The Indian Express*, 18 May 2006.

24. K.C. Suri (1995); Krishna Thummala (1995: 500).

25. Interview with Arjun Singh, *Outlook*, 22–28 April 2008.

26. Rochna Bajpai (2006: 329).

27. V.P. Singh, Rajya Sabha Debates, 7 August 1990. Speech cited in Rochna Bajpai (2006).

28. Ibid., p. 329.

29. P. Radhakrishnan (1997: 208–9).

30. For a critique of caste as the basis of reservations, see I.P. Desai (1984); for a contrary view, see Ghanshyam Shah (1985) and D.L. Sheth (2004a).

31. Ornit Shani (2007: 133–44).

32. Several court verdicts have upheld the lists of Hindu castes declared backward. For example, in *Ramakrishna Singh* v. *State of Mysore*, 1963 AIR 338, 349, the Mysore High Court held that class included persons grouped on the basis of their castes. A series of Supreme Court cases have further refined the provision. This was reaffirmed in *U.S.V. Balaram* v. *State of Andhra Pradesh*, AIR 1968 AP 165, where the Supreme Court scrapped the Andhra Pradesh High Court ruling and allowed the use of caste as a determinant to define backwardness. In *Balaji* v. *State of Mysore,* the Supreme Court put a ceiling on the total quota for affirmative action at 50 per cent. It was critical of using the caste criterion, and one of the reasons cited was its inapplicability to non-Hindu groups.

33. *Indra Sawhney* v. *Union of India*, AIR 1993 SC 477: 1992 Supp (3) SCC 217.

34. Ibid.

35. Ibid.

36. National Commission for Backward Classes, *Annual Report* (2005).

37. Justice T.K. Thommen's comment, cited in Sukumar Murlidharan (1999).

38. Ibid.

39. Figures cited by the Solicitor General of India, G.E. Vahanvati in *Ashoka Kumar Thakur* v. *Union of India*. Reported in V. Venkatesan (2008).

40. Manoj Mitta (2003).

41. Clark Cunningham and N.R. Madhava Menon (1999).

42. Ibid.

43. Interview of Rudhra Gangadharan, Director, Lal Bahadur Shastri National Academy of Administration (LBSNAA), quoted in report on the changing face of the IAS. See Anjali Puri (2007).

44. Santosh Goyal (1989: 429, 430).

45. Ibid., p. 430.

46. Ornit Shani (2007: 59–60).

47. Ibid., p. 61.

48. Jayati Ghosh (2006).

49. *P.A. Inamdar & Others* v. *State of Maharashtra*, 2005, AIR (SC) 3226.

50. *Islamic Academy of Education + 1* v. *State of Karnataka & Others*, 2003, 6 SCC 697. Reviewing the role of private higher education providers, an eleven-member bench of the Supreme Court in the *T.M.A. Pai Foundation & Others* v. *State of Karnataka & Others*, AIR, 1994, SC 13, judgment had ruled that fees charged by unaided institutions cannot be regulated but no capitation can be charged. This was once again challenged in the Supreme Court, which reiterated the concept of keeping fees imposed by private education providers within 'reasonable' limits. The key part of the judgment was that opportunities for the poorer and backward sections of society to enter unaided professional colleges should be provided and that the state government should, according to local needs, draw up a prescription for the percentage of seats in these colleges. Consequent to *Islamic Academy*, some state governments, notably Karnataka and Kerala, sought to tighten controls on unaided private colleges, and enacted legislation to this effect. Their enactments were, however, struck down by the courts and, at the education ministers' conferences held in 2004 and early 2005, the state ministers asked the Central government to enact legislation which would enable them to exercise the powers they wanted.

51. For a discussion of unequal access, see Satish Deshpande (2006: 2438–44).

52. According to the NSSO, upper castes are 37 per cent of the population of urban India but they accounted for almost 66 per cent of

all non-technical subject graduates, more than 65 per cent of medical graduates, almost 67 per cent of engineering graduates, and about 62 per cent of graduates in agricultural sciences. Ibid., p. 2438.

53. In Article 15, after Clause (4), the following clause was inserted: '(5). Nothing in this article or in sub-clause (g) of clause (1) of Article 19 shall prevent the State from making any special provision, by law, for the advancement of any socially and educationally backward classes of citizens or for the SCs or the STs in so far as such provisions relate to their admission to educational institutions including private educational institutions, *whether aided or unaided* [emphasis added] by the State, other than the minority educational institutions referred to in Clause (1) of Article 30.'

54. Dipankar Gupta (2007).

55. Pratap Bhanu Mehta (2006a).

56. *The Hindu*, 11 June 2006.

57. Report of the Committee to Enquire into the Allegations of Differential Treatment of Scheduled Castes/Scheduled Tribes Students in AIIMS (2007). This committee consisted of UGC Chairman S.K. Thorat; K.M. Shyamprasad, vice-president of the National Board of Examinations; and R.K. Srivastava, director general of Health Services. The report provides a detailed account of the role of AIIMS doctors in the anti-quota agitation (pp. 56–9).

58. 'The involvement of the administration in supporting the agitation was evident from the fact that the same administration had strictly applied a court order banning agitations within 500 metres of the AIIMS on previous occasions when workers went on strike, whereas this time the striking doctors and students had parked themselves in the central lawns. A tent was installed at the site during the night. At any time 50–100 persons were on hunger strike at this venue. The erection of the *shamiana*, provision of electricity for coolers, and other comforts such as mattresses and pillows would not have been possible without the support of the administration.' Ibid., p. 57.

59. Ibid., p. 67.

60. These colleges admit over 530,000 students and charge capitation fees upwards of Rs 50 lakh for admission to professional colleges, such as medical and engineering colleges.

61. For instance, during the agitation, upper-caste student protestors blocked busy streets and started polishing shoes (imitating shoeshine boys) with placards that read: 'This is what we will be reduced to because of the reservation system.' Notice the implication: the occupation that they (the

upper castes) would be reduced to was a 'Dalit occupation'. In other words, it is all right for Dalits to continue to do the menial jobs, but if upper castes have to descend to this low level, it is unacceptable. Needless to add, the belief that reservations would push the upper castes down to the menial jobs was only a presumption, not supported by any evidence.

62. Editorial, *Hindustan Times*, 3 June 2006.

63. The National Knowledge Commission is a high-level advisory body to the prime minister set up with the objective of transforming India into a knowledge society.

64. CNN-IBN poll conducted by A.G. Nielsen reported in *The Indian Express*, 25 July 2006.

65. Jayati Ghosh (2004).

66. Ibid.

67. There are repeated reports in newspapers that executives in the Indian private sector get the highest salaries in Asia. The prime minister urged the corporate sector to exercise restraint with regard to their salaries and lifestyle, which he said can lead to conflict and even violence. Prime minister's speech to the Confederation of Indian Industry, reported in *The Times of India*, 30 May 2007.

68. Meira Kumar, Minister for Social Justice, called this the 'Dronacharya mindset'—the mindset which systematically deprives groups of people of the very capacity to compete, and then cites performance in a limited arena of competition as proof of superiority. 'The continuance of the Dronacharya mindset in India is undoubtedly a result of thousands of years of caste-linked occupational reservation.' *The Times of India*, 11 July 2006.

69. Satish Deshpande (2006: 2442–3).

70. Praful Bidwai (2006c).

71. Pratap Bhanu Mehta (2006b).

72. For a discussion on the First Amendment, see Granville Austin (1999: 69–86).

73. Rajiv Gandhi's speech on the Mandal Commission in the Lok Sabha, reproduced in *The Indian Express*, 9 June 2006.

74. *The Times of India*, 14 July 2006.

75. *The Hindu*, 23 April 2006.

76. Ibid.

77. Pratap Bhanu Mehta (2007).

78. Interview with Arjun Singh, *Outlook*, 22–28 April 2008.

79. V. Venkatesan (2006).

80. Editorial, *The Hindu*, 2 April 2007.

81. SC interim order, 29 March 2006, reported in *The Hindu*, 30 March 2007.

82. Additional Solicitor General Gopal Subramaniam argued that for the 'SCs and STs, and OBCs the possibility for admission in education is much narrower than, and hence incomparable to, the degree of latitude available and possible for prescribing qualifications for public employment. This narrow range of flexibility in respect of qualifying marks for admission, necessitated by the need of each institution to prescribe cut-off norms in order to maintain academic standards, will have the effect of reducing the chances of adequate number of OBC candidates for filling the entire quota of 27 per cent being available if Socially Advanced Persons (SAPs) or Creamy Layer (CL) is excluded.' Reported in *The Hindu*, 1 November 2007.

83. Venkitesh Ramakrishnan, 'Political Consensus', *Frontline*, 26 April–9 May 2008.

84. Arguments in the Supreme Court and final verdict reported in *The Hindu*, 12 April 2008.

85. *The Hindu*, 11 October 2007.

86. *The Hindu*, 11 April 2008.

87. In *Venkataramana* v. *State of Madras*, the Supreme Court upheld the list of Hindu castes declared as backward by the Madras government. In a landmark judgment, the Mysore High Court held that caste 'classification will only be open to challenge if it can be shown that the criterion adopted for determining their backwardness is useless as test of backwardness, so that the preference would amount to preference on grounds of caste alone.' These judgments effectively set aside the constitutional objection in *Balaji* v. *The State of Mysore* to the use of caste as a unit, although it could not be the sole or dominant test of backwardness.

88. *The Times of India*, 25 October 2007.

89. Anuradha Raman (2007).

90. K. Venugopal, appearing for the Resident Doctors Association, stated in his submission on the 93rd Constitution Amendment and the OBC quota that the Hindi version of the bill specifically excluded the creamy layer but the English version curiously did not. *The Hindu*, 14 September 2007.

91. Satish Deshpande (2008).

92. Note Submitted by the NCM to the Rajya Sabha Department Related Parliamentary Standing Committee of the MHRD, 186th Report on the Central Educational Institutions (Reservation in Admission) Bill, 2006.

93. Bhiku Parekh (2006: 441).

94. Rajiv Gandhi's speech, reproduced in *The Indian Express*, 9 June 2006.

95. Excerpted from the *Report of the Backward Classes Commission* (1955).

96. Rajeev Dhavan (2003).

97. D.L. Sheth (2002).

5

Politics of Representation and Under-representation

Political representation like reservation has been at the centre of political debates in India in recent times. A fundamental issue in democracies is the extent to which the political system facilitates representation of multiple interests; in particular, the degree to which the diversity of both the interests and the characteristics of the electorate are represented in legislatures is a basic concern.[1] The legitimacy and stability of any democracy depends to a large extent upon its ability to accomplish this aim. Liberal approaches to representation have traditionally been concerned with what might be termed a strictly electoral theory of representation, wherein political legitimacy is seen to depend primarily upon elected status. On the other hand, a basic premise of representative democracy is that all those subject to policy should have a voice in its making. In electoral democracies, important changes in public policy depend critically on the presence of legislators and decision makers from disadvantaged groups, who can then use the legislative and policy arenas to bring about improvements.[2]

For the past few decades, scholars and politicians have recognized that the democratic system in India does not provide adequate representation to certain groups, especially ethnic minorities. Today, even equitable and fair-minded policies can be objected to because the processes by which they were arrived at were undemocratic and excluded certain groups—women and minorities, for instance.[3] In India, religious minorities and women have not yet made gains towards more equitable political representation. This chapter focuses on political representation, which has been helped along by policies of reservations discussed in previous chapters, enabling a steady increase in the legislative representation of backward castes, in contrast to the persistent under-representation of Muslims in Central and state legislatures. It provides a broad overview of the political context of these changes, which have promoted the representation of lower castes generally and more particularly in legislatures. It is when the close relationship between caste, politics, reservations, and the impact of the reservation regime on party political processes is examined that we can see how this relationship works to the advantage of backward-caste groups. It explores the role and effect of the policy of reservations on identity construction and on the political representation of the OBCs. This stands in contrast to the minorities, whose representation has been stationary through these turbulent changes. It seeks to foreground the evolution and progression of the representation of backward castes and under-representation of minorities in legislatures, focusing on political processes that can enhance or constrain their political representation. It examines why legislative representation has been low and how it can be increased.

Political parties generally tend to under-nominate minorities and lack the will to counter unsubstantiated assumptions with regard to political opposition of voters to minority candidates, who presumably cannot win elections owing to this opposition. It is clear from the contrasting political fortunes of the OBCs and minorities that institutional design, type of electoral system, and similar factors may have some impact on representational outcomes, but in the end it is party processes and political leadership that play the most important role in influencing outcomes. In short, it is political processes rather than institutional design that can better explain the differences and inequalities in representational patterns.

THE POLITICS OF REPRESENTATION

The centrality of caste in Indian politics was felt in the very first general election, and increasingly with each successive election.

The issue is not just the centrality of caste in electoral politics but its changed meaning and legitimacy for different sections of society since the 1980s that accounts for the huge increase in the legislative presence of OBCs. Caste-based mobilization has always been a marked feature of Indian politics, but it is much stronger today than when India became independent. A change in the orientation started in the 1970s, when the politics of backwardness took a new turn with the installation of the first non-Congress ministry at the Centre in 1977. It began to be argued that caste was important in public life on grounds of social justice. Lower castes exploited and humiliated in the past should be given special protection through quotas in the government. This was largely due to the reservation policy of the state, which had, despite slow and tardy implementation, created a significant section of lower castes that had acquired education and had joined non-traditional occupations and professions. This formed the nucleus of a small but highly vocal political leadership among the lower castes, which began to change the political discourse.

The Constitution and the dominant political discourse in the 1950s installed a specific view of representation, derived from the notion that representatives were supposed to be acting on behalf of society as a whole or the geographical constituency they represented. This was a conception widely shared by the Congress leadership; it allowed no space for descriptive representation. Jawaharlal Nehru was the most eloquent spokesperson of the strongly held belief that politicians should work in favour of larger social interests that were not their own. This view dominated the first phase of democratic politics. It extended to the end of 1960s, over four general elections.[4]

Political representation appeared to reflect the liberal-individualist format of constitutional arrangements, and debates were carried out in terms of conflicts between political ideals of laissez-faire and state intervention, or capitalist development and socialist redistribution. Social classes like the industrialists, managerial elites, and middle classes were central to political life and representation. Political parties throughout this period were supposed to be a crucial aggregative medium for the articulation of collective interests. Parties in office believed that they should intervene to reform the position of the socially and economically underprivileged. Underpinning these concerns was a consensus that the state was the most important means for the promotion of public good and well-being. This conception had its origins in ideas and principles of developmental democracy.

In the 1950s and 1960s issues of land reforms, nationalization of large industry, building the public sector, and alternative strategies for the development of industry and agriculture were central issues. Even the movements of that period, right up to the mid-1970s, were largely movements on economic issues and focused on questions of corruption, black-marketeering, hoarding, land reforms, and food shortages. By the early 1970s the importance of class-based movements and class politics was declining and being replaced by mass movements against corruption and nepotism. From the 1980s, there was a gradual erosion of the Nehruvian secular-nationalist imagination, and one factor responsible for it was the emergence of caste as an important feature of public discourse. The 1990s saw massive convulsions in the sphere of identity politics and the Congress, buffeted between contending positions, was unable to take clear-cut positions on some of the key issues like the secular–communal divide in the polity and reservations for the backward castes in the policy realm which we noted in the previous chapter.

During more than four decades of Congress dominance, political institutions were dominated by upper-caste elites. These upper-caste elites and the dominant classes, along with the bureaucratic interests, were keen to establish their control over political representation. This approach was challenged by subsequent political events from the late 1960s. Political discourse came to be increasingly influenced by ethnic inequalities, which also dictated the pattern of mobilization, considerably weakening the earlier language of class interests, capitalism, and socialism. The emphasis shifted from objectively defined interests to a much greater focus on identity and distribution of patronage to certain groups. This privileged political presence over common interests.

The breakdown of the Congress system was starkly evident after Indira Gandhi's disastrous Emergency experiment, which resulted in a sharp and substantial drop in its vote base. It was clear that Indira Gandhi's lurch towards authoritarian rule had cost the party heavily in terms of popular credibility in north India, which suffered the worst excesses of the Emergency. It was a blow that the Congress never really recovered from. Its uninterrupted three-decade-long rule at the Centre was broken when the 1977 elections brought the Janata Party to power. After the defeat of the Congress in the 1977 elections and the formation of the first non-Congress government at the Centre led by the Janata Party, a conglomeration of four parties (Jana Sangh, Bhartiya Lok Dal, Congress [O], and Socialist Party) emerged as a major force in national politics. However, as late as the 1980s the decline of the Congress was far from definitive. The disenchantment with the Janata Party's uninspiring leadership and its internecine squabbling brought Indira Gandhi back to power in 1980. In the 1984 elections, held after her assassination, the Congress polled the highest vote and seat tally ever as a sympathy vote swept the country and brought her young son Rajiv to power. But the underlying trends signified the collapse of one-party dominance and the end of the Congress epoch in Indian politics. It also signalled the decline of upper-caste dominance through the vehicle of the Congress party.

By the early 1980s, the Congress found itself at variance with the contradictory changes its own control over the state had brought about. Within the Congress itself multiple sources of power had developed, thanks to the formation of linguistic states and the emergence of regional elites. In later years these regional leaders challenged the hegemony of the Centre as well as the domination of the upper castes. They favoured rural interests, especially agriculture, and preferred to stress caste rather than class issues.[5] Three decades of economic growth had created opportunities, jobs, and public employment for the educated upper-caste/class English-speaking elite, and left behind the educated sections of the backward and lower castes. The Congress was unable to satisfy the growing aspirations of the lower castes that had been excluded from leadership positions. Even though the upper castes dominated the party, it was projecting itself as a party of the disadvantaged, poor, and landless.

Political parties like the Congress took to ethnic politics as a substitute for pro-poor mobilization and policies. For other parties, which were either breakaway factions of the Congress or new parties established to represent the aspirations of the lower castes, it was a platform for assertion of specific lower-caste interests that had less chance of articulation under the upper-caste hegemony of the Congress party. Large sections of the lower strata of social groups abandoned the Congress and constituted themselves into shifting alliances of their own separate political parties. The national parties had to now negotiate for political support directly with the social–political collectivities of the backward castes, the SCs, and the STs, or with the regional-caste parties constituted by them. The upper-caste hegemony over national politics began to be progressively challenged.

This process came to a head in the course of the Mandal Commission's proposal to extend reservations in jobs and education to the OBCs. This proposal was opposed by sections of the upper-caste middle classes. They saw the newly mobilized lower castes finding their way into the middle classes, not through open competition but through reservation. Notwithstanding the bitterness, this led to a resurgence of lower castes in national and state politics, even as it fuelled a conflict of interests between upper and lower castes. Nonetheless, loosely speaking, class and caste continued to roughly correspond. But over time, the middle and lower-middle class have developed a more diverse caste character through lower-caste incorporation as well as the presence of upper and forward castes among the lower-middle class.

The point to note is that lower-caste groups were no longer prepared to accept a Brahminical ordering of caste hierarchy and status. In fact there was an even greater emphasis on caste identity and consequent mobilization based on it. The categories of OBCs, SCs, and STs had acquired a strong social and political content, and there are now parties which specifically represent them. Self-representation was the epitome of representation, and reservation the singular scheme for promoting it. Within this form of representation, the political actor claims to act on behalf of his own group, or even simply for himself/herself. This was distinct from the earlier form of representation in which the elected politicians self-consciously acted on behalf of a larger group of which they were not a part and whose identity or interests they did not share.

Significant changes in the caste system also provided the impetus for these transformations, the most significant being the formation of a new trans-local identity among lower castes oppressed by the traditional system of hierarchy. A new form of caste politics emerged, in which larger agglomerations of castes and sub-castes have become the operative units. Several castes occupying more or less similar locations in different hierarchies began to organize themselves horizontally as it became necessary for them to negotiate with the state and in the process project a larger social identity and numerical strength.[6] The aim of this politics was to use the numerical weight of lower castes in electoral politics to restructure power and thus challenge the caste and class privileges of upper castes. With the growing awareness of their numerical strength and the important role this could play in achieving political representation, their aspirations took the form of political action and mobilization. The nexus of caste and ritual was broken down and caste groupings now exist as socio-cultural entities detached from the traditional ritual statuses.[7] The reservation policy itself, by providing special educational and occupational opportunities to members of the numerous lower castes, converted their traditional disability of low ritual status into an asset for acquiring new means for upward social mobility. As a result, caste assumed a new importance in political mobilization, and, as the basis of political representation far exceeded its role as the signifier of ritual hierarchy.

These trends were of greater relevance in north India. In the earlier part of the twentieth century, southern and western India had experienced caste-based politics with a long history of anti-Brahmin movements and struggles which was to become the vehicle for the empowerment of the lower castes. Reservation policies have played a considerable part in the crystallization of lower-caste movements and identities in south India as well, but in these regions this process was sustained and supported by non-Brahmin ideologies. Additionally, in south India, the mobilization of the non-Brahmin castes happened earlier than in the north.

Though backward-caste movements in Tamil Nadu and Karnataka were not radical, the political mobilization of lower castes was an important vehicle for social transformation and the consequent decrease in common indignities, as well as the rapid displacement of upper castes from positions of power in the administration and legislatures. An important factor in the rising political consciousness and organization of the lower castes was the widespread rejection of the ideological foundations of the hierarchical social order. The deconstruction of the ideology underlying caste politicized the lower castes. Some groups sought equality through Sanskritization, but the main strategy was that of proclaiming their status as backward castes and demanding greater political power. The north was 'catching up' with this trend, as it were.[8] One of the biggest successes of reservation policy and politics, therefore, lay in reshaping the very character of legislative representation and democratic politics. The formation of caste-based parties gave an impetus to this process in north India where reservation policies were more or less the starting point for the process of political mobilization.[9] It led to a resurgence of lower castes in north Indian politics, riding on feelings of resentment over their exclusion despite having numbers on their side. Backed by the OBCs, the political space for the non-Congress parties increased because lower-caste voters decided to no longer vote for upper-caste candidates put up by parties such as the Congress. The new development lay in the fact that these groups were not content with representation by upper-caste elites and wanted more direct representation.[10]

The push for reservations for backward castes in the wake of V.P. Singh's sudden decision to implement reservations in Central and state government jobs underlined the crucial role of the state's conception of backwardness. The state had succeeded in encouraging through preferential policies a structure of political representation tied to notions of proportionality. There is a political logic to preferential policies that shapes public debates and political responses. The social construction of target groups becomes embedded in policy as messages that are absorbed by citizens and affect their orientation and participation patterns.[11] Reservation policy sends messages not only about which citizens are disadvantaged and therefore deserving of state support but also regarding what kinds of identities and participatory patterns are appropriate and legitimate in a democratic society. These policies are often important in shaping the identity of an ethnic group and determining who a member is; state actions intentionally and unintentionally influence the identification and formation of groups, as well as the demands and accommodation of various sectors of society everywhere in the world. Directly and indirectly, state policies offer incentives and opportunities for mobilization of influence of some groups, while simultaneously denying these to others. The key point is that state institutions and state policies inevitably affect decisions about types of groups that gain representation. In India's electoral democracy, however, policies differ according to the identity in question. Therefore, institutional interventions for caste groups and religious minorities assume distinct forms and distinct political consequences.

The reservation policy was critical to the increased political representation of backward caste groups. It created a powerful inducement for political mobilization on caste lines, as it grouped members of diverse castes together under a backward-caste identity. It provided political and economic incentives to mobilize around this identity, which has been sustained not only by affirmative action programmes of the government but also by social and political organizations that evolved in response to government's willingness to reward claims on the basis of backwardness. Its main contribution was to club together a broad range of castes together under the OBC label. The new unity helped the backward castes to organize themselves as a powerful group outside the Congress system by leveraging their main asset at the time of elections—their massive numbers. This strategy of political mobilization reached its apogee in the aftermath of the Mandal decision to implement 27 per cent quotas for backward castes in the Central government.

Reservations have had a cumulative impact on India's political system. The beneficiaries of affirmative action are now occupying important positions in legislatures, the Cabinet, and the bureaucracy. Reservations have contributed to changing the balance of power in government and legislatures. The political inclusion of the excluded groups encouraged by social policy and facilitated by democratic politics has resulted in changing the social relations of power. This has produced a shift in the balance of political power in governments and legislatures, with a new downward thrust, which coincides with similar trends and patterns in south and west India which were well established by the late 1960s.[12] The growing clout of backward castes has been largely due to the politicization and mobilization of the OBCs in favour of reservations, and their increased democratic participation and assertiveness has in turn changed the political attitudes of most political parties towards them.

Post-Mandal all major parties (including, notably, the BJP) have accommodated the ambitions of backward castes and facilitated their entry in the corridors of power. By giving the lower castes a large number of tickets and the possibility of a share in power, non-Congress parties addressed the critical issue of the representational blockage in political institutions.[13] Henceforth, political power passed into the hands of the less socially and educationally advanced group.

Changes in Caste Composition of Legislatures

A brief comparison of the caste composition of national and state legislatures today with the situation soon after Independence reveals significant change in the political representation of backward castes. In the 1950s, India's national politics were dominated by English-speaking, upper-caste urban politicians who constituted two-thirds of the Lok Sabha.[14] Even the lower-level political leadership tended to come from the upper castes in north India. There is now much greater diversity in public institutions, as can be seen from the major increase in the number of lower-caste legislators and senior civil servants in influential government positions.

Based on the percentage of their population in each state, the Constitution explicitly permits reservations for SCs and STs in Parliament and state assemblies. Both the national and state electoral systems use single-member constituencies with FPTP, winner-takes-all majority elections. Overall, the proportion of SCs and STs in Parliament is approximately at the level of the reservation for them, though in the case of STs it has exceeded this figure by about 2 per cent over the last decade, and stands at 9 per cent in the case of the SCs.[15]

The gap between the upper and lower castes narrowed during the 1980s and 1990s and the share of lower castes shot up when lower-caste parties began to grow and acquire power.[16] With the increase in mobilization of backward castes, there has been a substantial rise in the representation of the OBCs in legislatures. The proportion of upper-caste MPs fell below 50 per cent for the first time in 1977 (Table 5.1). More than 60 per cent of north Indian MPs in the first Lok Sabha came from the upper castes and only 4.5 per cent from the OBCs; by 1996, the share of OBC MPs had increased to over 25 per cent. The emergence of the Janata Dal in the late 1980s produced a bigger change: the percentage of backward-caste MPs doubled in 1989 from 11 to 21 per cent; by 1996, the share of OBC MPs had increased to over 25 per cent.[17] V.P. Singh called this gradual transfer of power a 'silent social revolution'.[18] This shift was, however, under way in the state legislatures much before it occurred in the Lok Sabha (Table 5.2). It was most discernible in Uttar Pradesh and Madhya Pradesh, despite their rather different demographic patterns and distinct political traditions.

The rise of the backward castes is the most striking feature of Madhya Pradesh and Uttar Pradesh politics, even though conservative influence has dominated the former while socialist currents dominated the latter. The interesting feature is that despite these contrasting political legacies the rise of backward-caste mobilization changed the social profile of representation in both states. The political trajectories of these two states have produced more or less parallel outcomes even though different political parties have ruled them throughout the 1990s, with the BJP, BSP, and Samajwadi Party in power in Uttar Pradesh, and the Congress and BJP in control of Madhya Pradesh. Indeed, the success of the BJP in Madhya Pradesh and Uttar Pradesh is attributable in part to the rise of backward castes in the party.[19] In other words, both states converged in the 1980s in terms of the social profiles of their ruling elites. The overall picture of political representation in Madhya Pradesh is similar to that of the other Hindi-speaking states. Upper-caste MLAs declined from one-half in the early 1970s to one-third in 1998, while backward castes have risen from one-tenth to one-fifth in the same period.[20] To some extent this is true of Uttar Pradesh as well, although in this state the representation of backward castes varies according to which party wins elections. In Uttar Pradesh, the share of upper-caste MLAs declined from 58 per cent in 1962 to 37.7 per cent in 1996, whereas the proportion of backward castes grew from 9 per cent to 30 per cent in 1993. The biggest change was witnessed in Bihar. Here, the number of MPs rose from 17 per cent to 40 per cent—comparatively the biggest increase in any state in this period; while the backward castes rose from 26 to 35 per cent in the same period.[21] The proportion of backward-caste MLAs has doubled from 20.6 per cent in 1952 to 42 per cent in 2005 while the percentage of upper-caste MLAs was down from 46 to 26 per cent.[22]

In Tamil Nadu it is well known that backward castes have been in a dominant position in the legislature since the early 1960s. The share of backward castes has never dropped much below 60 per cent since then, although it has dipped slightly and gone up again in 1989.[23] In Karnataka, Lingayats and Vokkaligas have traditionally been the dominant players in state politics. The backward castes emerged as a major political force ever since the first non-dominant-caste chief minister Devraj Urs forged unity among them to break the hegemony of the dominant castes. Since then the backward castes have had a powerful impact on electoral outcomes, resulting in an increase in their representation in parties and legislatures. Congress chief ministers between 1989 and 1994 had failed to resolve the issue of which caste groups (and in what proportion) would continue to enjoy reservation benefits.[24] This was necessary in view of the Supreme Court's creamy layer decision, which required exclusion of such members as had already advanced in class terms from both the backward and scheduled communities. In July 1993 when 12 per cent of the members of Lingayats and Vokkaligas were excluded from benefits by the Congress government, it posed a threat to the privileges of the most prosperous members of both castes. The government was compelled to back down and in the end actually raised reservations from 50 to 57 per cent.[25] The subsequent success of the Janata Dal compared to its main competitor, the Congress party, among the dominant castes was contingent upon the resolution of the reservation issue to the advantage of dominant and non-dominant backward castes. In Andhra Pradesh, Kammas and Reddys are quite prominent as they represent more than 50 per cent of MLAs, at the expense of both the upper and backward castes. In fact, in Andhra the share of backward-caste MLAs has declined from 20 per cent to 12 per cent.[26] The increasing importance of backward castes is evident in the relatively more class- and ideology-driven politics of Kerala as well. There is high representation of backward castes in the Muslim League, the RSP, the CPI (M), and the CPI. Over the years, the Congress, which had given lesser tickets to them, has also increased their percentage of tickets. The percentage of upper-caste MLAs decreased from 49 per cent in 1957 to 40 per cent in 1996.[27] The increase in non-upper-caste representation has much to do with the sizeable presence of the Izhava community and the close proximity of the Sree Narayana Dharma Paripalana (SNDP) Yogam, an Izhava organization, to the communist parties in Kerala.

All in all, the most dramatic change has clearly taken place in politics and the social background of political personnel at the state level rather than at the Central level, but Christophe Jaffrelot points out that 'it is an uneven pattern of political empowerment.'[28] The biggest change has taken place in Uttar Pradesh, which was for more than three decades an upper-caste stronghold. Here the rise of lower caste has been at the expense of the upper castes in the last two decades, and most noticeably in the 1990s. West Bengal and the dominant caste-oriented states of Gujarat and Rajasthan are exceptions to the forward march of the backwards; these are the only states where backward castes have not made a big headway. But in most other states the OBCs and SCs are in a majority.

In the 2004 Lok Sabha, the backward castes, SCs, and Muslims together constitute almost 50 per cent, while upper castes constitute the rest.[29] The 'fifty-fifty' distribution of seats between upper and lower castes signaled the emergence of disadvantaged castes as a major force in politics and governance in India. Its biggest effect was felt on mainstream parties such as the Congress and BJP, which have offered tickets to a larger number of OBC candidates.

Indeed, because of the existence of democracy and the electoral value attached to large numbers, it has been possible for OBCs to use the political process to assert their collective power and to try and change the social, ideological, and economic underpinnings of the caste system in their favour. This has completely altered the architecture of political representation in India.

Backward-Caste Ascendancy and Other Marginalized Groups

Democratic participation in the past two to three decades has seen a transfer of power from the upper castes/classes to the middle and backward castes, but it has not produced a structure of power sharing that fully reflects the pattern of social diversity in India. The new pattern of political representation has principally benefited the backward castes, whereas minorities and women have failed to get adequate representation in legislatures and higher echelons of decision making, with or without quotas. As mentioned earlier, the backward castes, with no legislative reservations, constitute more than a quarter of the Lok Sabha today. On the other hand, formal equality has obscured the conspicuous under-representation of minorities in legislatures. Yet, there is very little debate or thinking about the under-representation of minorities, as much of the discussion on political reforms has been restricted for the most part to reform of the electoral system to make it free and fair.

The substantial increase in the representation of backward castes has encouraged an escalation of demands from other excluded groups—notably, women and minorities. However, in India, the caste system is the 'steel frame' that has underpinned society and the polity in the past several decades and particularly the last two. From 1996, when the 81st Constitutional Amendment Bill, called the Women's Reservation Bill was first announced, proposing a reservation of 33 per cent in Parliament for women, the Bill has not been passed, owing to opposition that emanates largely from parties representing backward castes and Dalits. The party consensus that had allowed the smooth passage of the historic 73rd Amendment Act reserving 33 per cent of seats for women in local bodies broke down on the question of backward-caste and Dalit representation within the quota for women. Caste-based parties argued fiercely for a quota within the women's quota. This has effectively stalled women's reservation in legislatures ever since the Bill for 33 per cent reservations for women in legislatures was introduced in 1996. The saga of women's reservation shows the power of the backward-caste groups in the political system, which has given them a virtual veto on the question of representation of other marginalized and excluded groups. Despite the political pressure mounted by women's groups they have not succeeded in getting the legislation passed. This is because the question of caste remains predominant in the structure of representation.

However, the success of representative politics is to be judged by the extent to which political mobilization and electoral processes generate the representation of a diverse range of groups and interests. From 1947 to 1966, despite Nehru's sincere efforts to include minorities in the government at all levels, Muslims did not get adequate representation in state institutions. Although the Constitution does not require that minorities will be included in government, there appears to be a national common sense that the dominance of the Congress party after Independence allowed minorities to gain effective representation in governance.[30] It has been argued that the Congress party, functioning as an inclusive 'grand coalition', accommodated minorities by granting cultural autonomy, ensuring minority proportionality in politics, education, and government employment, and giving them a veto over important social legislation.[31] Many advocates of secularism share the belief that these policies were responsible for India's relative stability and success in managing ethnic and communal conflict. While the Congress governments regularly offered positions to Muslims (and certainly much more than other parties have done), it was nowhere near proportional to their population.[32] Moreover, these men and women were kept away from positions of real power. Given the inflated ideas about the role of Muslims in public life, it is hardly surprising that the issue of Muslim under-representation has gone unnoticed.

The Congress party has historically projected itself as the patron and protector of Muslims, and as the guarantor of the secular state that recognizes minority rights. The Congress, especially Nehru's Congress, was the party of choice for Muslims. In the first general elections, Muslims voted en bloc for the Congress, and yet the number of Muslims elected to the Lok Sabha was by no means in proportion to their population and entitlement. The fundamental premise of joint electorates was the expectation that they would usher in a non-communal and non-sectarian environment which would be conducive to equal opportunities for all. But this did not happen—in fact, political exclusion was to become the order of the day. Representation of Muslims under Congress and non-Congress rule remained roughly the same.

However, the secular credentials of the Congress have been compromised in recent years as the party diluted its secular commitment for the sake of electoral calculations. After 1983, the party under the leadership of Indira Gandhi actively courted the vote of the majority community to undercut the growing influence of the BJP.[33] The Congress also tried to woo and pander to the religious sentiments of the Muslim clerics in order to ensure that the electoral reverses suffered by the party in by-elections were not repeated on a national scale—hence the controversial decision of the government to reverse the Supreme Court verdict in the Shah Bano case in 1986. The attempt to please majority and minority sentiment was evident when the Congress government led by Rajiv Gandhi enacted a legislation—the Muslim Women's Act in 1986—declaring that Muslim women would not have access to civil law in matters of marriage and divorce. These campaigns made the status of Muslims a leading political question in the parliamentary elections of 1989 and 1991 and the state assembly election of 1993–4 in north India.

The shift in the Muslim voting pattern was even more striking in the wake of the Ayodhya controversy and the failure to prevent the demolition of the Babri mosque in Ayodhya in December 1992 and the subsequent violence in which hundreds of Muslims lost their lives. Muslims turned away from the Congress party when it allowed the foundation stone of a new Ram temple on the disputed site in Ayodhya. Before this event, Muslim leaders had been demanding that the government should stop the foundation ceremony, and they used the potential loss of Muslim vote to bargain with the Congress on the matter. The Congress government ignored the Muslim plea, resulting in a loss of their support. This proved to be a turning point in the Muslim backlash against the Congress as they blamed the party for its failure to protect the mosque. Their collective frustration was expressed in the vote against the Congress in the 1991 parliamentary election. The Shah Bano and Babri mosque controversies have seen the re-emergence of Muslims as a factor of tremendous importance in India's electoral politics.

The Congress was unable to address issues of security and equity, especially livelihood, education, and employment. Most of all, it did not address the vital issue of security which remained a major concern for ordinary Muslims as the incidence of violence against minorities showed a marked increase throughout the country. Several communal riots left behind a disproportionately large number of Muslim victims. Muslims recognized the relevance of secularism and used it effectively for the acceptance of Muslim identity, which they had at first apprehended would be diminished by it. But in the new political context, secularism was reduced to an identity-constituting ideology that offered Muslims an identity as citizens without the substantive rights that frequently go with it. This was despite the fact that there was evidence that the socio-economic condition of Muslims was extremely bad. They had a negligible political representation in legislatures. Ordinary Muslims began to lose faith in the Congress, as the party was unable to address their basic needs.[34]

Importantly, Muslim political behaviour is quite similar to that of other groups.[35] The degree of Muslim concentration and the political context does play a part in determining their electoral preferences. With the exception of a few elections in which Muslims have displayed solidarity, their political support is fragmented. They have not voted en bloc for any single party and have changed their preferences from election to election; rather they have voted for whichever party was likely to offer them economic and physical security. This is particularly true of non-elite Muslims, as their energies are focused principally on the problems of economic deprivation, educational backwardness, and the insecurity produced by frequent communal riots, which affect their livelihood. Muslim support varied from region to region and sometimes even from constituency to constituency. No non-BJP party was in a position to claim their total support.

As Dalits responded to the disintegration of their vertical ties to national parties by pursuing laterally integrated political mobilization, Muslims too have forged links with regional parties such as the Telugu Desam Party in Andhra Pradesh, the DMK in Tamil Nadu, and caste-based parties such as the BSP, RJD, and Samajwadi Party in Uttar Pradesh. This notwithstanding the fact that many of them have joined the BJP-led coalition. Regionalization of the Muslim vote reduces its importance as an all-India political force at the same time, as it is useful for gaining access to the material benefits of development.

Overall, it is important to note the three currents in Indian politics that have affected the interests and representation of Muslims. The trends consisted of the decline of Congress dominance, the intensified assertion of backward castes and regional parties, and the steady rise of the BJP as a major force in the polity, culminating in the formation of a BJP-led government in 1998 and 1999 at the Centre and in several states in north and north-western India in the past decade.

Minority participation in electoral politics measured in terms of participation as voters and attendees in public meetings and campaigns has been on the increase. But political equality as implying a roughly proportionate distribution of political activity rarely extends to the sphere of representation in governance and public institutions. That is to say, there is no tendency towards equality when it comes to the distribution of power or membership of representative bodies.

The increasing involvement of Muslims in electoral processes has not enhanced their representation in the legislature, both state and national. Muslims have been consistently under-represented in Parliament. The representation of Sikhs, Christians, and Jains is roughly in proportion to their population. In fact, only Muslim representation, averaging between 4 to 5.7 per cent, continues to be appreciably lower than their proportion in the population. Table 5.3

shows that the overall average representation approximates 5.79 per cent, which is less than half their share in the population. Within this range we can see that Muslim representation has fluctuated. In the first Lok Sabha they constituted 4.3 per cent of the house, and in the 14th (2004) Lok Sabha they formed 6.4 per cent.

In 1980 the total number of Muslims elected was the highest ever at 9.2 per cent. In other words, low percentages in the 1950s and 1960s increased slowly and reached a high of 9 per cent in the 1980s, after which Muslim representation has remained stuck at roughly 5 per cent. But the overall proportion of Muslims who actually get elected does not change very significantly—it was 6.6 per cent of the Lok Sabha in the 2004 elections, which is slightly higher than in previous three elections. In other words, there was no consistent upward trend in the political representation of Muslims, which on the whole remains low, with the exception of 1980 elections. Also while the number of Muslim contestants has gone up considerably, the success ratio has gone down, which is an indication that most of these candidates were contesting from less winnable seats. In the Lok Sabha, the success ratio of Muslim candidates has slipped from 61 per cent in 1952 to 18–20 per cent in 1991–9 (Table 5.4).

The under-representation is doubly evident from the minuscule presence of Muslim women in legislatures, both at the state and national levels.[36] Of the 406 Muslim candidates elected to the last thirteen Lok Sabhas, only twelve have been women; their record in elections to Vidhan Sabhas is not much better. The percentage of Muslim women who win elections to the Vidhan Sabhas (5.5 per cent) is roughly half the average for all women (10.62 per cent); although this is better than their performance in the Lok Sabha, it is still only half that of women in general, bolstering the view that Muslim women find it even harder to get elected. Discrimination on the part of political parties or the electorate at large may play a role in the lower electoral success rates of Muslim women. Their participation has been hampered both by their gender as well as their minority religious status, as both women and Muslims have traditionally been under-represented in the formal structures of politics. Even before the rise of BJP their presence was miniscule.

Muslim representation in Vidhan Sabhas is not much better (Table 5.5). Regional and party breakdown of candidates reveals that Muslims have tended to be elected from a small selection of states. Uttar Pradesh is overwhelmingly dominant, with 98 candidates (24 per cent of the total), followed by West Bengal with 56 candidates (14 per cent of the total), Bihar with 47 candidates (12 per cent of the total), and Jammu and Kashmir with 40 (10 per cent of the total).[37] Among the state legislative assemblies, in Uttar Pradesh, with a Muslim population of 19 per cent, the proportion of Muslim MLAs was 8–10 per cent, decreasing quite significantly to 5–6 per cent in the 1990s marked by communal politics and violence surrounding the Ayodhya movement. The representation of Muslims in the states of Assam and Kerala is quite low compared to the proportion of their population but much better than other states. The states which have significant Muslim population but under-represented Muslims in the legislature are Andhra Pradesh, Maharashtra, Gujarat, and Karnataka. Overall, the number of Muslim candidates elected to the Vidhan Sabhas remains far lower than the proportion of Muslims in the population might warrant. Iqbal Ansari's analysis shows that in Andhra Pradesh, Muslim under-representation in the Legislative Assembly is 61 per cent (much higher than in the Lok Sabha, 41 per cent), in Bihar 47 per cent, Gujarat 79 per cent, Karnataka 71 per cent, Madhya Pradesh 69 per cent, and Maharashtra 62 per cent. Rajasthan shows an improved index (56 per cent) over its Lok Sabha score. But Uttar Pradesh shows a decline from 39 to 46 per cent.[38]

Between 1952 and 2004, of the 441 elected Muslim MPs only 24 per cent were elected from Muslim-majority constituencies, whereas 76 per cent were elected from non-Muslim majority constituencies, indicating that significant proportions of non-Muslims are voting for them (Table 5.6).[39] This pattern suggests two important trends. Muslims are usually given nominations from constituencies with sizeable Muslim votes. However, constituencies with marginal Muslim presence have regularly returned Muslim candidates, indicating that Muslims can and do win from non-Muslim majority constituencies despite the Hindu–Muslim polarization since 1989.[40] This underlines that voting is on party lines, which suggests that voters have no hesitation in voting for Muslims simply because party identification is generally more significant than the identity of the candidates. This pattern holds good even after 1989–99—a period marked by the escalation of communal polarization, and yet the majority of Muslims were elected from non-Muslim constituencies. Muslims themselves invariably vote for secular and centrist parties that dominate in constituencies with a Muslim population of 30–50 per cent.

Despite this non-sectarian trend in voting, parties often tend to look at electoral politics from an identity angle and are unwilling to give tickets to minorities for fear of giving an advantage to their rivals. Party leaders and managers assume that identities influence voting behaviour and that voters prefer candidates from their own community. Parties disregard minority claims to tickets because they fear their rivals would rally the majority of voters against the minority candidate. In other words, party managers worry that members of their own group will vote on non-ethnic lines or for a party that represents a competing ethnic identity.[41] In the event, even secular parties go out of their way to woo the majority community by giving tickets on caste rather than community lines. Thus, even Abul Kalam Azad, one of the tallest leaders of the nationalist movement, who spoke eloquently of Muslims being an inseparable part of the unity of India, had to contest elections from the Muslim-majority constituency of Rampur in Uttar Pradesh in 1952 and 1957, even though he hailed from Calcutta, as the Congress Parliamentary Board was not confident of his election from his home constituency. Few Muslims are given tickets, and those who get tickets lose elections because of the split vote. In consequence there is a divergence between the Muslim vote (a little over 60 per cent), which is the same as the national average, and their political representation, which is nowhere near proportional to their population.

Persistent Under-representation of Muslims

This under-representation in Parliament and state legislatures may be due to a combination of the FPTP electoral system (single-member district, simple plurality, or SMSP) and the dispersion of Muslims demographically in a way that they are a minority in all but about eleven out of 543 Lok Sabha constituencies and most assembly constituencies (besides some such constituencies in which Muslims are concentrated being reserved for SCs, for example, Bijnor and Karimganj). India's electoral system is unlike most electoral systems.[42] The single-member district majoritarian systems favour minorities that are geographically concentrated, and conversely disfavour minorities that are not demographically concentrated. This can partially explain the under-representation of Muslims, as they are geographically dispersed. By contrast the STs do manage to win seats in excess of their population, largely due to the concentrated character of their population in central India and the northeast, where they are in significant numbers. This is, however, not the case with the SCs, who are, like the Muslims, distributed across the country.

In addition to the territorial dispersal of the Muslim population, Muslim representation is likely to have been affected by one additional factor, namely, the choice and selection of reserved constituencies. The choice of reserved constituencies was from the beginning a complex procedure with no clear criteria for the choice of particular constituencies for reservation.[43] Although the rules for the allocation of reserved constituencies are riddled with contradictions, the underlying ideas are clear enough. There is a direct connection between the MP/MLA from reserved constituency and the SC and ST voters in that constituency. In other words, reserved constituencies should be located in areas of high SC and ST concentration. The Delimitation Act of 1972 has given wide discretion for the allocation of SC seats, formalizing the idea that the distribution of reserved constituencies should be in some way representative of all of a state's SC population, rather than categorizing seats purely on the proportion of SC population of the constituency. But this consideration should not override the principal justification for reserved constituencies, which is that they should have a relatively high proportion of SC or ST population in order that the MPs or MLAs elected from reserved seats could be seen as in some way representing the SCs or STs.[44] This highlights the importance of geographical location of the reserved constituencies, but the selection and choice of reserved constituencies appears to give no consideration to the proportion of population of SCs or of non-SCs/non-STs in the constituency. This creates two problems: on the one hand, the link between the SC/ST voter and the candidates in reserved seats is weaker, and on the other this reduces the opportunities for non-SC candidates to stand for elections in these constituencies.

The problem is evident in the case in Uttar Pradesh, Bihar, and West Bengal.[45] The notification of reserved constituencies in these three states indicates a pattern where several reserved constituencies with high concentrations of Muslims were selected for reservation and where only SC candidates can contest elections while constituencies with high concentration of SCs were not reserved.[46] In a list of constituencies attached to the SCR, it has also listed nine constituencies each in Uttar Pradesh and Bihar and ten in West Bengal which were not reserved for SCs, although they form a majority there. On the other hand, a number of Muslim-dominated constituencies have been reserved for the SCs which would doubtless undercut the chances of Muslims being able to contest from these constituencies. T.K. Oommen, a member of the Sachar Committee, remarked:

> There is a feeling that selecting constituencies with high proportion of Muslims for reservation could be blocking the claims of representation of non-SCs most notably Muslims in areas where they could expect nomination owing to high concentration of population. You can never reserve a ST-dominated constituency for SCs. It may not be deliberate. But unwittingly it has reduced the representation of Muslims.[47]

A 'more rational delimitation policy' would ensure that constituencies where Muslims number more than SCs would be declared general. Reservation would be warranted where the concentration of SC or ST population was sufficient for the claims of non-SCs/non-STs to be overridden, but this is not the case in several of these constituencies which have below 20 per cent SC population and have yet been selected for reservation (Tables 5.7 and 5.8). The data marshalled by the SCR suggests that the distribution and categorization of reserved seats within states can be questioned. The issue is whether the selection of constituencies with high Muslim populations for reservation is intentional or simply that the proportion of minorities in a constituency is irrelevant to the decision to reserve a constituency. It is unlikely that this is a deliberate and calculated move intended to keep Muslims out of the political process. But this distortion could have been corrected by the Delimitation Commission (2007) without diminishing the existing number of reserved constituencies. The Delimitation Commission does redefine constituencies from time to time, though the total number of Lok Sabha and Vidhan Sabha constituencies will remain the same in each state, owing to the 91st Constitutional Amendment (2001) which froze the number of total and state-wise seats in the Lok Sabha and the number of seats in the Vidhan Sabhas at the existing level until 2026.

One year after the Sachar Committee had drawn attention to the anomalies of reservation, the gazette notification of delimitation of constituencies in twenty-five states was placed in Parliament at the end of November 2007. As a result, the boundaries of approximately half the 543 Lok Sabha constituencies have been redrawn. The reserved seats for SCs and STs will increase from 116 to 126. Several constituencies have been newly reserved, while some others have been dereserved.[48] But this elaborate exercise of redrawing of constituencies appeared to have passed over the need to dereserve constituencies that do not have a comparatively large SC population. This was partly because the Delimitation Commission did not have reliable religion-wise data on the constituency population. But there is adequate data on SC populations of various constituencies to enable categorization of reserved constituencies in relation to the population of SCs and such that these can rotate at least after every two elections. But rotation has been a contentious issue since Independence. The SC MPs and MLAs who win from reserved constituencies are opposed to rotation because it would undermine their legislative careers, as they would only represent a particular constituency for one term and would have to move to another reserved constituency. On this issue they act in unison, not on party lines but as a bloc, to safeguard their turf.

However, the under-representation of Muslims can only partially be explained by institutional factors. Caste and communal factors play an equally if not more important role in their under-representation. When it comes to distribution of tickets there is little evidence that parties are keen to give tickets to Muslims in the way they have given tickets to the OBCs, for example. Political leaders make distinctions between caste and minority identity in deciding on tickets, and caste invariably trumps all other identities. Within the caste frame, the majority community obviously gets preference.

The overall approach towards representation has been shaped by political factors—most notably, the two mainstream ideologies. The first is the policy of Congress benevolence or paternalism towards Muslims that treats them as a separate entity to be cajoled at election time. The other is majoritarian politics, which sees any preference to minorities as appeasement and a concession given to them at the expense of the majority and hence worthy of opposition. Both paternalism and majoritarianism have ended up excluding Muslims from the political system.

Another important reason is the under-nomination of minority candidates by parties which tend to favour the candidates of the majority community. The critical issue is that few Muslims have been given tickets, and those who managed to get tickets have not been able to win elections because of the split vote. Despite the strong political influence of Muslims within the Congress, it did not favour them with nominations on a large scale. In the first five general elections (1952–71), Muslim nomination by the party ranged between 4.29 per cent and 5.74 per cent. In all these elections Muslim candidates managed to win from constituencies with Muslim population ranging from a low of 3 per cent to a high of 18 per cent. In 1977, the Congress increased the nomination to 7.52 per cent. In the 2004 Lok Sabha, of 143 Congress members, only nine were Muslims. In the Congress Working Committee, the highest and most powerful decision-making body of the Congress, there are only five Muslims in forty-seven members. But, on the whole, the Congress was and remains the natural party of Muslim affiliation. Its policies in favour of autonomy for minorities—for example, the decision not to reform personal law—were a means of moderating conflict and a source of appeal to the minorities.

The Congress has on an average nominated 7 per cent Muslim candidates, which is slightly below the 8.8 per cent nominated by the CPI (M).[49] The caste-based parties give tickets to large number of Muslims, but often from constituencies where they are unlikely to win. With increasing competition, minority votes are more important than before, but this has not translated into enhanced representation for Muslims. There are 70 parliamentary constituencies with substantial Muslim population, which means the Muslim vote can influence the electoral outcome. Political parties could field Muslim candidates in these constituencies just as they put up backward castes in constituencies where they predominate.

The rise of the BJP and the sharply polarized communal situation since the early 1990s diminished the prospects for any improvement in Muslim representation. The increased appeal of communal platforms was helped in a large measure by the disaffection of the upper castes in north India as a result of the anti-reservation stir of 1990. Furthermore, the rise of Hindutva politics, based on the strategic decision of the BJP to make the critique of the secular ethos the centrepiece of its campaign, paid off in the expansion of the BJP's influence among middle-class constituencies.[50] It held responsible the minorities for India's problems and its disunity, and promised a resurgent strong India in which everyone could take pride. It argued that the Congress has manipulated minorities in order to consolidate its vote bank. A substantive part of the strategic focus in this period after the demolition of the Babri mosque was on vote-bank politics and how that was endangering national security.

The stigmatization of Muslims is a critical component of the Hindutva strategy. These ideological campaigns, against the backdrop of constant ridiculing of secularism and minorities, generally provided conducive conditions for the violent campaigns carried out in Gujarat in 2002 and elsewhere. As we have seen in preceding chapters, the BJP has refused to be persuaded by the SCR on institutional deficits and under-representation of Muslims, and has in fact attacked the report as another instance of appeasement. Drawing a line between the Muslim minority and the Hindu majority, the BJP made no significant effort to mobilize Muslims. In Uttar Pradesh, with a Muslim population of 19 per cent, the proportion of Muslim MLAs was earlier between 8–10 per cent, decreasing quite significantly to 5–6 per cent in the 1990s (in the middle of the communal politics and violence surrounding the Ayodhya movement), but it has increased to 11.2 per cent in 2002 assembly elections. The BJP did not put up a single Muslim candidate in the Uttar Pradesh and Gujarat Assembly elections in 2007, perhaps because it is unlikely to get a large chunk of their vote or because it believes it can do without it.

All in all, Muslim representation in legislatures was nowhere near what their numbers warrant or political justice dictates or what is required for an articulation of their concerns and interests. For their part Muslim voters are less demanding than other politically mobilized groups. The primary focus of Muslim voters, especially in the north Indian states where there is a higher degree of social polarization, is identity and security. Secular political formations too find it convenient to stress these issues, as it does not cut into the demands of other groups for resources, seats in government and legislatures, etc. Parties prefer to give tickets to non-Muslim candidates, as it prevents polarization along communal lines. The support for these demands for more representation has widened considerably over the years.

The experience of backward-caste politics has underlined the importance of political mobilization at different levels—local, state, and national—for the increase in the political representation of the OBCs. It is through these movements and assertions that backward castes have been able to stake a claim to citizenship and equal representation in political life and political institutions. The increase in representation of OBCs shows that sustained pressure from groups within parties can help in increasing the number of candidates on party lists. The contrast between OBCs and Muslims is instructive because it shows that although Muslims are a numerically large minority, they have not been able to harness their numbers in the absence of political mobilization and readiness of political parties to give them nominations. Indeed, the political empowerment of OBCs is a significant reminder in this regard because it shows that they first mobilized through political formations and then went on to demand reservations. When we look at the problem in a larger time frame, we can see that reservations also play the role of a catalyst in the construction of political identities.

The case for fair representation of Muslims is obvious. Political representation is valuable not only in itself—it can give a legitimate voice to minorities in the political arena, something with intrinsic expressive value—but also has instrumental value because it can help them to influence policy decisions that can decrease the marginalization and exclusion of minority communities. Rajeev Bhargava argues:

> Inclusion in the political process is important for the legitimacy of decisions arrived at through the process. Even if the decision goes against the interests of the minority, the chances are that they would be gracefully accepted if the process through which they were made has included them in a meaningful way and given them an effective voice.[51]

However, the interest on the part of parties in finding ways of increasing their representation is rather limited. After nearly 50 years of silence on this issue, at a convention held in New Delhi in 1989 a group of Muslims protested against their under-representation and demanded the introduction of a system of proportional representation in elections at all levels. But support for this demand has not widened. Over the past few years there has been considerable debate on the electoral system in relation to the vote-to-seat disproportionalities of the FPTP system, which can over-represent certain parties and groups. There have also been debates in relation to stability of coalitions as against single-party rule. Unlike the under-representation of women—which became a slogan of considerable discursive power, resulting in policy initiatives at every level of the political system, from 33 per cent reservations for women at the local level in panchayats to the proposed legislation to reserve 33 per cent seats in legislatures at the state and national level—minority under-representation could not gain much significance in political discourse. Even though top leaders from time to time express their concern, there is no serious attempt to rectify the under-representation of Muslims. The two recent documents on reform of the electoral system—the Law Commission's Report (May 1999) and the two consultation papers on the subject issued by the National Commission to

Review the Working of the Constitution in 2002—did not take up the issue of under-representation of Muslims. On the contrary, both are inspired by a kind of vision of the national polity which delegitimizes all electoral devices which seek to provide due representation to smaller political parties or weaker social groups, regional interests, or religious minorities. Even secular parties have not paid much attention to the representation deficit in legislative bodies.

International experience has shown that the only way to significantly increase the numbers of under-represented groups in legislative assemblies is to use positive action measures. This has been done to increase the representation of women through shortlists or by selecting women for winnable seats, for instance.[52] One way of increasing the representation of minorities is by changing the electoral system to proportional representation in which parties win seats in proportion to the votes they poll.[53] Evidence from different parts of the world indicates that proportional representation (PR) can produce better representation for both ethnic minorities and women.[54] Of the ten countries with highest ranking in terms of women's representation, all use PR electoral systems. PR systems are supposed to be 'more inclusive, they promote power-sharing, and thus provide a greater voice for marginalized groups.'[55]

The principle of fair political representation for Muslims is best fulfilled either by a switch to proportional representation and/or more nominations in proportion to the overall population of Muslims in the country. Under PR systems, parties are allocated seats in proportion to the votes that they get. PR is a category of electoral formula aiming at a close match between the percentage of votes that groups of candidates (grouped by a certain measure) obtain in elections and the percentage of seats they receive in legislative assemblies. It is often contrasted to plurality voting systems, where disproportional seat distribution results from the division of voters into multiple electoral districts, especially 'winner takes all' plurality (FPTP) districts.[56] A variant of PR can ensure better representation of dispersed minorities which are most vulnerable to under-representation, and at the same time ensure that the governments elected are more representative of the popular vote and possibly more coherent in terms of policy and governance. E. Sridharan suggests that PR in India would necessitate a complex process of social coalition-building and pre-election alliances; otherwise, there would be a danger of splintering of the state-level party system into caste- and religion-based parties. This is because most significant castes or religious communities in each state would be assured of representation even when they compete essentially on caste and communal lines, since most of these groups would be over 5 per cent in the statewide population (which assures them a threshold of support) and much higher in their areas of concentration. But there has been no serious debate on alternative electoral systems and much less debate or support for a switch to PR. Both the Congress party and the BJP are vehemently opposed to it. Among major parties only the Left parties seem to support it.

In the present circumstances, the most effective way of ensuring better representation is for parties to nominate more Muslims. Political parties have to summon the resolve to give a larger number of nominations to minority candidates in party lists and from winnable constituencies. The legislative representation of backward castes has gone up through this route. In short, parties have to do for minorities what they have done with regard to backward castes. This will encourage the political process to internalize minority concerns and in the process bring them into the mainstream of the polity and economy. This can be buttressed by better-defined minority rights and, above all, inclusion of minorities in the development process through affirmative action. There must also be space for the idea that, regardless of ascriptive identities, people have shared experiences and concerns that are best represented by candidates and parties that share those interests. This would help to shift focus from minority candidates to making institutions and policies inclusive so that they can protect minority interests.

With or without change in the electoral system, the role of political parties appears to be critical in enhancing representation. Thus the focus of attention should be on both the electoral system and the party system. Only political parties committed to higher representation for excluded groups can ensure it. Political parties have to start with the incorporation of excluded groups into positions of real power in the party hierarchy where they can influence decision making. But none of this will work unless political parties are committed to increasing the representation of minorities. Parties have to take the initiative by giving tickets and party positions to excluded groups even in the face of opposition from party managers who generally adopt a conservative approach in such matters. Globally, it has been recognized that parties have an important role to play in the representation of disadvantaged groups in governance. The political presence of these groups can be enhanced only by the active intervention of parties. On balance, increasing political representation is an important and worthwhile objective, but it should be seen as one of the multiple strategies required to achieve substantive equality and policy outcomes.

Notes

1. Hanna Pitkin (1967); Anne Phillips (1999); Iris Marion Young (1990); Melissa Williams (1998); Jane Mansbridge (2003: 515–28); Geoffrey Brennan and Alan Hamlin (1999: 109–27).
2. Rohini Pande (2003).
3. Anne Phillips (1999: 25).
4. Zoya Hasan (2006: 54–60).
5. Radhika Desai (1999).
6. D.L. Sheth (2000: 211).
7. Ibid., p. 230.
8. Ashutosh Varshney (2000).
9. Christophe Jaffrelot (2003: 147–53).
10. Ibid.
11. Anne Schneider and Helen Ingram (1993: 334).
12. Ashutosh Varshney (2000).
13. Kanchan Chandra (2000: 12–14).
14. Ashutosh Varshney (2000).
15. Alistair McMillan (2005).
16. Stephanie Tawa Lama-Rewal (2005).
17. Christophe Jaffrelot and Sanjay Kumar (2008).
18. Christophe Jaffrelot (2003).
19. Christophe Jaffrelot (2000).
20. Ibid., p. 151.
21. Ibid., p. 98.
22. Christophe Jaffrelot (2008).

23. Ibid.
24. Harold Gould (1999: 189–90).
25. Ibid., p. 190.
26. Christophe Jaffrelot (2008).
27. Ibid.
28. Ibid.
29. Ibid., p. 46.
30. Arendt Lijphart (1996).
31. Ibid.
32. Steven Wilkinson (2005: 108–10).
33. Mushirul Hasan (1998: 320–4).
34. Ibid.
35. On Muslim political behaviour, see Javeed Alam (2004).
36. Karin Deutsch Karlekar (2004).
37. Iqbal Ansari (2006).
38. Ibid. p. 27.
39. E. Sridharan (2006: 409).
40. There are eleven constituencies with Muslim majorities, including Dhubri, Kishanganj, Anantnag, Baramula, Srinagar, Manjeri, and Ponnani. The six constituencies having over 40 per cent Muslim population are Ladakh, Amroha, Moradabad, Basirhat, Berhampore, and Malda.
41. E. Sridharan (2006: 790).
42. E. Sridharan (2002).
43. Alistair Mcmillan (2005).
44. The allocation of reserved seats in Vidhan Sabhas is decided on the basis of the proportion of SCs in the state. First, the size of the assembly is fixed, and then the number of reserved seats on the basis of population. However, the procedure used for allocating reserved seats in the Lok Sabha is entirely different, since reserved seats are meant to be at the state level and in line with the state population.
45. *SCR* (2006: 25).
46. Ibid.
47. Ibid.
48. *The Times of India*, 29 November 2007.
49. Iqbal Ansari (2006).
50. Malini Parthasarathy (2008).
51. Rajeev Bhargava (2007).
52. The Labour Party policy of selecting candidates from all-women shortlists for half the winnable seats resulted in the number of women in Parliament doubling from 62 to 121 in 2001.

53. Congress leader Salman Khurshid, president of the UPCC, has been advocating a change to PR. *The Hindu*, 25 January 2005.

54. Susan A. Banducci (2004).

55. S. Childs, *et al.* (2006).

56. Various forms of proportional representation exist, such as party-list proportional representation. Within this form a further distinction can be made depending on whether or not a voter can influence the election of candidates within a party list (open list and closed list respectively). Another kind of electoral system covered under the term PR is the single transferable vote (STV), which, in turn, does not depend on the existence of political parties. Elections for the Australian Senate use what is referred to as above-the-line voting where candidates belonging to registered political parties are grouped together on the ballot paper with the voter provided with the option of 'group voting' a semi-open party list/individual candidate system.

6

Muslim Backwardness and the Elusive Promise of Affirmative Action

India's vast array of policies of affirmative action and reservations do not cover religious minorities per se. Political transformations around the world have led, however, to various innovations, including the establishment of quotas for minority groups. Virtually everywhere in the world there is now a demand for greater equality and equality of treatment among ethnic groups.[1] Educationally and economically disadvantaged groups and minorities the world over are demanding governmental intervention on their behalf. Most governments have responded positively to these demands either out of concern for social justice—as the Indian government has done with regard to the SCs, STs, and OBCs—or to mitigate political conflict between competing interests.[2] Whatever the causes, what is striking is the growing worldwide concern for the removal of inter-group inequalities.

There is a widespread recognition that unless nation-states become more sensitive to the concerns of and the need for minority voices in decision making, strategies of inclusion cannot have any chance of success. The critical issue in this regard is the ways and methods through which minorities can be included in public institutions. Until recently, however, policy makers in India did not view these inequalities in regard to the under-participation of minorities in governance as a problem. Under-representation was seen to be a consequence of the historical legacy of Partition or due to the differences in job preferences and educational backwardness. But in recent years, coalition governments at the Centre have responded positively by expanding the range of targeted policies for a variety of disadvantaged groups. Caste and women's groups have received guaranteed seats in local government (though women have experienced difficulties at the legislative level, primarily due to questions of how to resolve caste reservations demanded by caste-based parties and organizations) and a range of special measures for their advancement.[3] Minority groups, on the other hand, have been refused reservations on the grounds that it would be discriminatory and violate the fundamental right to equality.[4] The reluctance stemmed from a larger concern that this would hamper national unity, undermine secularism, and engender communal discord.

India's caste, class, and community spectrum is complex and multifaceted but official group-based policies frequently fail to capture this complexity. The Indian debate has covered a wide range of issues from who should be targeted, why they should be targeted and how they should be targeted, to merit, and the economic criteria for reservations. However, this debate has for the most part skirted the question of application of affirmative action to minorities in areas of employment or education. One important issue in this debate is with regard to the import of caste in the conception of disadvantage in the formulation of affirmative action policies. An alternative view implicit in the discussion in this chapter would make caste only one consideration and would move towards a principle which is sensitive to different layers of deprivation that stand in the way of equal opportunity. Examining the pros and cons of affirmative action for minorities in public employment is instructive in this regard because it draws attention to the deprivation of other groups and hence the need to be sensitive to multiple dimensions of disadvantage.[5]

This brings to the forefront the question of which identities count in affirmative action for the disadvantaged, and whether public policies take into account the complexities in the relationship of caste and minority on the one hand, and minority and class on the other, or the overlap between cultural and socio-economic inequalities. There is also the issue of the ways in which state-driven conceptions of backwardness tend to equivocate on the complex relationship between these categories. Minorities suffer in varying degrees from discrimination and deprivation. These inequalities can be gleaned from NSSO data (discussed in Chapter 3), which clearly show that the SCs, STs, and Muslims are among the most deprived groups and that there is not much difference between these groups in terms of levels of deprivation and disadvantage. But India's affirmative action policies are yet to take this social reality into account. Many of the policy interventions have frequently revealed an inability to comprehend the various facets of disadvantage as they occur within and between groups. Today social and political exclusion can no longer be understood, if it ever could be, by narrowly assessing the situation of upper and lower castes without taking into account other social inequalities and oppressions.

The two key issues with regard to inclusion are backwardness (which in principle covers the Muslim community but is not specific to it) and under-representation (which is more specific to the Muslim community). This chapter focuses on the specific issues of under-representation and of affirmative action measures needed to redress this imbalance. In this context, it more specifically focuses on the merits and demerits of minority versus backward-caste reservations in the context of differences amongst Muslim groups on the issue and the wider debate on minority versus caste quotas and the demand for sub-quotas for Muslim OBCs. This must be read in conjunction with the discussion on the demand for SC status for Muslim and Christian Dalits in the next chapter, which highlights the exclusion of these two doubly disadvantaged groups from the purview of reservation. Neither affirmative action for minorities nor sub-quotas for Muslim OBCs or legal recognition for Muslim and Christian Dalits has made any headway. The concentration of the benefits of affirmative action among members of the majority community and the virtual exclusion of the minorities from these benefits has therefore become a source of resentment.

There are two broad issues here. One, how does a society ensure fairness where unfairness reflects not only long-standing, systemic discrimination but also deprivation arising from different dimensions of disadvantage? The second issue is whether Muslims deserve affirmative action, and, if so, on what basis. While there is no consensus in the political system on the issue, there is also no unanimity among Muslims either on caste versus minority status as the basis for making claims of affirmative action on the state. Sharp disagreements have come to light among Muslims after the Mandal Commission recommendations to include certain backward Muslim groups in the OBC list and after several state governments decided to extend reservations in principle on this basis to Muslims by classifying sections of them in the backward-class category.[6] Different organizations representing divergent positions have raised competing demands on reservation, as Muslims are clearly at odds over this issue.

Representation in Public Employment

After India's Independence in 1947, most Muslims in India decided to stay on in the country despite large-scale killing, dislocation, and violence. However, social stagnation and educational backwardness cumulatively resulted in growing socio-economic deprivation and marginalization of Muslims. The NSSO data across different groups show that they suffer substantial material deprivation and also face greater under-representation in jobs, education, and material resources than any other population group demarcated by religion. They constitute the poorest sections of society, with income well below the national average, and face relatively higher material deprivation in urban areas. The SCR's analysis of the distribution of population in different expenditure classes shows that in urban areas the largest numbers of Muslims are in the expenditure range of Rs 400–500 and about half are in the range of Rs 300–600. Over time the economic condition of Muslims has not improved as much as other groups.[7] The SCs/STs show slightly better distribution of consumption compared to Muslims, followed by the OBCs.[8]

A study of the civil service published in 1989 showed an overwhelming preponderance of Hindus in government employment, particularly in the higher level: 75 per cent of IAS officers were Hindu, 5.3 per cent Sikh, 2.1 per cent Muslim, and 2 per cent Christian.[9] More than two decades ago, the Gopal

Singh Committee Report on Minorities (1983) showed the percentage of Muslims in the IAS in 1980 to be 3.22 per cent (Table 6.1). It is useful to compare this with the data marshalled by the SCR, which show no major increase in their representation twenty-five years later. The SCR's chapter on Government Employment and Programmes begins with the observation that 'in a pluralistic society, a reasonable representation of various communities in government sector employment is necessary to enhance participatory governance.' The data show that the country is far from attaining such a goal. In 2006, Muslims constituted barely 3.2 per cent of the IAS, IFS, and IPS (Table 6.2). Muslim under-representation appears stark because India has become much more proportional in its approach than it was under Nehru or Indira Gandhi.[10]

The absence of Muslims in the corridors of power and decision making is just as marked today as when Nehru had drawn attention to it fifty-five years ago. From time to time there have been government instructions sensitizing selection boards about the need to select minority candidates for public employment and public sector jobs. In 1975, Indira Gandhi had directed all the Central ministries and departments and the state governments to nominate...a member of the minority community in the selection committee/board for recruitment to group 'C' and group 'D' posts within the overall sanctioned strength of the committee/board. In August 1990 all the ministries and departments were asked to conform to the above-mentioned original notification on selection boards as there was very little compliance since 1975. This position was reiterated in January 2007 by the Department of Personnel and Training to all Central and state departments to include one member from the minorities in recruitment boards/selection committees.[11] But these instructions are invariably ignored by recruitment boards for public employment.

With low levels of education and no affirmative action in the sphere of public employment, Muslims are mostly in self-employment. Although they are a distant third compared to the upper- and backward-caste Hindus, they are over-represented in self-employment, given that they are a smaller proportion of the population. The SCR showed that only 8 per cent of urban Muslims are part of the salaried classes compared to the national average of 21 per cent for urban India. In 2005–6 about 27 million persons were employed in the organized sector; of these 18.6 million were employed by government departments and public sector undertakings (PSUs) and the remaining were in the organized private sector. The SCR received data pertaining to 88 lakh employees of which only 4.4 lakh were Muslims.[12] Though Muslims have a share of 13.4 per cent in the country's population, their share in government jobs is a mere 4.9 per cent. Of the fourteen lakh PSU workers, Muslims constituted 3.3 per cent of Central PSUs and 10.8 per cent of state-level PSUs (Table 6.3). They are very poorly represented in the armed forces, where their proportion is believed to be just 2 per cent, and in paramilitary agencies it is nominal (between 1 and 5 per cent).[13] The Indian Railways is one of the largest employers in the country, employing about fourteen lakh people; of these only 4.5 per cent are Muslims. Even among these, 98.7 per cent occupy lower-level positions and officers are only 1.3 per cent. In the Group A category in the railways, Hindus (General) and Hindus (OBCs) hold 72 per cent of the jobs, followed by SCs/STs at 18 per cent, and Muslims a mere 2.5 per cent (Table 6.4).

The SCR reported severe under-representation in government jobs even in states in which Muslims constitute large minorities (Tables 6.5 and 6.6). In states like Uttar Pradesh, Bihar, and West Bengal with large Muslim populations, their proportion in state employment is less than a third of their population share. In West Bengal, despite the Left Front's three decades in power, their share in government employment is an abysmal 4.2 per cent, a fraction of their population share (25.2 per cent).[14] In Bihar and Uttar Pradesh too, the number of Muslims employed in the government is less than a third of their share of the total population. Uttar Pradesh and Bihar have 18.5 per cent and 16.5 per cent Muslims, but only 5.1 per cent and 7.6 per cent Muslims in government jobs. Among all states which shared data with the SCR, the highest percentage of Muslims employed in the government is in Assam, at 11.2 per cent. This is still way below their 30.9 per cent population share.

Andhra Pradesh is the only state which shows representation that is fairly close, but there too it is less than the population share in the state. Three other states that show relatively better Muslim representation in state government jobs are Karnataka (Muslim population share 12.2 per cent, share in jobs 8.5 per cent), Gujarat (Muslim population share 9.1 per cent, share in jobs 5.4 per cent), and Tamil Nadu (Muslim population share 5.6 per cent, share in jobs 3.2 per cent). The highest percentage of Muslims in higher positions in state public sector undertakings is in Kerala with 9.5 per cent, but this is also less than half the share of Muslims in the population of the state.[15] The recent data on recruitment by the State Public Service Commissions from 2001 to 2006 from Uttar Pradesh, Assam, Gujarat, Delhi, Rajasthan, Orissa, and Himachal Pradesh show that the share of Muslims in all recruitments is about 2.1 per cent.[16]

The situation is conceivably worse in the private sector. The proportion of Muslim directors in the private corporate sector is very low. Apart from a few exceptions, the corporate sector appears to have an unofficial policy of keeping the minorities out, especially Muslims.[17] One survey showed that just over 1 per cent of corporate executives are Muslim.[18] One effect of this exclusion in the economic sphere has been the slowing down of the emergence of a Muslim middle class.

This brief description shows that Muslims have on the whole not done well since Independence in public institutions and government jobs. Apart from having a long-term regular income and retirement benefits and providing economic security, higher positions in government jobs offer the employee privileged positions in society through ascribed and sometimes assumed status; they are also accorded privileges as members of governmental institutions. Besides regular employment in the government sector can also influence the distribution of goods and access to public services in several ways which affect different sections of the population.[19] Job reservation has succeeded in raising the representation of the SCs/STs by at least 5 percentage points.[20] Without reservation, the representation of these two groups in regular salaried and wage employment might have been even lower than that of Muslims, and the estimated gain of five points therefore underestimates the true gain from job reservation policies.[21] The importance of reservations in enhancing the political representation of SCs is obvious from the near absence of SCs in the Rajya Sabha, which has no reservations. This is perhaps the most telling instance of under-representation in the absence of reservations for a disadvantaged group.

The key question in this regard is how much of Muslim under-representation is attributable to educational backwardness and how much is due to discrimination and bias in public employment on the part of those who control the avenues of employment in government and the public and private sectors. Historical factors have played a major role—Partition was accompanied by mass migration of the Muslim elite to Pakistan, including government servants, businessmen and the affluent sections, and educated youth. This inhibited the growth of a Muslim middle class for the first few decades after Independence.[22] As a consequence, the Muslim middle class is still weak and relatively small and hesitant to act as an agent of change to provide leadership to the community in its search for equity and justice.

A second set of factors has to do with the nature of Muslim communities. This has been discussed in detail by numerous sociologists.[23] A large proportion of Muslims are descendants of converts from various 'low' castes, whose social and economic conditions remained largely unchanged even after conversion. The third factor relates to the influence of conservative sections of the *ulema* and the paucity of civil society groups and initiatives working for educational and economic development and empowerment.[24] Most organizations associated with Muslims in north India and influential sections of the Muslim elite have focused on identity issues rather than education and empowerment, as it shores up their claims to authority and enables them to deliver votes in return for being treated by the state and political parties as the 'representatives' of the community. Many others feared that they would be branded communal and hence did not want to work exclusively among or for Muslims. Until quite recently, Muslim legislators avoided raising issues that were considered to be exclusively Muslim. This is not surprising. Negative stereotypes abound in India not the least because of the historical legacy of Partition, and post-9/11, after the terrorist attacks on New York's twin towers and in different parts of the country in the past few years.

The educational backwardness of Muslims is an important reason for their under-representation in public employment and decision-making structures. More than six decades after Independence they are among the most educationally backward groups in both school and higher education. The gap between Muslims and the advantaged sections has actually widened, particularly since the 1980s. In fact, the traditionally underprivileged SCs/STs are overtaking them in several areas. The last point is of special importance, as at the time of Independence the socio-economic position of SCs/STs was recognized to be inferior to that of Muslims. One important reason for the low participation of Muslims in higher education is their significantly low achievement level in higher secondary education.

There is a positive link between education and employment. Human resource capital, especially education, not only affects employment opportunities but also determines occupational patterns. Without economic returns to education provided in the form of a higher probability of getting employment or earning higher income, investment in education may not occur. In this vicious circle, both education and employment suffer. Education also creates social linkages and networks necessary for gaining employment. But the widespread perception that Muslims will not get government jobs acts as a deterrent and also leads them to attach less importance to education because they assume that they will not be able to get government jobs in comparison to other communities and hence there is no incentive to complete higher education, in fact it encourages them to drop out and take up self-employment.

Discrimination is another possible reason for the under-representation of Muslims in public employment. This is hard to establish, however, because there is obviously no discrimination at the level of rules of recruitment at the formal level. But there could be discrimination or a perception of discrimination in interviews for selection for civil services. This perception is evident from a number of court cases indicating that Muslims feel that they are adversely affected by selection biases.[25] Whether true or not the fact is that a large section of the Muslim community harbours a perception of discrimination against it. The SCR cites a number of instances of discrimination against the Muslim community. For example, many Muslims complained to the Sachar Committee in the course of its meetings with stakeholders in different parts of the country that they were not able to get bank loans from nationalized banks, while others said that it was difficult to sell or buy property. While educational backwardness is certainly an important factor, it cannot be responsible for the huge extent of under-representation of Muslims in the public services, especially at lower levels which do not require major educational qualifications. It can explain to some extent the under-representation in the higher levels of jobs but it cannot account for their near-complete absence from the lower levels of employment, for instance, at the level of Class IV jobs of drivers, messengers, constables, etc. For example, in 2003 when the Archaeological Survey of India (ASI) was asked to excavate the Babri mosque site at Ayodhya on the Allahabad High Court orders, it turned out that out of the 55 or so diggers whom it engaged, not one was a Muslim. The court's intervention resulted in the hiring of a few Muslims by the ASI. If the court had not expressed its concern over the complete absence of Muslims, the ASI would not have recruited Muslims and their exclusion would have gone unnoticed.[26]

The ASI instance is indicative of a pattern of exclusion operating at different levels of employment, even though it is not acknowledged. The scope for the operation of partiality on the basis of connections can work to the detriment of groups who do not have such connections and networks within the system. This is a major drawback for groups such as Muslims who are virtually absent in so many sectors of the government. The existence of networks within the government system would enable aspirants to gain access to information and connections to influential people that are necessary for getting jobs in India. All in all, at times Muslims lack education and skills required to compete for jobs at the higher levels of the civil service and at other times they lose out in the competition due to the lack of required networks and influence for lower-level positions too. Furthermore, because the political participation of

Muslims has also been low, there have been very few to raise their voice in favour of Muslims.

S.K. Thorat and Paul Attewell's study of job discrimination indicates the existence of discrimination against Muslims. This study demonstrates that religious identity, along with other identities, affects patterns of employment and exclusion in India. The analysis of differential pathways of Dalit and Muslim students from comparable elite backgrounds found that applicants with Dalit or Muslim names applying for private sector jobs are significantly less likely to have a positive outcome in response to applications than people with equivalent qualifications from a high-caste Hindu background.[27] More significantly, the study also reported that of these two disadvantaged groups, the probability of Muslim applicants getting a positive response was half that of Dalits.[28] It found a pattern of decision making by private sector employers that repeatedly disadvantages low-caste and Muslim job applicants with equal qualifications in comparison with job applicants from Hindu higher-caste backgrounds.

Although there is no direct relationship between minority presence in the administration and welfare of minorities, the presence of disadvantaged groups in office and political positions provides opportunities to incorporate the concerns and interests of these groups in the calculations of politicians belonging to a variety of groups. Several governments around the world have made efforts to promote the participation of ethnic minorities because the lack of representation in public institutions and the hierarchies of power make such groups vulnerable to exclusion from the broader policy discourse.[29] The experience of SCs and STs shows that presence in public institutions can offset some of the disadvantage that these groups otherwise face. The presence of legislators and administrators belonging to the SCs has promoted policies that reflect the interests of these disadvantaged groups, and legislators have used this influence to increase the incidence of targeted redistribution. Furthermore, it is because of reservation in public employment that a middle class has emerged among them, and this has in turn provided a measure of energy and leadership to the community in its struggle for equity, dignity, and justice.

Disadvantaged Muslims

Affirmative action for minorities has always been a controversial issue in India. Historically, the hegemonic majority–minority syndrome and the controversies surrounding Partition have fundamentally shaped how we think about and engage with this policy in relation to religious minorities. This thinking significantly obscures the changing pattern of social stratification and the positioning of various groups (including Muslims) over time. But it is important to bear in mind the historical context and constitutional debates discussed in Chapter 2, as they underline the political–ideological roots of this opposition. These ideological misgivings emerged vividly in the course of the public debate as well as the debate in government and policy-making institutions over the recommendations of the SCR, which indicates that to a large extent the contemporary response is very similar to the arguments and positions taken against affirmative action for minorities during the framing of the Constitution. The hesitation and the sense of uneasiness articulated at that time continues to reflect in political circles and has led to concerns that reservation for minorities—indeed, any form of special treatment and not just reservation—might again give an impetus to division and separation.

However, promoting the welfare of the disadvantaged is a central responsibility of the state. The founding fathers treated this as a foundational philosophy. This obligation was part of the Objectives Resolution and was later incorporated in the Preamble of the Constitution. Equality and justice have since then been the two central concerns of the Indian state. The Constitution specifically allows for special provisions and enactment of welfare measures for SCs, STs, and socially and educationally backward classes in education or jobs. This has been interpreted as permitting the inclusion of any group regardless of religion, provided there is adequate evidence of their social and educational backwardness. According to this understanding, any community comprises backward and non-backward sections; as there are castes among Hindus there are caste-like formations among Muslims and Christians that have a low social status within the community.

The category of OBC provides a window of opportunity through which disadvantaged groups among the minorities can gain access to public jobs and other social benefits. For the first time, the Kaka Kalelkar Commission declared certain castes/communities among Muslims (and other religious minorities) as backward, and thus brought them within the purview of the official framework of disadvantage.[30] The Kalelkar report was rejected by the Central government on the ground that it used caste rather than economic criteria for identifying backward classes. Like the Kalelkar Commission before it, the Mandal Commission noted the incidence of caste-like features among Muslims, and hence the OBC category included Muslims. At the same time, the Commission refrained from using caste as a criterion to identify non-Hindu OBCs as these religions are egalitarian in their outlook. The criteria evolved for this purpose had two conditions: (1) all untouchables converted to any non-Hindu religion; (2) such occupational communities which are known by their traditional occupation and whose Hindu counterparts have been included in the list of Hindu OBCs.[31] Based on the data provided by the 1931 census and field survey conducted by the Commission, over 80 groups among Muslims were declared backward. According to the data used, Muslims constituted a little over 8 per cent of the 27 per cent of the OBC population; backward-caste Muslims were over half of the total Muslim population. Various states were directed to implement these provisions with the proportion of reserved positions that would go to them left to state governments to decide.

At the state level, there are three different models for affirmative action for the Muslims/Muslim backward groups. These can be classified into three types: (1) reservation of seats for the entire Muslim community (excluding the creamy layer): Kerala and Karnataka; (2) reservation on the basis of backward caste/*biradari*, but most of the Muslim groups included, covering 95 per cent of the Muslim population: Tamil Nadu; (3) bifurcation of OBCs into backwards and most backward classes (MBCs), with most of the Muslim backwards in the MBC list: Bihar.[32] In other words, in Kerala and Karnataka all non-*ashraf* Muslims (about 80–90 per cent of the total Muslim population) qualify as backwards whereas in the Hindi-speaking states only a few politically and numerically dominant communities (roughly 30–40 per cent of the total Muslim population) qualify.

Most states have no separate quota for Muslims. Karnataka and Kerala are an exception to this pattern, as they have included a very large proportion of Muslims in the backward classes. This has been achieved by including Muslims (minus the creamy layer) as a distinct group within the broad category of Backward Classes and then providing them with an exclusive quota. In Karnataka, when Veerappa Moily was chief minister, the entire community was declared backward and a 4 per cent reservation package within the OBC reservation was given to Muslims in 1994 under II B category. The state classified Backward Classes into three categories: (a) Most Backward, (b) More Backward, and (c) Backward. No one has questioned this. This measure has led to a substantive rise in Muslim share in the state government services. Within the OBC quota 10–12 per cent was fixed exclusively for Muslims at different levels.

As we have noted in the preceding sections of this chapter, states with high demographic concentration of Muslims have not been able to provide adequate representation of Muslim OBCs in government employment, but by and large all the states have listed backward Muslim groups as OBCs. The inclusion of Muslims in the OBC list marks a significant shift in established patterns of thinking on affirmative action and also dents and undercuts the concept of a monolithic Muslim identity.[33]

Multiple Identities and Minority Quotas

Against the backdrop of the acceptance of the Mandal Commission's recommendations for reservations for OBCs in government employment, campaigns for the inclusion of Muslims in quota regimes began to emerge in the early 1990s. Almost at the same time, there was counter-pressure building up to implement caste-based reservations. During this time, the actors involved in the campaigns included civil society groups like NGOs, Muslim backward-caste and Dalit organizations, Muslim organizations, and political parties such as the Congress, Samajwadi Party, Rashtriya

Janata Dal (RJD), and the Left parties. Involved in various ways, several Muslim organizations have been vying with each other to gain recognition, either individually or collectively, as backward caste or SC or simply as Muslim.[34] Among the most outspoken of these groups are the Pasmanda Mahaz and the All India Muslim Backward Classes Organization. These demands sparked strong disagreements within Muslim communities, in addition to the well-known opposition from right-wing Hindu organizations to any suggestion of affirmative action for Muslims.

A strong and influential section of Muslim leaders favoured reservations for Muslims on a community qua community basis, because in their view 'the entire Muslim community forms a backward class.' This group raised several objections against caste-based reservations for Muslims, as they felt that Muslims did not fit into the OBC category because they are not a caste. They do not accept that caste is more significant than the overall unity of the community. They believe that the philosophy and structure of caste as a superstructure of social discrimination is wholly contradictory to the basic beliefs of Islam, which implicitly emphasize equality and universal brotherhood.[35] They want the entire Muslim community to be declared a 'backward class' and given reservations on that basis. These leaders have repeatedly emphasized the necessity of 'cutting the cake' not just horizontally by class and caste but also vertically by religion so as to evenly distribute opportunities in administrative positions, as this is one way of increasing the presence of minorities in the public domain. Since political power resides in the administrative system, it is important that the Muslims too should be given a proportionate share of administrative positions. Basically, the inclusion of Muslims in the OBC list would exclude them and they would stand to lose unless the entire community was declared backward.[36]

In a memorandum submitted to the National Commission for Religious and Linguistic Minorities (NCRLM) in 2006, the All India Muslim Majlis-e-Mushawarat (AIMMM) suggested that it is impossible to identify and quantify the backward sections of the Muslim community since there was 'simply no authentic data to indicate the population of various religious sub-communities, far less to quantify the relative backwardness of Muslim sub-communities among the Muslims or in relation to the other 100 per cent backward communities like the SCs or STs.'[37] The AIMMM's basic contention was that:

> While the so-called low castes among the Muslims in any case enjoy the benefit of reservation as OBCs, though the real problem is faced by the so-called high castes among Muslims i.e. Syeds, Shaikhs, Pathans and so on who were dependent on government employment and on landholdings which they lost since 1947. This problem of the backward sections among the Muslims, not covered by reservations, is the same as those faced by the Hindu high castes cited above. All these 'high castes', Hindu or Muslim, have their share of poverty, unemployment and economic distress and deprivation, and pockets of backwardness. However, poverty and backwardness are much more endemic and widespread among the Muslim upper castes because of relatively lower levels of participation in governance and administration.[38]

Simultaneously, during this period a number of Muslim OBC organizations emerged to challenge this position. Their demand for inclusion of Muslims in the OBC list brought them into direct confrontation with Muslim leaders who were demanding reservation for minorities qua minorities. Belonging to the lower and backward castes, the Muslim OBC organizations have led and participated in a movement for recognition of lower-caste Muslims on par with the lower castes in the Hindu society. These groups prefer to press for a caste quota for OBC and Dalit Muslims within the OBC and SC reservations.

Their basic contention was that caste exists among Muslims; it has been a pervasive reality for centuries and is not the result of colonial government policies which favoured the so-called upper-caste Muslims.[39] In opposing minority reservations, the OBC Muslim leaders point out that elite Muslims have consciously played identity politics to restrict minority politics to issues such as the Aligarh Muslim University, Urdu, and Muslim Personal Law, while marginalizing the backward classes among Muslims and sidelining the more important issues of educational, social, and economic development of the Muslim masses.[40] This political strategy designed to perpetuate the semblance of collective monolithic identity is deliberate and helps to project the upper-caste/class Muslims as the representatives of the community. It enjoyed the support of the Congress leadership which backed these sections at the expense of backward-caste Muslims, even though the backward-caste Muslims form the majority of the Muslim population. As a result, the backward-caste Muslims find themselves left out of such government employment as have come the way of Muslims. Thus, they strongly opposed the proposal put forward by some Muslim leaders that all Muslims be declared a backward class and on this basis become eligible for reservations in government jobs and education. This is precisely what the Andhra Pradesh government attempted to do in 2004 and the courts had turned it down.

The debate over stratification patterns among Muslims and who should be included in the officially designated backward categories and benefit from these schemes hinges on the recognition of caste in Muslim society. The heterogeneity of Muslims in India and the existence of caste-like features and status distinctions based on it are well known. There are two aspects to the social stratification pattern which are relevant for assessing the competing demands. The first relates to their disadvantaged position vis-à-vis the larger society. The second relates to the disadvantaged position of sections within the Muslim community that underlines the relevance of internal differentiation in the Muslim communities. Generally, Muslim elites have emphasized the first position. This situation has changed somewhat as disadvantaged groups within the Muslim community have questioned the representation of Muslims as a monolithic community. On the other hand, Muslim elites altogether deny the existence of caste among Muslims, arguing that Islam is an egalitarian religion and does not recognize distinctions of caste and status.

Sociological studies of social structure have emphasized the existence of descent-based social stratification among Muslims. Sociologist Imtiaz Ahmad notes that empirical studies which initially took the form of decennial censuses adduced considerable evidence that caste (or caste-like groupings, which is a much later categorization) existed among Muslims and could be identified through a hierarchy of status orders.[41] Before him, anthropologist Ghaus Ansari, using evidence from decennial censuses, argued that Muslims were divided into three broad categories that he called the *ashraf* (noble born), *ajlaf* (mean and lowly) and *arzal* (excluded). Each of these categories was further divided into a number of groups, which, following the practice of the decennial censuses, he chose to designate as castes.[42]

Evidence brought together by Ahmad as well as subsequent research demonstrates that Muslim groups, which are the point of reference here (and for which the words *biradari* and *jat* or *jati* are commonly used), are local and corporate entities.[43] The broad categories identified constitute a hierarchy in which the sub-communities called castes were ranked in an order of social precedence. Additional evidence regarding the close mutual interaction of castes also pointed out the differences between the Hindu and Muslim caste systems, but it nonetheless pointed to the existence of caste-like features in the Muslim stratification system. In other words, Muslims may be a faith community, but in sociological and even theological terms they are not homogeneous,[44] being divided into numerous sects and, in India, into various caste groups as well. Therefore, to treat them as a single entity and to deny internal differentiation would only perpetuate inequalities and further reinforce structures of marginalization. Moreover, most Muslims are from lower-caste backgrounds and the majority are descendants of converts to Islam—known as *ajlaf* (meaning base or lowly).[45] In this context, the SCR points out: 'Features of the Hindu caste system, such as hierarchical ordering of social groups based on descent, endogamy and hereditary occupation leading to each caste confining marriages to its members, and differential access to economic resources and power have been found to be amply present among Muslims as well.'[46] Muslims who claim foreign descent assert a superior status for themselves as *ashraf* or 'noble'.[47] Going by this classification, an overwhelming 75 per cent of Muslim population of India would fall into the *ajlaf* category. This large group of *ajlaf* continues to be discriminated against by the so-called *ashraf* groups and also by their counterparts in the majority community.

The orthodox Muslim organizations and the Sangh Parivar share certain misconceptions about the innate unity and immanent quality of Muslim identity. The former perceive Muslims as united and integrated by their adherence to Islam, while the latter is prone to paying more heed to religious identity than to other identity markers.[48] In both cases religion is designated as an all-encompassing identity to the exclusion of other factors, discounting influences from the cultural and socio-political environment wherein Muslims live and practise their faith.[49] A neglect of the societal context of which Muslims have been a part for centuries results in giving an image of Muslims as unchanging, rigid, and beyond liberal influences.

Many Muslims who admit that caste or caste-like groupings exist in their community are nevertheless ambivalent with regard to the precise relevance of caste among them.[50] This ambivalence has resulted in two distinct tendencies among them. Those who admit that caste differences obtain among them often come up with the plea that a term other than 'caste' should be used to designate and differentiate Muslim groups. Accordingly, ethnic groups, *biradaris*, or caste-like groupings have been considered and used as substitutes. Others deny the existence of caste among Muslims altogether, saying that Islam is an egalitarian religion and does not recognize distinctions of caste and status. This tendency refuses to recognize that Islam and Muslims are not necessarily one and the same, and that there might be a gap between Islamic beliefs and ideology and actual social behaviour.[51]

Arguably, both tendencies arise from Muslim anxieties about their minority status in India and the vulnerability associated with this identity. Even those Muslims who deny the existence of caste tend to do so out of a need for protecting the community in the context of its standing as a minority in India. Many Muslims argue that some word other than caste should be used to designate social divisions among them are guided by the unease that if caste was accorded recognition it would suggest similarity and resemblance with the Hindus, which they are keen to deny. This concern also arises from the recognition that the Muslim community was very substantially formed through conversion from the indigenous groups and there is an apprehension that it might relapse back into

Hinduism (much like the fear expressed by Sikh leaders). This has prompted large sections of the Muslim community, particularly the elite and middle classes, to clearly distinguish themselves from Hindus by evolving distinctions that they feel are more Islamic and set them apart from Hindus. Accordingly, while they are willing to admit that caste-like formations exist among Muslims, they would much rather use some other word to designate Muslim castes.

The other important issue regarding differentiation within the Muslim population relates to regional and class differences, which both advocates and opponents of caste reservation are reluctant to recognize as it would deflect attention from their claims to minority or caste reservation, as the case may be.[52] Muslims are not a monolithic community: there is class variability and internal class differentiation among them. A large majority of Muslims are in the unskilled labour category or in small businesses or self-employment and definitely not in the top-end occupations and employment, which are confined to the Hindu upper castes but a section of Muslims are well off. Apart from the differentiation in terms of class and income, their socio-economic status also varies from region to region, which means that the entire community is not uniformly disadvantaged across the country.

The socio-economic differentiation of the Muslim community undermines the idea of a monolithic community and hence renders the proposal for minority reservations completely untenable. Repeated failure of the Andhra Pradesh government in extending reservations to Muslims qua Muslims underlines the constitutional problems of instituting it on a minority basis. The Congress government in Andhra Pradesh provided 5 per cent reservations for Muslims in 2004, which was struck down by the High Court of that state ruling that reservations could not be given on the basis of religion and that the total quantum of reservations could not exceed 50 per cent.[53] The SC/ST and OBC quotas in the state already add up to 46 per cent. In view of the successive failures of the government in 1968, 1982, and 2004, the Andhra Pradesh government referred the matter to the Backward Classes Commission. The state government appointed a committee in 2007 headed by P.S. Krishnan, former member secretary, NCBC, to suggest ways of providing reservations within the constitutional framework, which in effect required recognition of caste and caste-based entitlements. The committee repackaged reservations on Mandal lines: about fifteen OBC Muslim groups were recognized for the purpose of reservations while ten sub-castes were excluded.[54] Based on this recommendation, the state government decided to bring in legislation to provide 4 per cent quotas for 'socially and educationally backward Muslims in education and employment'. The Sangh Parivar had earlier criticized this, terming the decision 'divisive and communal' and even 'a prelude to Partition'.[55] For the Congress, on the other hand, it was an important move in the process of building its support base among Muslims. It fits into a pattern of decisions taken by the Congress government of Andhra Pradesh to rebuild its support base among the social constituency of the poor, lower-caste, and minority populations. Following up on the advice of the committee headed by Krishnan, the Andhra Pradesh government devised criteria to classify Muslims as a backward class and finally succeeded in implementing 4 per cent reservations for backward Muslims in February 2008 in government employment subject to the final verdict of the court in the matter.

Muslim Under-representation and Affirmative Action

So, is affirmative action possible for Muslims? There is no easy answer to this question. The issue is complicated for two reasons: on the one hand, the SCR clearly demonstrates the huge institutional deficit with regard to representation as well as socio-economic backwardness of Muslims as a whole, and on the other, it also shows that the community is differentiated and divided into sub-groups and caste groupings which have different capacities to access opportunities. The point to note is that the categorization of sub-groups among religious groups as a backward class was fully consistent with the original concept as advocated on the floor of the Constituent Assembly by the entire spectrum of political opinion (including Ambedkar himself), with subsequent judicial pronouncements, and finally with executive dispensation in force in several states. This view was upheld by the Venkatachalliah

Commission, which stated that grant of reservation to Muslims, if they constitute a backward class, does not require any amendment to the Constitution but is a matter of government policy.[56]

To sum up, affirmative action is possible on the basis of social backwardness defined in caste terms but not on the basis of minority identity. The Mandal Commission and some state governments have adopted this approach. Caste groups listed in both the Mandal Commission and the state list have been included in the Central list. Hence a large number of groups listed in Mandal but not in the state list were left out. But the fact is that Muslim OBCs have not benefited from their inclusion in the OBC list. It has had no significant impact on their access to jobs, education, or generally in improving their welfare. This much was apparent from the findings of the SCR.[57]

According to the 55th round of the NSS, Muslim OBCs constitute 31.7 per cent of the Muslim population, whereas the 61st round of the NSS shows them at 40.7 per cent. Among the total OBCs of the country, the Muslim OBC share stands at 15.7 per cent. But this is not reflected in their representation, either in public employment or educational institutions. The social composition of public sector undertakings, the railways, and the Central security agencies indicates that out of every hundred workers about eleven are Hindu OBCs while only three are Muslim (General) and one is a Muslim OBC. This includes even the lowest level of Group D employees. The Muslim OBC representation did not exceed 3 per cent on average.[58] The SCR data shows that the proportion of Muslims in general and Muslim OBCs in particular in the formal sector is below the corresponding proportion for similar Hindu categories. Within the formal sector, non-OBC Muslims do better than OBC Muslims but hardly better than Hindu OBCs. The lower employment status of Muslim OBCs vis-à-vis the other two groups is also reflected in the fact that a much smaller proportion of workers among them are engaged in regular wage/salaried jobs, especially in urban areas. In general, Muslim OBCs were lagging behind Muslim (general) category and Hindu OBCs in terms of participation in the formal sector and jobs that provide regular employment (both waged and salaried). The under-representation of Muslim OBCs is highest in the railways.[59] While Hindu OBCs are also under-represented, it is less than that of Muslim OBCs in five out of the six agencies, and less than that of Muslim (General) in three out of the six agencies. In the states the situation is better for the Hindu OBCs. Although still short of proportionate representation, their share in the upper and middle levels is much higher than that in the Central organizations. While Muslim OBCs have a comparatively better representation in Group A posts of state services, their presence is insignificant at all other levels.

A small number of Muslims have benefited from reservations, but nowhere near the extent of the benefits derived by the Hindu OBCs. They have made gains in the southern states, but there are hardly any benefits at the Central level and in most other states. According to a recent study, government facilities for the OBCs had been cornered almost entirely by more numerous and powerful Hindu backward castes.[60] In Rajasthan, for instance, only thirty-eight Muslims have been appointed under the OBC category, although it is possible that some OBC Muslims have been selected in the general quota as well. This very low figure clearly suggests that Muslim OBCs have not gained much from the state's policy of positive discrimination for the OBCs.

The problem is partly inherent in the adoption of a caste-based approach for minorities; a large number of Muslims, though socially and economically backward, cannot be covered under the Mandal system. This is because Muslims do not easily fit into the OBC caste categorization. Besides, the Muslim OBC list does not distinguish between backward castes and Dalits among them and includes both in the same category. Even those Muslim sub-communities that have the same vocations as the SCs are included in the OBC list.

The main problem with the Mandal paradigm is that it has generally assumed the absence of internal differentiation in the backward castes. As a rule, the benefits of reservations have generally gone to the dominant sections of the backward castes, with the result that a few forward groups have over-benefited in comparison to their population while most of the other OBCs (including non-Muslim OBCs) have not gained much. It has been argued that: 'This is a natural consequence of bundling unequals together. This is why Muslim OBCs cannot receive their due share as part of a conglomerate because they suffer under double jeopardy—backwardness and communal prejudice.'[61] In other words, occupational categories have generally not been able to compete with the landed communities, which have cornered the benefits of reservations even among the Hindu OBCs. Muslims are concentrated in the lower-backward category, which means it is more difficult for them to access the provisions of reservations. It is doubtful if they can receive a fair share in the absence of affirmative action or a Central directive for a distribution of proportional share among eligible backward groups at the operational level. But there is no fixed numerical quota for backward-class Muslims in the Central services. One option is a classification of backwards on the basis of relative backwardness, cutting across religion, into three–four categories and then distributing the 27 per cent quota on the basis of the proportion of the relatively backward in the states. Alternatively, there can be a separate sub-quota for Muslims in the OBC quota. Since the bulk of Muslim OBCs are in the lower-backward category they would stand to gain from the implementation of the sub-quota option. Several Muslim organizations, including the Jamiat Ulema-i-Hind (JUH) and AIMMM are in favour of a sub-quota.

The additional problem in the case of Muslim OBCs is that the classification has not been done uniformly in different states. The Central list of OBCs was initially prepared on the principle of 'commonality' between the Central and state lists. Thus, only those castes/communities listed both in the state list and also in the list prepared by the Mandal Commission were included in the Central list. As a result, a number of castes/communities that had either been listed only in the Mandal list or only in the state list were left out. There are many OBC groups, irrespective of their religion, that are present in the state list but missing in the Central list.[62] There are a few groups of Muslims who have found a place in the Central OBC list but are yet to be included in the state lists. The reconciliation of discrepancies between various state lists and the Central list was supposed to be solved by the NCBC. Some of the groups which have been left out have made representations to the NCBC for their inclusion.

Arguments against Minority Quotas

Since the early 1990s, especially in the past few years, several Muslim leaders and organizations have made renewed calls for minority reservations. The OBC Muslim organizations, on the other hand, have confined their claims to the demand for a sub-quota for the Muslim OBCs within the OBC quota. Several influential politicians have extended support to Muslim reservations. For instance, Railway Minister Lalu Prasad Yadav expressed his support for reservation for Muslims in government jobs.[63] However, Law Minister H.R. Bharadwaj termed Prasad's suggestion as 'fanciful'. 'There are several ideas, including this, and these can be described as fanciful. Islam believes in equality for all and does not discriminate against caste or creed like in Hinduism.'[64] He was replying to a question on Prasad's demand that the UPA government should provide reservations for Muslims for various posts.

Minority reservations have been opposed principally on three grounds: (1) they are incompatible with the constitutional project of secularism; (2) in the absence of a caste system among Muslims there is no overt discrimination suffered by them to justify special measures; and (3) it would undermine national unity. The substantive issue is that affirmative action is valid in case of historically oppressed groups which have faced systematic discrimination over a long period of time, but that it is not valid in the case of marginalized groups.[65] Reservations were principally a matter of social justice or reparation for those who were the victims of oppression and discrimination arising out of the Hindu caste system.[66] Hence, special treatment is only applicable to caste groups and not religion-based groups. Even though some remedial measures may be needed for minorities, these mechanisms should not take the form of reservations. Thus, according to this argument, deprivation suffered by minorities cannot be put in this category of exclusion, and consequently, the same remedies will not work for them. The second set of objection stems from the fear of social and political Balkanization. This apprehension—that it would sharpen communal differences and is bound to generate a communal backlash—continues to dog any proposal for affirmative action and finds reflection in the opposition to preferential treatment for minorities. In this context, the identification of Hindu disadvantaged groups as more vulnerable and deprived than Muslims plays into the popular construction of Muslims as an 'appeased' group that is taking away jobs that should go to more disadvantaged castes. Further, there is a strong belief that Muslims are really not backward and if they have been left behind it is due to their own faults and the internal social milieu of the community; that is, they were neither historically disadvantaged nor unable to voice their demands but have simply manufactured the myth of backwardness. There is also sometimes an attempt to ascribe the glaring under-representation of minorities in sectors like the army and bureaucracy to personal choices and preferences.[67] This kind of thinking fails to factor in the lack of 'real choices'.[68] Yet others question the efficacy of state intervention in bringing about structural changes, which according to them is limited; in fact, community initiatives are more important and the key to their mobility and success. All these arguments clearly absolve the state of its responsibility to evolve inclusive policies and promote participation in governance, blame minorities for their exclusion, and foreclose state intervention to ensure equitable access to opportunities. Moreover, such an approach allows the critical issues of deprivation and exclusion of minorities to be sidelined while an agenda of social justice on the basis of caste can be promoted.[69]

Both sides to this dispute have focused primarily on the political implications of reservations, with opponents bolstering their position with reference to this legal position, and supporters highlighting the fact that the categorization of sub-groups among religious groups as 'backward' is fully consistent with the original concept and with subsequent judicial pronouncements, and also with executive dispensation in force in several states. To most Muslims, the opposition to the demand for reservations or at least a sub-quota reinforced the feeling that governments were simply unwilling to grant benefits to minorities because of a mindset that was ill-disposed towards them. In this vein, M.J. Akbar, editor of *The Asian Age*, comments:

If this is the way the political game is being played, then why should Muslims and Christians be excluded from the game? Almost everyone else has been allotted a piece of the cake, so why not them? Are they paying the price for being 'foreign faiths', that is, religions that originated outside the Indian subcontinent? If that is the truth, then the establishment should change the truth before the people change the establishment. If that is not the truth, then someone should let us know what the truth is.[70]

Dilemmas of Muslim Reservation

To find a resolution to these contending claims, Prime Minister Manmohan Singh had appointed the Sachar Committee to form an opinion on the questions of reservation and representation, and recommend remedial measures. The Committee heard arguments for and against affirmative action for Muslims at consultations organized by it in different parts of the country. It made seventeen recommendations, most of which relate to the Muslim community as a whole despite the SCR's attempt to disaggregate Muslims in caste terms, as evident from a separate chapter on OBCs in the text of the report. The SCR recommended 'equitable' distribution of available jobs in the 'formal sector' for Muslims and 'incentives to the private sector to encourage diversity in the work force', but it did not recommend reservation for Muslims, not even for Muslims with traditional occupations comparable to those of SCs and STs.

The SCR recommended several special measures for the Muslim community as a whole. For example, it recommended a special package for the development of districts with more than 25 per cent Muslim population. From this it appears that the Committee made a distinction between affirmative action and reservation. While it recommended special measures and targeted intervention to help the disadvantaged minority, it was not in favour of reservation for the community as a whole because the selection of a religious minority as a target group for reservation in jobs lacks legitimacy as against caste groupings.

Despite its reluctance to recommend reservations, the SCR's emphasis on the institutional deficit of Muslims bolstered the long-standing claim of the Muslim community that it has been the recipient of unfair treatment from successive governments of every political colour. It provided fresh ammunition to the claims of Muslim organizations that the Muslim community as a whole was backward and must be given quotas on this basis. As a result, the under-representation of Muslims is increasingly regarded as a problem which a significant number of political parties are concerned about. Many parties went on to advocate the urgent need to increase the proportion of minorities in government jobs but few have had the political will to initiate effective measures to bring this about.

Addressing the Annual Conference of State Minorities Commissions on 2 November 2006, the prime minister had underlined the need to provide a 'fair and legitimate share for minorities in Central and state governments and in the private sector jobs'.[71] The BJP condemned this as nothing but 'vote-bank politics' and 'minority appeasement'.[72] Describing 'fair share of minorities in government' as a 'dangerous doctrine', the BJP spokespersons said that any such move had the potential to divide the nation and that 'the party would fight it tooth and nail.'[73] The party categorically rejected the idea of 'fair share' because the Constitution did not envisage parity on the basis of religion. It accused the Congress of completely surrendering itself to the politics of minorityism and lending support to this divisive demand either overtly or covertly. By raising the issue of communal divisions, the BJP leadership once again sidetracked the issue of institutionalized bias and inequalities.

The Congress was in favour of affirmative action measures for all minorities, including religious and linguistic minorities. But there was a big gap between Congressmen who were in favour of affirmative action measures for Muslims as a whole and those who argued that these should be limited to listing them under existing OBC schemes. Several Congress leaders, especially from south India, stressed the point that the party had taken the lead to introduce reservations for Muslims in Kerala and Karnataka in government employment and education on the basis of social and educational backwardness of Muslims. Even before the SCR had been submitted, Veerappa Moily said: 'If Muslims fulfill the criteria for backward class, they should definitely be put in the mainstream with OBCs.'[74] He referred to the Karnataka model where 4 per cent quotas are given to Muslims from the quota reserved for OBCs. Other voices in the political arena, notably the Left parties, also spoke up in support of state intervention for minorities to improve their social and economic conditions. Another Congress leader Salman Khurshid conceded:

> Muslims cannot be given reservation on religious lines but it's possible on grounds of being a backward class. The central list of OBCs contains innumerable Muslim communities (most Muslims in India are OBCs) who are entitled to reservation. The problem is that most of them can't take advantage of this provision as the principal OBC groups gobble up the benefits. A solution is to segregate the less advantaged as was done in states like Bihar so that more backward Muslims can get a share. This is constitutionally valid. No one has challenged the list of communities. So nothing prevents the government from passing an order that Muslim communities named as backward be given benefits on a priority basis.[75]

On the whole, with the exception of a few initiatives such as a centrally sponsored scheme of merit-cum-means scholarships for students from minority communities to pursue professional and technical courses at under-graduate and post-graduate levels and infrastructure development and welfare schemes in minority-concentration districts, the UPA government did not move forward with regard to affirmative action in recruitment to government. Even though Congress leaders had expressed concern over the exclusion of minorities from public institutions, their government was reluctant to implement any positive proposals because of the communal backlash it feared it could engender.[76] The hesitation has much to do with the propaganda of Hindu nationalists who are hostile to any positive discrimination in favour of Muslims. Driven by the need to counter the charge of tokenism as also the need to defuse Muslim resentment which may lead to conflicts, even as it had to deal with the real possibility that affirmative action for minorities would give impetus to the BJP's propaganda of minority appeasement, the Congress staged a virtual retreat. In the event, it was vulnerable to the charge of grandstanding or, at best, making meaningless promises of good intent.

The Sangh Parivar was opposed to affirmative action and more so to reservations for minorities. Its opposition was summed up by L.K. Advani when he said that the principle of minority proportionality must be stopped as it represents a harmful mindset and a separatist attitude. He argued that communal reservations are violative of the letter and spirit of the Constitution.[77] Referring to the Andhra Pradesh government's decision in particular, he said '...it will legitimise and in course of time, revive the very same communal and separatist tendency that developed into the two-nation theory and led to the partition of our motherland.'[78] At the same time, he argued that positive discrimination for SCs and STs was justified, as it took into account thousands of years of discrimination, marginalization, and atrocities heaped on them, but this was not the case with Muslims. Besides, Muslims are already included in the OBC category and enjoy reservation on that basis and a Muslim quota will be cornered by the creamy layer among them. Detailing this concern further, BJP leader Arif Mohammed Khan observed: 'This will mean inclusion of creamy layer which...will make things even more difficult for the really depressed sections of Muslims to compete against the Muslim creamy layer when today they find it hard to secure a fair share for themselves while competing against the depressed sections of other religious denominations.'[79]

The Sangh Parivar's opposition is typically couched in the language of constitutionalism, even though it seems to derive its force from prejudice. This political language does not allow Muslims to make claims on the state in the way that other disadvantaged groups can make claims and assert their rights. Such opposition draws on a specific re-articulation of the concept of affirmative action in a manner that serves to buttress the primacy of its caste underpinnings and the constitutional illegitimacy of the category of 'minority' for this purpose. The particular effect of this articulation was to provide a broader location for the conception of disadvantage in terms of social justice, past oppression, and historical disadvantage, which excludes consideration of contemporary forms of discrimination and deprivation that other groups may suffer.

Affirmative Action for Minorities

The preceding section points out that over the past decade numerous activists and leaders have argued that institutional deficits with regard to minorities can only be remedied through minority reservations while others have favoured backward-caste reservations for them. Two decisions of the UPA government—the appointment of the Sachar Committee and then the National Commission for Religious and Linguistic Minorities (NCRLM) headed by Ranganath Misra and its recommendation to provide reservations to minorities, particularly Dalits, in the SC quota—recharged this debate. In this regard, Home Minister Shivraj Patil's sudden observation in support of minority reservations at the inauguration of the Annual Conference of State Commissions for Minorities (2008) added fuel to the controversy. He emphasized the need for 'ingenious' steps to achieve minority reservations.[80] But minority reservations are neither feasible nor desirable, since it is well-nigh impossible to build a national consensus on them.

Besides political problems, there are practical constraints, most obviously the Supreme Court-approved ceiling on the quantum of reservations which cannot exceed 50 per cent. The 50 per cent ceiling established in 1992 makes it impossible to go beyond this maximum without a constitutional amendment, although states like Tamil Nadu and Karnataka have had reservations far in excess of 50 per cent and courts have not been able to stop them. Reservation for minorities was unlikely to be conceded because it would go beyond the ceiling. Moreover, mandatory reservations are not the best solution to problems of institutional deficit, which is serious and needs to be addressed but not necessarily through reservations. Besides, the number of government jobs is limited and declining in the face of neo-liberal economic reforms and the rapid growth of the private sector. Moreover, in this context it is also worth pointing out that a minority reservation of say 4 to 5 per cent would not significantly enhance their representation which stands roughly at 3 per cent in the IAS and 5 per cent in the state services. On several counts it would be controversial and fraught with communally charged tensions and conflict.

All in all, it is not easy to make headway with regard to reservations for minorities because of the constitutional bar and because of the strong opposition to it from several different quarters. Even in the case of OBCs, the UPA government could ultimately implement reservations in higher education only when the court pronounced a verdict in its favour in April 2008. Unlike affirmative action for minorities there was no serious opposition from political parties, in fact, there was a strong cross-party consensus on quotas for SCs/STs and OBCs. Yet the government had to wait for two years before it could implement a law passed unanimously by Parliament. In Mandal I, the government had to wait for four years to roll out reservations for OBCs in government jobs. The political consensus on OBC or SC/ST reservations stands in sharp contrast to the rancour and stereotyping with regard to minority reservations, ranging from caution to outright hostility to any proposal for affirmative action or sub-quotas within the OBC quotas. To cut through this welter of arguments and counter-arguments it is important to grapple with the problem of inter-group disparity and institutional deficits. The data in the SCR lead one to conclude that minority deficits have not withered away with development, but that, in fact, some form of affirmative action might be necessary to tackle institutional deficits. For this to happen it is important not to conflate reservations with affirmative action, as is commonly done, as this tends to undercut the possibility of affirmative action. Affirmative action need not be synonymous with reservations; we must recognize that different groups of the disadvantaged warrant different kinds of affirmative action. All things being equal, in the sense of qualifications of candidates, affirmative action can give preference to minorities in public institutions and higher education. Muslims need affirmative action in the above sense to increase their representation in government in view of the severe deficit in institutional representation. In this regard, it is important to keep in mind the objectives of the state, specified not only in the Constitution but also arising out of other values that are basic to any modern democratic society, such as social equality and equal treatment. We might, with some justification, say that making political elites and legislatures more representative is an important objective that stands on its own, and even if it does not result in increasing the weight attached to the concerns of the disadvantaged, it has an independent symbolic weight in making the polity more representative and pluralistic.

Although demands for affirmative action or a sub-quota for Muslim OBCs are not very radical steps, the fact remains that they can have a vital role in widening the reach and application of affirmative action. For the state, conceding one or both the demands would indicate a tangible commitment to the provision of a 'fair share' of jobs to all disadvantaged groups. More importantly, it would signal a major conceptual shift in the approach towards minorities, particularly Muslims, who have been outside both the development and constitutional discourse of social justice and equity. It would also help to facilitate a radical shift in the very terms of political discourse of the Muslim leadership, which has since Independence occupied itself with identity issues. For both reasons it would signify an integration of Muslims into the national mainstream, build bridges with other oppressed sections, and thus bring an end to their treatment as the historical 'Other'.

Notes

1. Equality of treatment suggests that individuals, regardless of the ethnic group they belong to, are treated alike, and have a right to live a life of dignity. Equality of outcome, in the context of ethnicity, means that distribution of income, wealth, and occupations among individuals be in proportion to the population of each group in the country. Siddharth Varadarajan (2006).

2. Myron Weiner (1983: 36).

3. Laura D. Jenkins (2003).

4. Theodore Wright (1997); Zoya Hasan (2005); A.R. Momin (2004).

5. Satish Deshpande and Yogendra Yadav (2006: 2420–1).

6. Laura D. Jenkins (2003).

7. *SCR* (2006: 153).

8. Ibid.

9. Santosh Goyal (1989: 429).

10. Steven Wilkinson (2005).

11. Government order clearly states: 'Whenever a Selection Committee/

Board exists or has to be constituted for making recruitment to 10 or more vacancies in Group "C" or Group "D" posts/services, it shall be mandatory to have one member belonging to SC/ST/OBC and one member belonging to minority community on such Committees/Boards.' Report of Ministry of Personnel, Public Grievances and Pensions (2007).

12. *SCR* (2006: 165–75).

13. One place where Muslims are over-represented is prisons. Barring Assam, the proportion of Muslims in prison is considerably higher than their share in the population. In Maharashtra, Muslims account for 10.6 per cent of the population, but they form 40.6 per cent of all prisoners. In Delhi, the respective figures are 11.7 and 27.9 per cent, in Gujarat 9.1 and 25.1 per cent, and in Tamil Nadu 5.6 and 9.6 per cent. Reported in *The Indian Express*, 20 October 2006.

14. *SCR* (2006: 17–71).

15. Ibid.

16. Ibid.

17. Harish Khare (2002).

18. Barbara Harris-White (2002).

19. A recent study on the social, economic, and educational conditions of Muslims notes that even in Muslim-majority areas there are hardly any Muslim employees in government departments, even in junior posts such as drivers, cleaners, and clerks, for which higher educational qualifications are not required. The study also observes that basic infrastructural facilities, such as proper roads, sewage systems, banks, dispensaries, health facilities, and schools, are largely conspicuous by their absence in these localities. The respondents claimed that while they, like others, are also taxpayers, government departments consistently ignore them. Imran Ali and Yoginder Sikand (2006).

20. According to a recent study, it has raised employment by at least by about five percentage points. Vani Barooah, *et al.* (2007).

21. Ibid.

22. Mushirul Hasan (1998).

23. On the nature of social stratification among Indian Muslims, see essays in Imtiaz Ahmad (1978).

24. Rowena Robinson (2005).

25. Omar Khalidi (2005).

26. Irfan Habib (2006).

27. A study by S.K. Thorat and Paul Attewell (2007) of private sector hiring done on the basis of correspondence methodology of sending five applications—a Muslim, a Dalit, a high-caste (all qualifying), one

overqualified Dalit and one underqualified high-caste—for each job advertisement. The authors made 4,808 applications in response to 548 job advertisements over 66 weeks. They found that discriminatory processes operate even at the first stage of the application process. Their field experiment shows that on an average college-educated lower-caste and Muslim job applicants fare less well than equivalently qualified applicants with high caste names in the modern private sector. Thorat and Attewell (2007: 4144).

28. Ibid.

29. Steven Wilkinson (2005) and Rohini Pande (2003) develop an important argument along these lines.

30. *Report of the Backward Classes Commission* (1955). The Mandal Commission too relied on the caste criterion; however, the tangible indicators to ascertain a caste or any social group as 'backward' included a lower position in the caste hierarchy, lower age at marriage within the group, higher female work participation, higher school dropout rate, inaccessibility to drinking water, lower average value of family assets, higher occurrence of *kutcha* houses, and so on.

31. Ibid.

32. *SCR* (2006: 198).

33. On this controversy, see the debate between D.L. Sheth (2004b) and Syed Shahabuddin (2004).

34. Laura D. Jenkins (2003).

35. Shabbir Ansari of the All India Muslim OBC Organization, quoted in Laura D. Jenkins (2003: 116).

36. Theodore Wright (1997: 853–4).

37. AIMMM Memorandum submitted to NCRLM, *The Milli Gazette*, Delhi, 10 February 2006.

38. Ibid.

39. Ali Anwar (2001).

40. Anwar Alam (2003); Irfan Ahmad (2003).

41. Imtiaz Ahmad (2007).

42. Ghaus Ansari (1959).

43. Imtiaz Ahmad (1978).

44. Ibid.

45. Imtiaz Ahmad (1978: 13).

46. *SCR* (2006: 192).

47. One can discern three groups among Muslims: (1) those without any social disabilities—the *Ashrafs*; (2) those equivalent to Hindu OBCs—the *Ajlafs*, and (3) those equivalent to Hindu SCs—the *Arzals*.

The OBCs among Muslims constitute two broad categories. The Halalkhors, Helas, Lalbegis or Bhangis (scavengers), Dhobis (washermen), Nais or Hajjams (barbers), Chiks (butchers), Faqirs (beggars), etc., are *Arzals*, the 'untouchable converts' to Islam that have found their way into the OBC list. The Momins or Julahas (weavers), Darzi or Idiris (tailors), Rayeens or Kunjaras (vegetable sellers), etc., are *Ajlafs* or converts from 'clean' occupational castes.

48. Mushirul Hasan (1998).

49. Susan Bayly (1999).

50. Imtiaz Ahmad (2007).

51. Ibid.

52. On social differentiation, see Chapter 1 on 'Socioeconomic Status of Muslims' in Zoya Hasan and Ritu Menon (2004); Rakesh Basant (2007a).

53. Report of the Ex-Officio Commissionerate of Minorities Welfare, Backward Classes Welfare Department, Government of Andhra Pradesh, No. 33 (G.O. 33), 12 July 2004.

54. *The Indian Express*, 23 June 2007.

55. Aniket Alam (2004).

56. Cited in Syed Shahabuddin (2004).

57. See Chapter 10 in *SCR* on the Muslim OBCs.

58. For a detailed comparison see *SCR* (2006: 210–14).

59. Ibid., p. 211.

60. Imran Ali and Yoginder Sikand (2006).

61. Syed Shahabuddin (2004).

62. *SCR* (2006: 200–1).

63. *Manorama*, 28 October 2005.

64. H.R. Bharadwaj, Law Minister, quoted in *Manorama*, 28 October 2005.

65. Some of these objections are discussed in Rajeev Bhargava (2007: 102–4).

66. Ibid.

67. Jaya Jaitley makes the argument that if the SCR had studied the preferred occupations of Muslims it would have come to a different conclusion on the status of Muslims, which is that Muslims have a preference for artisanal and craft-based occupations. See Jaya Jaitley (2007).

68. This thinking is similar to white racist beliefs that African Americans are born singers and artists and prefer to dance instead of becoming lawyers or bureaucrats; and that since some Blacks have made it big, the status of

Blacks is not bad. In the same vein, some would like to believe that Muslims are good tailors, cooks, carpenters, artisans, and craftsmen, and therefore prefer self-employment to public employment or becoming administrators, doctors, and company managers. On this, see Mona Mehta (2007).

69. I am grateful to Professor Suhas Palshikar for drawing my attention to the importance of why the caste question assumed greater political salience and traction in India's democratic politics in contrast to the Muslim question. He suggests this was because the caste question was from the beginning squarely located in the framework of social justice, equality, and democracy. This lent primacy and ideological superiority to the issue of handling the caste question, while the minority question remained trapped in identity politics.

70. M.J. Akbar (2006).

71. *The Times of India*, 3 November 2006.

72. *The Hindu*, 25 January 2007.

73. *The Indian Express*, 6 November 2006.

74. *The Deccan Chronicle*, 13 November 2006.

75. *Outlook*, 14 November 2006.

76. For example, the Central government issued instructions to states to ensure adequate representation of Muslims in police stations, education, and health departments, *The Times of India*, 6 September 2007. Criticizing the move, BJP spokesperson Ravi Shankar Prasad said: 'The directive, apart from its serious constitutional vulnerability, has very dangerous and sinister implications for the unity and integrity of India. In fact this directive is reminiscent of the frequent demand which the Muslim League used to raise during the pre-Partition days.' *Hindustan Times*, 7 September 2007.

77. L.K. Advani, 'Why We Are Opposed to Communal Reservations', www.bjp.org/Publication/LKA/1404E.pdf (n.d.).

78. Ibid.

79. *Organiser*, 3 December 2006.

80. *The Times of India*, 19 January 2008.

7

Social Discrimination and the Reservation Claims of Muslim and Christian Dalits

In June 2006, newspapers reported the case of a Dalit woman, Rima Singh, whose husband, Mukesh Kumar, had converted to Islam and taken the name of Muhammad Sadiq. The woman had recently been elected as a *sarpanch* on a reserved seat in a village in Uttar Pradesh and wanted to follow her husband and become a Muslim. However, if she did so, she would have to resign from her post because, as the law stands, Dalit Muslims (as well as Dalit Christians) are not considered Scheduled Castes by the state. A bench of the Supreme Court issued a notice in response to the writ petition filed by the couple asking the government to explain why Dalit Muslims are denied reservation benefits.

Such an uneven approach towards disadvantaged groups has created new arenas of conflict not just on the desirability of reservations and defining the relevant groups based on concepts such as caste and caste-based discrimination but also with regard to the fairness of these policies and the exclusion of non-Hindu groups. Dalit Christians and Dalits Muslims have for several years been demanding inclusion in the SC category; however, successive governments have not paid heed to these demands.[1] These groups claim to occupy a position comparable to those officially designated as SCs, but the official framework looks upon caste as a feature of Hindu society and hence excludes them. This has led to controversies regarding the nature of social disabilities and the framework of special treatment arising out of it. It would appear that officially some identities count for the purpose of reservation, and the recognition of these identities is implicitly or explicitly linked to the non-recognition of others.[2]

In India, the definition of backwardness remains contested despite attempts to list groups in schedules with justifications invoking a set of normative concepts of social justice, equality, and secularism.[3] The process of identification of these groups and how they are categorized by the government has an impact on the allocation of opportunities and access to government jobs and resources. Such groups have a vital interest in inclusion in the SC and ST lists, as it affects their access to education and government employment. Falling outside the ambit of reservations, they face marginalization in politics and in the distribution of benefits.

At a basic level, the controversies are fuelled by the belief that official categorization and reservations are not based on just criteria but on the assertion of power and clout.[4] This interpretation of course depends on one's reading of the state in India and whether it is seen as a fairly neutral arbiter of interests or as a set of agencies pushing their own agenda and often that of specific groups. To pose the question differently, does state policy reflect objective realities or does it reinforce and privilege certain categories over others? Although reservations on the basis of religion remain highly controversial, there are questions with regard to the concept of backwardness which by privileging certain identities can end up communalizing deprivation and disadvantage.

Can a Dalit Muslim or Dalit Christian be a Scheduled Caste? This is an important question which is at the heart of the debate on affirmative action. This chapter examines the question in the light of the claims and counter-claims of Dalits in the Muslim and Christian communities for SC status. It also looks at the response of various institutions of the state and political parties to these contentious claims. Despite a long campaign by Christian organizations and NGOs, Dalit Christians (and Dalit Muslims) have not been able to gain official recognition as SCs. These efforts have led to tensions between SCs, on the one hand, and Christian and Muslim Dalits, on the other, and also to tensions within these groups. Most notably this demand challenges the widely held assumption about the non-religious basis of reservation policies, and the link between the evidence of social inequalities and reservations and distribution of benefits.

There is resistance to reservation for religious minorities on the grounds that religion-based reservations are unconstitutional. But the SC category is for the purpose of reservation mainly a Hindu category. This raises important questions with regard to the neutrality of reservation policies as claimed by those who support this position. The second and more important issue pertains to the relative importance of ritual aspects of social disabilities and discrimination in the definition of SCs. This issue is significant because it relates to the primacy of caste inequalities relative to a socially grounded notion of discrimination and deprivation for the purpose of reservations. The third issue concerns the position of various groups in this conflict. Dalit Hindus are apparently opposed to the inclusion of Dalit Christians and Dalit Muslims because they fear that their benefits and entitlements would be diluted with an increase in the number of claimants. Sections of Christians and Muslims themselves are opposed to recognizing caste within their religions because they believe their faiths are egalitarian, while the Dalits among them insist that caste inequalities are rampant in these theoretically egalitarian religions.

Classification of Scheduled Castes

Scheduled Caste is a legal and administrative category. It is intended to comprise those groups isolated and disadvantaged by their untouchability—that is, their low status in the traditional Hindu caste hierarchy, engagement in traditionally defiling occupations, exclusion from residential areas within localities, and untouchability practised against them by other castes owing to their presumed superiority of status. The Constitution does not provide a standard for selection of groups as SCs, except for the general understanding that they were untouchables.[5] It provides a procedure and agency for designating them. The president is empowered to specify 'the castes, races or tribes or parts of or groups within castes, races and tribes which shall for the purposes of the Constitution be deemed to be SCs in relation to the state' for reservation and other state actions to ameliorate their condition. This can be changed only by an Act of Parliament.

In 1950 the president issued the Constitution (SC) Order specifying the definition of SCs. The Order states: '...no person professing a religion different from the Hinduism shall be deemed to be a member of a Scheduled Caste.'[6] This Order has been amended twice, once in 1956 to include Sikhs and again in 1990 to include the neo-Buddhists. The Sikh demand was accepted on the ground that Sikh untouchables were originally SC Hindus who had only recently converted to the Sikh faith and had suffered from the same disabilities as the Hindu SCs, and that this was true of the neo-Buddhists as well as they were subjected to social ostracism similar to their counterparts among Hindus. With regard to Sikhs, Vallabhai Patel conceded in his intervention on the subject in the Constituent Assembly that 'as a matter of fact, these converts are not SCs or ought not to be SCs, because in the Sikh religion, there is no such thing as untouchability or any classification or difference of classes.'[7] But Sikh leaders feared that if the Dalit Sikhs who were originally SCs were denied SC status they would reconvert to Hinduism, and hence the Congress leadership was willing to make a generous political concession to accommodate their anxieties. This was because they belonged to the 'reformed community of the Hindus, called the Sikhs', as Patel conceded.[8]

The SC Order of 1950 promulgated by the president established state-specific lists which identified castes that fell into these categories. This Order basically re-enacted the Imperial (SC) Order of 1935 that did not include Christians and Buddhists (in Bengal) in the list of SCs. Until 1947, several kinds of communities (not necessarily defined by religion) were given reserved political representation in India: Muslims, women, Europeans, Dalits, and so on. With two exceptions, such reservations were abolished after Independence. The major purpose of the earlier imperial list was to provide for electoral reservation, including for Christians and Muslims who were the beneficiaries of special treatment as minorities. Hence, they had to be excluded from the SC list to avoid double reservations for them as SCs and as minority groups before Independence. But after the elimination of separate representation for minorities and the change in the purpose of affirmative action from political reservation to a much broader purpose of administration of policies for the social welfare of disadvantaged groups, the retention of the religious qualification was unjustified.

Under this scheme, all SCs are assumed to be Hindus; hence, any individuals converting to Islam or Christianity were no longer entitled to the benefits that accrue from being an SC. As early as in 1950, Christian leaders questioned both the prime minister and the president on the exclusion of Christian Dalits from the SC group and by implication the discrepancy that this represents between the secular nature of the Constitution and the religious bias of the presidential order. For both Jawaharlal Nehru and Rajendra Prasad, however, the distinction between Hindu and non-Hindu SCs was limited to political reservations. They did not envisage barring converts to other religions from enjoying all the other benefits of affirmative action or to make differentiations on grounds of religion and caste. However, the Central government did not press the issue outlined by the president and prime minister, and instead accepted the dominant view that SCs meant only Hindu SCs. This position was confirmed in 1956 when Parliament decided to exclude converts to Christianity and Islam from the list of SCs. Since 1950 the criteria for inclusion of any community is that it should suffer from extreme social, educational, and economic backwardness arising out of traditional practices of untouchability.

In 1956, the Constitution (SCs) Order was extended to include Dalits professing Sikhism and again in 1990 to include neo-Buddhists. Neither the original order nor the two amendments to the presidential order offered any explicit justification or rationale. The apparent justification was that they were recent converts and hence caste was still the key basis of their social identity. But the same argument does not seem to be applied to Dalit converts to Islam and Christianity. They were included in the OBC list, which failed to make a significant impact as they were clubbed along with the relatively more advanced groups of backward castes/classes which were in a better position to avail the benefits of reservations.

This exclusion, many have argued, is inconsistent with Articles 14, 15, 16, and 25 of the Constitution that guarantee equality of opportunity, freedom of conscience, and protection of the citizens from discrimination by the state on grounds of religion, caste, or creed.

Judicial Perspectives

Courts have by and large deferred to the executive and upheld the exclusion of non-Hindus and the established criteria of low social and ritual standing for the definition of SCs.[9] As a result, converts to Islam or Christianity have not been included in the SC list. Courts have sustained this exclusion on the grounds that 'acceptance of a non-Hindu religion operates as a loss of caste.'[10] Additionally, judicial approaches have been shaped by legal theories of caste and untouchability as distinct features of Hindu society.[11] The courts have been concerned mainly with three issues: (1) the caste status of converts from Hinduism; (2) the specific nature of social disabilities; and (3) the fact that the extension of SC status hinges on the nature of evidence of social disability in this regard.

A Christian petitioner from Tamil Nadu filed a petition before the Supreme Court to seek benefits as SCs (and not OBCs) for converts on the grounds that the 1950 Order discriminated against Christians and was violative of their fundamental rights guaranteed in Articles 14 and 15 of the Constitution. The principal point of the petitioner was that social and economic disabilities do not cease after conversion, and that such conversion cannot be a legal basis for denying them the benefits available to other SC persons. The court rejected the petition in the *Soosai & Others* v. *Union of India & Others* judgment in 1985 and ruled that a person belonging to a SC is not entitled to welfare assistance after conversion to Christianity because there is insufficient evidence of discrimination and degradation in Christian society after conversion. For them to gain recognition as SCs, they would have to establish that converts suffer from comparable social and economic disabilities, cultural and educational backwardness, and similar levels of degradation within the Christian community necessitating intervention by the state under the provisions of the Constitution. The judgment says: 'It is not sufficient to show that the same caste continues after conversion. It is necessary to establish further that the disabilities and handicaps suffered from such caste's membership in the social order of its origin—Hinduism—continue in their oppressive severity in the new environment of a different religious community.'[12]

The basic issue pertains to social disability and how it is to be established. In addition to their caste identity, the claimant groups need to establish that they are worse-off than their co-religionists, that this is due to their caste status, and that this is comparable in status to the Hindu, Sikh, and Buddhist Dalits.[13] The question is complicated by the need to establish a causal link between caste inequalities and social disabilities. In other words, it is not enough to say that Dalit Christians and Dalit Muslims share the same economic and social status; it is necessary to show that the similarity is due to their caste identity rather than other possible causes.

The evidence of social disability and its causes remains the most contentious issue. The courts now seem to be willing to concede the point that caste survives conversion, which means that conversion may not erase caste identity. But they want the claimants to demonstrate the extent and nature of social disability.[14] This was the court's response to a 2004 petition filed by the Centre for Public Interest Litigation which claimed that Dalit Christians suffered from 'double discrimination' as the government did not provide them with reservation even though the faith they had embraced was unable to ensure equal treatment.[15]

Political Campaigns and Challenges

Aware of the importance of affirmative action and the political and economic benefits that accrue from it, the Dalit movement has over the past two decades sought to establish and promote a much wider sense of Dalit identity. The resurgence of Dalit consciousness has not been limited to those defined according to the law as SCs but includes Dalits of all religions.[16]

Spearheaded by the All-India Christian Council and the Catholic Bishops Conference of India, several Christian groups have participated in the campaign in support of the demand that Dalit

Christians be recognized as SCs and given the benefits associated with this. Their contention for recognition is that there is no change in their social status after conversion.[17] For the past many decades, through memoranda, delegations, rallies, and conventions they have sought to convince the government to amend the Constitution to broaden the definition to include them in the SC category. They have made representations to all political parties and governments in the Centre and states to extend the concessions granted to SCs to Dalit converts to Christianity on the grounds that social disabilities and educational backwardness and not religion should be the basis for special treatment. Since the early 1990s Christian groups have intensified the campaign and organized numerous demonstrations and rallies in different parts of the country, not only for job reservation, but also to establish equal rights with other Dalits.

The Muslim Dalit campaign, though of more recent origin, has gained momentum from the early 1990s after the implementation of the Mandal Commission Report. The campaign has been led by the All India Backward Muslim Morcha (AIBMM) which was set up in 1994 by Ejaz Ali, a doctor from Bihar. The foremost objective of the AIBMM is to gain recognition of Dalit Muslims as SCs. While various Christian groups have been campaigning for SC status from the early 1950s, it was only with the emergence of the AIBMM that Dalit Muslims began to mobilize to demand what they see as their rights that have been denied to them by the law.[18] In 2000, the activists of AIBMM demonstrated before Parliament to press their demand for an amendment of the Constitution to provide for reservation in the SC category to Dalit Muslims.[19] Like their Christian counterparts, their basic contention is that no religious community in India is free of caste, and that hence all the Hindu caste groupings are present among Muslims and Christians. There are a substantial number of Muslims who are either converts from the outcastes or from other backward castes, and that the character of their oppression did not alter after their conversion. In this sense, these particular segments among Muslims have been historically marginalized. They contend that Dalit Muslims are descendants of low-caste converts with similar caste names as Hindu Dalits and backward-caste communities and continue to be engaged in the lowliest occupations such as scavenging and washing of clothes. They suffer from extreme marginalization and oppression, not only within Muslim society but also in the wider society, and suffer a social stigma closely comparable to that of the Hindu Dalits. Yet, they are denied SC facilities available to the Hindu Dalits and can get these facilities on their return to the Hindu fold. In this regard the AIMMM statement observed: The exclusion of persons of Dalit origin professing Christianity or Islam and their 'reinclusion' on returning to Hindu fold is not only discriminatory under Articles 14, 15, and 16 but is violative of the right to freely profess and practise one's religion under Article 25, as the Article provides disincentive to those who want to convert to Christianity or Islam, and provides inducements to Christian and Muslim Dalits to return to the Hindu fold.[20] Thus, even organizations such as the AIMMM which are dominated by *Ashrafs* demanded the removal of this anomaly so that Dalit Muslims can avail of the same benefits their counterparts among Hindu SCs enjoy. 'Thus exclusion of Christian and Dalit Muslims is not only unjust to concerned citizens but is also indirectly supportive of the Hindutva ideology,' says the AIMMM.[21]

Christian groups have been more proactive in protesting their exclusion from the SC list and continue to petition the government for inclusion, but they too have not succeeded in changing the Central government's stand on the issue and the state governments have taken a similar stand. The position of both Dalit Christians and Dalit Muslims boils down to the claim that social and educational backwardness persists even after conversion.[22] They claim that the state denies recognition to them only because the concerned groups profess Islam and Christianity. The National Council of Dalit Christians (NCDC) submitted a memorandum to the UPA government in 2006 to extend SC status to Dalits converted to Christianity. The memorandum states:

> The Constitution of India does not distinguish or discriminate the untouchables (Dalits) on the basis of religion. It clearly upholds secularism in India. But it is the Presidential Order (Scheduled Castes) 1950 which discriminated them on the basis of religion. If all religions are treated equal in the Constitution, then Dalits in all religions must be also treated

equal. The religious ban in the Presidential Order 1950, para-3 must be removed forthwith. The Union Government is saying that there should be no reservations based on religions, but based only on castes. Why then the Government delays (sic) to remove the discrimination on the basis of religion imposed by the Presidential Order (SC) 1950.[23]

Moreover, these benefits have been extended to converts from Hinduism to Sikhism and Buddhism even though both these religions do not recognize the caste system. The nub of the argument therefore is that the state discriminates on grounds of religion, which is violative of the fundamental rights enshrined in the Constitution.

At stake are major benefits that go with SC status such as reservation of jobs and seats in educational institutions. But receiving official SC status is not simply about gaining access to reserved government jobs and representation in state legislatures and Parliament, although these too are important. Muslim and Christian Dalit leaders point out that SC status brings various other benefits, which are now denied to them simply because of their religion. These include special development programmes, scholarships and hostels for students, reserved seats in educational institutions, special laws against atrocities on Dalits, and so on, all of which do not apply to Dalit Muslim and Christian communities.

Opposition to SC status for Dalit Muslims and Christians

Major political parties have expressed support for the campaign to recognize equal rights for Dalits in the Christian and Muslim communities. Meetings and demonstrations organized by the All-India Christian Council and the Catholic Bishops Conference of India have seen leaders from various parties pledge their support for legal and legislative action in favour of these groups. However, the BJP and certain segments of the Congress have opposed the inclusion of converts from Islam and Christianity in the SC list. The most organized and vocal opposition has come from Hindu nationalists, however. In 2002, the BJP-led National Democratic Alliance (NDA) rejected the demand to include Dalit Christians in the SC list. Building on a policy of selective inclusion, they favour inclusion of certain religions they consider Indian indigenous and therefore, whereas they oppose Islam and Christianity, constructed as foreign.[24] The party spokesmen argue that those who had opted out of Hinduism had done so because of their claim that the new religions they were converting into are not caste-based or discriminatory. Once the converts are out of caste-based society, they cannot revert and seek benefits from the same religion which they have given up. The legal recognition of Dalits in the Christian and Muslim communities as SCs would violate constitutional provisions and a Supreme Court judgment that 'caste discrimination and oppression was a feature unique to Hindu society, not applicable to Muslims or Christians.'[25] For them caste as a category is specific to Hindu society and hence SC is Hinduism-specific. In other words, when a Hindu Dalit converts to a new faith which professes to possess a casteless character, the stigma of being a Dalit disappears. In this view, reservations were principally reparations for those who were the victims of discrimination and injustice in the Hindu caste system.[26]

At the same time, the BJP was eager to marshall support among lower castes, and hence it was keen to separate Dalits of various faiths and thus draw the Hindu Dalits firmly into its fold by claiming to protect their entitlements.[27] By giving primacy to Hindu Dalits and their oppression and contrasting it with that of Muslims or Christians, Hindu nationalists could deflect charges that their opposition to affirmative action was basically communal. The emphasis on oppression and victimization of Hindu Dalits in this context was actually a strategic use of discrimination to sidetrack the issue of communal prejudice. The main purpose is to demonstrate that SCs will be hurt by such policies and the other is to draw boundaries between groups in order to protect them from encroachment by others. Such an ideological move allows communal prejudice to be sidetracked, while an agenda based on anti-discrimination, which supposedly subsumes all disadvantaged groups, is promoted. The BJP leadership warned the UPA government that it would have 'to reckon with a nationwide crisis' if it went ahead with their inclusion in the SCs.[28]

The most important reason for the hostility to reservations for Dalit Muslims and Christians stems from the fear of conversions.[29] In other words, the recognition of Christian and Muslim Dalits as SCs could encourage conversions to Islam and Christianity and this will be tantamount to providing incentives for conversion. Arguably, this implies that the restrictions in SC reservations are an inducement to keep Dalits in the Hindu fold, with the religion bar being a device to prevent Dalits from converting to other religions. Historically, in India, conversion to non-Hindu faiths, including Buddhism, Sikhism, Christianity, and Islam, has been a means for Dalits and other oppressed castes to overcome caste Hindu oppression. This is obvious from the fact that majority of Buddhists, Sikhs, Christians, and Muslims are descendants of converts from these castes.[30]

Although the fear of conversions remains an important focus of opposition, very few untouchables have actually converted, for example, to Islam, since Independence. Contrary to the eagerness of state governments to enact legislations seeking to regulate conversions on the premise that there is a rash of conversions, there have actually been very few conversions.[31] The demographic profile of various religious communities in India from 1961 to 2001 reveals no major increase in the population of religious minorities.[32] The only major conversions to Islam took place in Meenakshipuram in 1981, but overall, such conversions have generally been few and far between. There is no evidence that the conversions to Christianity that have taken place in some districts of Orissa, for example, have been caused by inducement or allurement.[33] Even so, the spectre of conversion looms large; it is one of the major reasons for the resistance to the expansion of the SC list. At the same time, it is interesting to note that mass conversion of 100,000 Hindu Dalits to Buddhism in Mumbai in 2006 did not cause a ripple, whereas the conversion of 2,000 Dalits to Islam in Meenakshipuram was a turning point in the emergence and expansion of the Hindu right in the 1980s.

The basic issue is not conversion but the discriminatory attitude towards indigenous and non-indigenous religions. Christianity and Islam are perceived as 'foreign' religions, and hence seen as a threat to Hinduism. In this framework, 'the very concept of Dalit or SC is Hindu specific.'[34] Muslims, Sikhs, Christians, Parsis, and Buddhists are all minorities, but four of these minorities are small in numbers and do not pose a threat; moreover, Sikhism and Buddhism were born and nurtured on Indian soil. In this context, Gyanendra Pandey points out that during the late 1940s, Hindus, Sikhs, and Buddhists were often spoken of as a unity and had been subsumed under Hinduism for legal purposes. According to him, this dimension of the controversy has to be seen in conjunction with notions of 'us' and 'them' that served to reinforce the conceptual split between the Hindu/Indian on the one hand, and the Muslim/foreigner on the other.[35] In this view, the other minorities belong here because they think of India as their native land; they treat India as the land of their birth because this is where they and their religious traditions were born. They are 'insiders', 'original', 'natural' Indians, whereas Muslims and Christians are 'outsiders' because their religions were born outside India. Exclusion of Dalit Muslims and Dalit Christians is in this sense based on the quintessential logic of majoritarianism.[36]

An important part of the opposition to legal recognition of Christian and Muslim Dalits has come from SCs who fear that their benefits would be threatened by the larger pool of beneficiaries, especially from religious minorities, which may cut into the shrinking cake of government jobs and coveted seats in medical and engineering colleges.[37] Dalit activists of the BJP SC/ST Morcha complained that, 'already many Dalits are facing problems because they are not getting the facilities provided by the government. When this is the situation, then providing facilities to those Dalits converting to Christianity will be a social injustice.'[38] Thus, by including Muslim or Christian Dalits in the OBC list, there is apparently an attempt to reduce the competition and concentrate the benefits among the existing beneficiaries, and at the same time, offer them the elusive benefits of inclusion in the OBC list. The SC leaders were worried about the inclusion of Christians because many of them have the advantage of education, which the vast majority of Hindu SCs still lack. They fear that better-educated Christians will cut into the 15 per cent quota for the SCs, whilst the entry of Muslims will increase the competition from below. Besides many SCs consider reservations to be their singular entitlement in view of the uniqueness and enormity of discrimination that they have faced and continue to face. Any new entrants would necessarily impinge on their benefits; thus, inclusion of more groups in the SC list is seen by them as an infringement or violation of the social compact between them and the state and their special political entitlement.

State Response

The dominant role in the designation of the SC list in 1950 and the subsequent decisions to include Sikhs and Buddhists has been played by the executive at the Centre. Formally, the power to make the change lies with the president, but the executive played the overriding role in regard to inclusion and exclusion of groups in the SC list in 1950 and subsequent decisions to include Sikhs and Buddhists and to exclude Christians and Muslims from this category. The list, therefore, designates all those groups which in the view of the executive require special protections provided by the Constitution. The Attorney General's submission to the petition filed by the Centre for Public Interest Litigation in the Supreme Court (2004) reiterated the primacy of the Central institutions in taking a decision on the issue, as it was a matter of policy. He stated: 'It was a matter of policy and legislation and the courts should keep out of it.'[39] In earlier rulings the court had pronounced that the list of entries in the SC and ST lists under the presidential order was final and the courts could not 'add or subtract'.[40] This position is different from the court's approach to the OBC category. In the case of OBCs, the use of social and ritual status as a criterion has been severely restricted by courts, which have generally been hands-on and quite willing to define the criteria of inclusion and exclusion and even prescribe the methodology for identification of beneficiaries.

The SC list is based on 'extreme social, educational and economic backwardness arising out of untouchability'. This dimension has been reiterated time and again—for instance, by the home minister in 1976, when he emphatically stated that the concept of SCs is one of backwardness stemming from untouchability.[41] This position 'reflects the continued force of a view of caste groups which sees them as units in an overarching sacral order of Hinduism.... From this view of caste derived the long-standing reluctance of the courts to give legal effect to caste standing among non-Hindu communities,' remarks Marc Galanter.[42] The exclusion of non-Hindu converts has been justified as they now fall outside the caste system. This doctrine disqualifies Dalits in Muslim and Christian communities from inclusion in the SC category. SC reservations are meant to redress the wrongs of the Hindu caste system and cannot cover Muslims and Christians; Muslim and Christian equivalents of the SCs can be included in the OBC list, but not the SC list. Most state institutions have adopted this view on the SC list. Legislative powers permit the use of broader benchmarks that can decrease the role of ritual standing and disabilities and increase the weight of educational, economic, and cultural criteria.[43] However, both executive and Parliament have chosen not to exercise this power and settled instead for primacy to ritual factors to the exclusion of economic and social backwardness. In the event, the SC category continues to be defined principally on the basis of ritual standing in the Hindu hierarchy, even though this criterion was supposed to be combined with economic, occupational, educational, residential, and religious tests.

The mix of ritual and other factors in the selection of SCs can be changed, but successive governments have chosen not to do so and have preferred to give priority to ritual factors. Opposition to altering the mix had become clear in 1965 when a committee under the chairmanship of Law Secretary B.N. Lokur was appointed by the government to advise on revision of the existing lists of SCs and STs. It found that in view of the constitutional abolition of untouchability 'it would indeed be inappropriate to apply the sole test of untouchability in preparing the list of SCs.'[44] But SC MPs rejected the report and refused to accept any exclusions or deletions based on these criteria. Another attempt in 1967 encountered the same angry resistance from SC MPs. The amended list was introduced in August 1967 and included all groups whose deletions had been recommended by the Lokur Committee, just as the MPs would have wanted. There was a suggestion during the parliamentary debate on the 1976 Amendment to the SC Order that 'it is basically the economic and social backwardness of a caste which should entitle it to be categorized as a SC.' The home minister however emphatically reiterated that 'the concept of SCs is one of backwardness stemming from untouchability. It is not neglect, it is not mere poverty, it is not mere backwardness that entitles a man to come under the SCs.'[45]

This position was restated in 2006 by the Ministry of Social Justice and Empowerment, which made a submission to the Parliamentary Standing Committee stating that 'The criteria applied for inclusion in the list of SCs is extreme social, educational and economic backwardness arising out of traditional practice of untouchability.'[46] However, the Report of the Standing Committee (2006) observed that though the test for inclusion is 'extreme social, educational and economic backwardness arising out of the practice of untouchability', the government has not evolved a yardstick to measure backwardness beyond untouchability. For purposes of identification, factors like literacy rate and per capita income are only taken as indicators, and not benchmarks.[47] The Committee urged the Ministry to take into account data on per capita income as well as literacy rates for all communities which it plans to include in the SC list. Most of the demands for inclusion of new castes fall within these criteria, and cover inclusion of synonymous communities in respect of a caste in the existing SC list. In the absence of any attempt to benchmark the description of social, educational, and economic backwardness, the likelihood of inclusion of other educationally and economically backward groups was very slim.

The emphasis on untouchability flies in the face of repeated claims that these practices have declined if not disappeared altogether. On the one hand, there is denial of untouchability in view of the laws against it, and on the other, its existence is readily accepted when it comes to the continuation of reservations for SC status for existing beneficiaries. The dominance of low ritual and social status or untouchability in the selection of SCs has endured despite the decline of untouchability mentioned in government reports, including the Sixth Report of the NCSC/ST and the NHRC Report on Atrocities Against Scheduled Castes.[48] 'If untouchablity is a useful criterion for identifying those groups which are at the bottom in terms of economic, educational, and cultural resources and opportunities, at the same time, the success of redistributive measures might lead to a discrepancy between ritual standing and the other indices of backwardness.'[49]

One of the important issues that the National Commission for Religious and Linguistic Minorities appointed by the UPA government was to evaluate the demand for extension of affirmative action to SC converts to Christianity and Islam. Headed by Justice Ranganath Mishra, the Commission was established in 2005 by the UPA government in fulfilment of its commitment in the National Common Minimum Programme (NCMP) to recommend administrative and constitutional solutions for the economic and social backwardness of minorities and to look into the criteria for defining backwardness among minorities. The additional term of reference on SC converts was added by the government to the original terms of reference several months after it began its work. Although the report was submitted in June 2007 it had not been adopted or released until 2008.

The media reports indicate that the Commission found substance in the points raised for granting SC status to Dalits who converted to Christianity and Islam. On the basis of a study of the prevalence of the caste system, it concluded that caste is a social phenomenon shared by almost all Indian communities irrespective of their religious persuasions. The caste system should be recognized as a general social characteristic of Indian society as a whole, without questioning whether the philosophy and teachings of any particular religion recognize it or not, because posing this question with regard to the caste system alone and singling it out for a differential treatment is unreasonable and unrealistic. Many of the caste groupings are found in various religious communities, and these groups face the same problems of social degradation and mistreatment both by their co-religionists and the others as do these groups in the Hindu community.[50]

The Commission was conscious of the fact that the Constitution prohibits any discrimination between the citizens on the basis of caste, and yet it sanctions special affirmative measures for the SCs. At the same time, it prohibits any discrimination on the ground of religion. Since the Constitution guarantees freedom of conscience and religious freedom as a Fundamental Right, once a person has been included in an SC list a wilful change of religion on his part should not affect adversely his or her SC status, as that would conflict with the basic constitutional provisions relating to equality, justice, and non-discrimination on religious grounds. Convinced that any religion-based discrimination in selecting particular castes for affirmative action will conflict with the letter and spirit of the constitutional provisions, the Commission recommended that Para 3 of the Constitution (Scheduled Castes) Order 1950—which originally restricted the SC net to the Hindus and later opened it to Sikhs and Buddhists, thus still excluding from its purview the Muslims, Christians, Jains, and Parsis, etc.—should be wholly deleted by appropriate action so as to completely delink the SC status from religion and make the SC net fully religion-neutral like that of the STs.[51]

In a strong dissenting note, the Commission's Member Secretary, Asha Das, a former secretary in the Ministry of Social Justice and Empowerment, opposed the legal recognition of Christian and Muslim Dalits as it will amount to changing the tenets of these egalitarian religions and inserting caste in religions that do not recognize it. In effect, she reiterated the position that the SC list was basically meant for Hindus and the condition of 'religion' in the Constitution (SCs) Order, 1950, should not be deleted.[52] Buddhism and Sikhism are doctrinally equally egalitarian religions, but law has taken into account the social reality of the existence of accumulated historical deprivation among sections of these two communities.

Even before adopting the report the government decided to seek the opinion of the NCSC and NCBC on the NCRLM's recommendation for amending the presidential order to include Dalit Christians and Dalit Muslims in the SC category. Initially, the NCSC completely opposed it on the ground that Dalit Christians and Dalit Muslims cannot be included in the SC list as they do not 'satisfactorily' fulfil the key criterion for being SC.[53] Buta Singh, the new chairman of the NCSC, appointed by the UPA government in 2007, did not formally oppose inclusion of Dalit Christians and Dalit Muslims in principle in the SC category, but he put in a caveat that they should not encroach on the 15 per cent reservations for SCs. In other words, the inclusion of these two groups should be in addition to the 15 per cent quota earmarked for SCs. An additional quota can be achieved only by exceeding the 50 per cent ceiling fixed by the Supreme Court or by reducing the 27 per cent OBC quota. Both these are difficult to achieve. Moreover, the real issue was not the ceiling on reservations but inclusion on the basis of recognition as SCs. The suggestion that the UPA government should have a separate quota underlines the notion of 'separate entitlements' for deprived groups, which in effect is a continuation of the status quo that these two groups are not part of the SCs.

The NCM has recommended amendments to the presidential order to include Dalit Muslims and Dalit Christians in the SC list. In 1995 and 1997, the NCM made positive recommendations. The first recommendation in 1995 states that SC/ST converts to Christianity and Islam should continue to enjoy all privileges and benefits as SCs/STs on par with SC/ST converts to Buddhism so as to remove this anomaly. The second, in 1997, recommends the outright removal of the religion criterion, which confines the SC status to three specified religions to the exclusion of other religions. The Commission justified it as necessary in order to fully implement the Constitution's stress on and guarantee of equality before law and equal protection of laws, and constitutional prohibition of all religion-based discrimination. But the NCSC was opposed to the NCM getting into the issue of SC status for Dalit Muslims and Dalit Christians, questioning the *locus standi* of the NCM in taking up the issue, which it believes falls strictly within its domain. While matters pertaining to SCs are certainly the concern of the NCSC, public institutions and policy makers treat Dalit Christians and Dalit Muslims as Muslims and Christians first, and as such the issue concerns both commissions.

Several political parties within the UPA support the inclusion of Dalits in the Muslim and Christian communities in the SC list but the Congress party leadership which took the initiative to set up the Ranganath Mishra Commission backtracked on the issue by the time the report was submitted in June 2007. Earlier, the Congress government in 1996 had brought a bill in the Lok Sabha to amend paragraph three of the Constitution (SCs) Order for extending benefits to Dalit Christians. Then too the Congress developed cold feet. This time too the Congress was reluctant to amend the presidential order. The government was also under pressure from its own MPs and ministers in the UPA government not to concede the demand of inclusion of Dalit Christians and Dalit Muslims in the SC list.[54] Also, many upper-caste MPs were against it, fearing that it might encourage Hindu Dalits to convert to Islam and Christianity. The Congress leadership and the UPA were thus on the horns of a dilemma as regards the Mishra Commission's recommendation that the two groups should be treated as SCs and that the quota facilities available to SCs should be extended to them. The government needed to either challenge the Supreme Court's ceiling of 50 per cent on all reservations or go to Parliament for new laws to circumvent the legal limitations. The UPA government simply shelved the issue.

The UPA government wanted to project its commitment to Dalit empowerment even as it was under pressure to extend the same to Dalits in the Muslim and Christian communities. But the Congress party simply could not afford to ignore the SC constituency, which once formed the core of its support. Until late 1977 the Congress was strongly dependent on Dalit support. With the emergence of Dalit parties, particularly the BSP, the Congress is not the preferred choice or the sole representative of SC interests and welfare. It is also no longer the chief beneficiary of their votes. It thus cannot afford to ignore the concerns of this important constituency. For the Congress, strengthening Dalit support assumed urgency after the inroads into its base by the BSP.

Caste Inequalities and Social Disabilities

There are two critical issues with regard to the inclusion of Dalit Muslims and Christians in the SC list. The first concerns the numbers of these two groups. There are no systematic statistical estimates of the numbers of Dalit Christians and Dalit Muslims. According to the 2001 census, the Christian population stands at 2.3 per cent, and although there is no official count of Christians of Dalit origin, they form roughly half of the Christian population. Dalit Christians are concentrated in parts of Tamil Nadu and Andhra Pradesh, as also in some districts of Punjab, Kerala, Maharashtra, Gujarat, Madhya Pradesh, Uttar Pradesh, and Bihar. But it is only in Andhra Pradesh and Tamil Nadu that they are of political significance. Dalit Muslims constitute a fraction of the Muslim population. According to the NSSO, they constitute 0.6 per cent of the Muslim population. Dalits are overwhelmingly Hindu. Within the SCs the share of Muslim and Christian Dalits amounts to 0.6 per cent and 9.4 per cent in rural India and 0.6 and 10.5 respectively in urban India. In the absence of official recognition and a census count of numbers, these estimates of their population are likely to be an undercount because the census list does not recognize their community as part of the SC category.[55]

Moreover, as many as twelve states accord recognition to sections of the Muslim and Christian populations in the OBC category. The Mandal Commission reinforced this trend. The Commission's task was to identify OBCs and to determine whether they should be eligible for reservation along the lines of the SCs and STs. There was no difficulty with respect to Hindu castes, because administrative policy clearly recognized a distinction between SCs and OBCs. When it came to religious minorities, the Commission lumped all the excluded groups among them (including the more severely stigmatized and excluded) with the OBCs for purposes of affirmative action. The Sachar Committee suggested bifurcation of the OBC category and putting Dalit Muslims in a separate Most Backward Class (MBC) category. Both ignored the fact that a Dalit Muslim stands a better chance of availing the benefits of reservations under the SC quota than under the OBC quota. The SCR's own data and analysis have shown that inclusion in the OBC list by several state governments and by the Mandal Commission has not helped them to gain access to education or employment because they are not in a position to compete with the more advanced backward castes.[56]

Despite this, it is quite likely that many Muslim and Christian Dalits report themselves as OBCs because they are recognized as such in their state or region. Since they are part of the OBC list, there is no incentive to self-report themselves as SC whereas there is an incentive to self-report as OBC. As of now, Muslim and Christian Dalits form a small proportion of the population; the share of Muslim and Christian Dalits is 1.2 per cent in rural India and 2.3 per cent in urban India.[57]

The second and more important set of issues pertains to the nature of social discrimination or disabilities faced by Dalits in the Muslim and Christian communities after conversion. There is a commonplace assumption that converts to these religions do not face social disabilities and discrimination after conversion as they did in the original religion of Hinduism. In the absence of the caste system, Dalits in the Muslim and Christian communities cannot claim that they suffer from social discrimination. Moreover, reservations were principally a form of compensatory justice for victims of discrimination arising out of the inequities of the Hindu caste system and therefore automatically exclude persons outside the caste system. Exclusion is justified on the grounds that the Hindu religion sanctioned untouchability, while egalitarian faiths like Christianity and Islam do not. Hence, according to this view, only Hindu Dalits can be given special treatment by the state and derive benefits from being categorized as SCs.[58] This approach ignores the fact that Dalit Christians also face similar forms of discrimination and that they [the opponents] failed to see the Christians of SC origin as dalits or SCs first and foremost, and then secondarily, only as converts to Christianity.[59]

Over the past two decades, social science scholarship and ethnographic materials have accumulated evidence to show the existence of caste among Muslims and Christians. Although Islam and Christianity are egalitarian religions, the practice of caste has penetrated both Christian and Muslim societies though it may not exist in its classic form.[60] Many recent sociological studies indicate that caste-like groups or social divisions displaying caste-like features are present in Muslim and Christian societies today.[61] The bulk of Muslims and Christians belong to groups traditionally considered low in the caste hierarchy, conversion to Islam or Christianity was a means for them to escape the excesses of Brahminical domination that sanctified caste. Yet, despite their conversion, their overall social condition did not improve much; they continue to face social discrimination after conversion. The specific notion of caste is unarguably different as it involved the notion of *jati* rather than *varna*. However, it has been observed that specific practices of untouchability are in some instances identical with Hindu practices, Kerala is a case in point. In other cases, specific belief in untouchabilty may be absent but 'Dalit castes are marked out in every other way.'[62] This suggests that the variations in the nature of caste among Hindu and Muslim and Christian Dalits do not significantly alter intra-group relations, and they make no significant difference to the socio-economic conditions of Dalits in comparison with others. Reports produced or sponsored by organizations that are actively working among Dalit Christians and Dalit Muslims indicate that they are treated as distinct groups within their own communities. They are invariably regarded as 'socially inferior' communities by their co-religionists.[63]

A report commissioned by the NCM presents evidence on social disabilities suffered by Dalits in the Christian and Muslim communities which broadly supports the assessment that while these religions do not practise untouchability, and caste as an institution may not exist in the definitional sense among Muslims and Christians in India, the Dalit adherents of these religions do face palpable social discrimination. The report observes: '…if Muslims and Christians "have" caste, then it is clear that Dalit Muslims and Christians have it most.' This study shows that compared to Dalit Christians, caste inequality is relatively low among Muslims, especially in rural India, but they also have a lower level of consumption.[64] But caste-like groupings and related social divisions are routinely present in both Muslim and Christian societies as they actually exist in practice.

Courts have repeatedly asked for objective evidence of social disadvantage suffered by these social groups. One important concern that has repeatedly arisen within the judicial verdicts relates to whether caste inequalities as well as cultural and educational backwardness suffered by Dalits in Christian and Muslim communities are comparable to their Hindu counterparts and, more importantly, whether these social disabilities are due to their caste identities or other possible causes. The critical issue is not with regard to the existence of caste per se but is related to the incidence and extent of social disabilities after conversion. The question is that if caste is a reality, as is widely accepted, does caste impose the same social disabilities on Muslims and Christians as are known to be imposed on Dalits of other religions?

The NCM report covering the nature of deprivation, discrimination, and exclusion suffered by these groups compared with their own community members and Dalit segments of other communities unambiguously demonstrates the extreme deprivation suffered by these groups. The four areas of comparison are: proportions of population in poverty; average consumption levels; broad occupational categories; and levels of education. The groups with whom Dalit Muslims and Dalit Christians were compared were Dalit castes of Hindus, Sikhs, and Buddhists; and non-Dalit castes among Muslims and Christians. The statistical material (NSSO, 61st Round, 2004–5) presented in this study shows that Muslim Dalits are socially and economically very deprived and poor in comparison with Dalits in other communities. Table 7.1 shows that in rural India less than 8 per cent of Dalit Sikhs are in the below-poverty-line category, compared to 30 per cent for all others. Buddhists are worst off, followed by Dalit Muslims. Dalit Christians have substantial numbers of poor people, but they also have a significant proportion in the affluent category.[65] Dalit Muslims are, on the other hand, significantly over-represented among the poorest in urban and rural India and completely absent in the affluent group. They are the worst off among urban Dalits, as almost 47 per cent are below the poverty line (Table 7.2). Also, Dalit Muslims are badly off compared to the OBC and upper castes in their community.[66] Likewise, Dalit Christians are worse off than their non-Dalit co-religionists.

The report notes an important trend: the low internal differentiation among Muslims. Dalit Muslims are only slightly worse off than non-Dalit Muslims. This is because, as the SCR has shown, non-Dalit Muslims are worse off than their non-Muslim counterparts. Much like the profile of the Muslim community, Dalit Muslims have more households in casual labour and fewer in the salaried segment (Tables 7.3 and 7.4). Dalit Muslims are by far the worst off in education in rural India (Tables 7.5 and 7.6). Tables 7.7 and 7.8 show that Dalit Christians are better off than Dalit Muslims and other groups, other than Dalit Sikhs who are the best off among urban Dalits. Dalit Christians are moderately better off but less so than the Dalit Sikhs.[67] The social and economic vulnerability of Dalit Muslims and Dalit Christians is similar to that of other Dalit groups. On all counts, Dalit Muslims are worst off among all Dalits in both the rural and urban sectors, being particularly badly off in urban areas. Since Hindu Dalits have received special status for decades and benefits from the state flowing from that status, it is obvious that their conditions are better. This makes the argument of differential treatment of Dalit Muslims and Dalit Christians as compared to Dalit Hindus and Dalit Sikhs hard to sustain.

Caste and Social Justice

The current controversies are reminiscent of the debates in the Constituent Assembly over the nature of religious and caste identities and primacy given to caste identity for the purpose of reservations. Various state institutions share certain common assumptions with regard to the intrinsic relationship between caste and social justice. These include the conception of discrimination and backwardness as a phenomenon of Hindu society, and hence fears of fragmentation and conversions from Hinduism by discontented Dalits to escape this. There is a concomitant reluctance to recognize the existence of discrimination and backwardness among other groups and, above all, the changing face of social disabilities which can weaken the established relationship between ritual standing and economic and social backwardness. Doing this would have required data on caste inequalities among other groups and data on the continuation of caste inequalities among groups classified as SCs, so as to exclude those who may not need it and include those who may need it owing to the social disabilities that they suffer from, albeit not exactly as prescribed in the presidential order. The ritualistic approach has, however, reinforced the centrality of the caste paradigm, thus underlining its importance as the lynchpin of the framework for reservations.

The belief that caste disabilities of Dalits in Muslim and Christian communities after conversion must resemble those of Hindus to entitle them to special treatment might be somewhat misplaced. More to the point is the fact that these benefits have been extended to converts from Hinduism to Sikhism and Buddhism, even though both religions do not recognize the caste system. If non-acceptance of the caste system by Islam and Christianity is the basis for disallowing benefits to those religions, the benefits cannot be extended to Sikhs and Buddhists.[68] If this denial is based on the argument that Christianity and Islam are egalitarian faiths and their adherents therefore have no caste, this applies equally to Sikhs and Buddhists, who belong to faiths as egalitarian as Islam and Christianity.[69] In fact, these two religions emerged as protest movements against the institution of caste in Hinduism. The reason for extending the benefits to Sikhs and Buddhists seems to be political and is motivated by the fact that these two religions are of indigenous origin, while Muslims and Christians are external to this fold simply because their religions originated outside India.

From the evidence marshalled in the NCM report (2008), there is a strong case for including Dalits in the Muslim and Christian communities in the SC category because, as the report says, they are Dalits first and Christians and Muslims only later. The report concludes that there are persuasive reasons in favour of such an inclusion based on principles of natural justice and fairness.[70] It points out that

> there is no compelling evidence to justify denying SC status to Dalit Muslims and Dalit Christians. If no community had already been given SC status, and if the decision to accord SC status to some communities were to be taken today through some evidence based approach, then it it is hard to imagine how Dalit Muslims and Dalit Christians could be excluded. Whether one looks at it positively (justifying inclusion) or negatively (justifying non-inclusion), the Dalit Muslims and Dalit Christians are not so distinct from other Dalit groups that an argument for treating them differently could be sustained. In sum, the actual situation that

exists today—denial of SC status to Dalit Muslims and Dalit Christians, but according it to Dalit Sikhs and Buddhists in addition to Hindu Dalits—could not be rationally defended if it did not already exist as a historical reality.[71]

Dalits, irrespective of religious faith, are the most deprived but the political will required for recognition of this social reality is absent. Since most of the claimants suffer from acute deprivation, inclusion in the SC list is of vital importance for them, as it critically affects their access to opportunities which reservations in education and government employment can facilitate. Entitlements of a particular group to benefits of special treatment are political decisions. The resolution of this problem therefore lies in the political domain because political factors, and not principle or lack of evidence of social disabilities, stand behind the denial of SC status to Dalit Christians and Dalit Muslims. Appearing for the All India United Christian Movement for Equal Rights, senior advocate Ram Jethmalani said the Congress government had brought in a bill in 1996 with the objective of giving Dalits equal rights irrespective of the religion they profess, but that 'it is only politics that has deprived the Dalit Christians their legitimate due.'[72] One basic problem is that the numbers of Christian and Muslim Dalits are small compared to the numbers of Dalits in other groups and hence they do not count in competitive politics. The government has not been able to take a positive decision on this controversial issue because of contending political pressures and expected the courts to settle it. But the courts which often overstep their bounds in many other areas have been reluctant to decide on a matter that falls in the domain of the political executive. Although reservations for Dalits in Muslim and Christian communities is not a solution to deprivation, given that the numbers of these two groups is small, legal recognition was important to promote secularization of affirmative action and democratization in the society and polity.

There is, therefore, merit in Mukul Kesavan's comment that 'SC reservations are in effect a system of reservation for Hindus.'[73] Denying SC status to these two groups can be construed as a form of discrimination. The ritual test is largely responsible for this as it operates as a disqualification for groups which may otherwise meet the criteria of social disabilities and economic and educational backwardness. In combating social discrimination of one kind, the ritual test is instituting 'social separation' of another kind. The contradiction arising out of this separation results in new forms of discrimination. As long as the religion bar remains in place, this category would only include Dalits of religions considered indigenous and exclude others regardless of their social disabilities and status. Such a conceptual grounding of the framework of affirmative action seems to undermine the secular thrust of such programmes. The state can ensure non-discrimination either by dropping the religious qualification or by specifying that SCs are to be designated in terms of an admixture of criteria that includes social disabilities and economic and educational backwardness. Evidence of the reality of economic and social backwardness of a group/caste should entitle it to be categorized as a SC. This would be a fulfilment of the constitutional promise and an avoidance of contradictions and disparities owing to differential treatment of the underprivileged. But this requires a framework of justice centred on a radically new paradigm of how we define and address deprivation and discrimination. The framework of justice must ensure that similarly placed groups are treated equally and evenly without religion being brought into play to deny some equal treatment under the law.

Notes

1. Prior to the designation of 'Scheduled Caste', adopted as part of the Government of India reforms, official documents referred to the term Depressed Classes and Outcastes. Gandhi used the term Harijans (people of God), which was seen as somewhat paternalistic. For the past few years the term Dalit has been widely used, embodying a sense of assertion. It is a term preferred by activists and SCs themselves.

2. Over the past few years, numerous groups have been lobbying for revisions in their classification (Malas and Madigas in Andhra Pradesh) or for changing their categorization (Gujjars in Rajasthan want to be classified as STs and not OBCs, Jats want inclusion in the OBC category, Christian SCs in Orissa want to be part of the ST category).

3. Rochna Bajpai (2006: 326).

4. For an analysis of these controversies, see Laura D. Jenkins (2003).

5. Marc Galanter (1984).

6. Ibid.

7. *CAD* (25 May 1949: 271).

8. Ibid.

9. Marc Galanter (1984: 135).

10. Ibid., p. 122.

11. Laura D. Jenkins (2003: 120).

12. *Soosai & Others* v. *Union of India & Others*, AIR, 1986 SC 733.

13. Report on Dalits in the Muslim and Christian Communities, NCM (2008: 63).

14. Ibid.

15. Civil Writ Petition No. 180 of 2004. *Centre for Public Interest Litigation* v. *Union of India*.

16. Barbara R. Joshi (1982).

17. For details of the campaign see, Jose Kananaikil (1983: 15); Godwin Shri (1997).

18. On AIBMM, see Yoginder Sikand (2004: 111–14).

19. *The Times of India*, 28 January 2001.

20. AIMMM Statement, *The Milli Gazette*, 23 May 2007.

21. Ibid.

22. Laura D. Jenkins (2001: 32–40).

23. Cited in Laura D. Jenkins (2003).

24. Ibid., p. 128.

25. Ibid.

26. L.K. Advani, 'Why We Are Opposed to Communal Reservations', www.bjp.org/Publication /LKA/1404E/pdf (n.d.).

27. Ibid.

28. Arun Jaitley, *The Indian Express*, 15 November 2006.

29. On conversions, see Rowena Robinson and S. Clarke (2003).

30. Laura D. Jenkins (2003: 132).

31. There are eight anti-conversion legislations: Orissa Freedom of Religion Act, 1967; Madhya Pradesh Dharma Swatantrya Adhiniyam, 1968; Chhattisgarh Freedom of Religion Act, 1968; Arunachal Pradesh Freedom of Religion Act, 1978; Tamil Nadu Prohibition of Forcible Conversions of Religion Act, 2002; Gujarat Freedom of Religion Act, 2003; Rajasthan Dharma Swatantrya (Freedom of Religion) Bill, 2006; and Himachal Pradesh Freedom of Religion Bill, 2006. With the exception of Chhattisgarh, no case of conversion has been reported from these states.

32. The NCM fact-finding team investigated the anti-Christian

violence in Orissa during Christmas 2007 (supposedly triggered by conversion activities of Christian missionaries) and found no evidence whatsoever of conversion. Report available at: http://www.ncm.nic.in/pdf/orissa%20report.pdf.

33. Ibid.

34. Gyanendra Pandey (1999).

35. Ibid., p. 621.

36. Yoginder Sikand (2004).

37. The NSSO put the SC population at 19.59 per cent, ST population at 8.63 per cent; and OBC population at 41 per cent. *The Times of India*, 1 September 2007.

38. *The Deccan Herald*, 5 September 2003.

39. *The Indian Express*, 19 September 2007.

40. Ibid.

41. Marc Galanter (1984: 144).

42. Ibid., p. 142.

43. Ibid.

44. Ibid.

45. Ibid.

46. Report of the Standing Committee on Social Justice and Empowerment (2006–2007).

47. Ibid., p. 12.

48. Sixth Report of the National Commission for Scheduled Castes and Scheduled Tribes (2004).

49. Ibid., p. 36.

50. Even though the NCRLM Report has not been released by the government, the main recommendations were widely reported in the print media. *The Times of India*, 22 May 2007.

51. Ibid.

52. Ibid.

53. *The Times of India*, 19 January 2008.

54. Subodh Ghildiyal (2006).

55. Nalini Taneja (2001). Taneja makes the additional point that two purposes are served here: inflating a 'Hindu majority' and reducing the liability of the state towards benefits to a section of society.

56. *SCR* (2006: 202).

57. NCM Report on Dalits in the Muslim and Christian Communities (2008).

58. Ibid.

59. Ibid.

60. On this, see Imtiaz Ahmad (1967); K.C. Alexander (1977); and Duncan B. Forrester (1980).

61. Prakash Louis (2003); Imtiaz Ahmed (1967, 2007).

62. NCM Report on Dalits in the Muslim and Christian Communities (2008).

63. Ibid., p. 75.

64. Ibid., p. 45.

65. Ibid., p. 29.

66. Ibid., p. 33.

67. Ibid., p. 60.

68. T.K. Oommen (1994).

69. Ibid.

70. NCM Report on Dalits in the Muslim and Christian Communities (2008: 78).

71. Ibid., pp. 78–9.

72. 'SC: Do Christians also Practice Caste System?', *The Times of India*, 20 July 2007.

73. Mukul Kesavan (2007).

8

Conclusion

The foregoing chapters have tried to provide an account of the policies and institutions of inclusion, designed to deal with disadvantage and backwardness and to enhance representation in public institutions and power structures. The state and policy makers have sought to promote and protect disadvantaged groups through a slew of policies of affirmative action and reservations. Despite the good intentions and positive commitments of many a secular government, minorities have been excluded from this framework of special treatment in the sphere of economic and social development, except in a few limited schemes. However, the past few years have witnessed a noticeable shift in the political thinking regarding minorities. The shift was prompted by the success of the Congress-led alliance in defeating the BJP-led NDA in the May 2004 elections. This signalled a repudiation of the politics of exclusion and a return to policies of inclusiveness. The UPA coalition government formed with the support of the Left parties and with substantial electoral support among the disadvantaged sections of society had promised the revival of the secular order and an inclusive agenda. Within months of assuming power the UPA government set in motion a large number of proposals for the welfare of disadvantaged and deprived groups. These included the National Rural Employment Guarantee Scheme, reservations for the OBCs in higher education, formation of the Sachar Committee, and the Prime Minister's New 15-Point Programme for Minorities, to mention just a few.

Three weeks after the submission of the Sachar Committee Report to the prime minister, Parliament unanimously passed the legislation on 27 per cent reservations for OBCs in higher education in December 2006, which we have analysed in Chapter 4. The OBC quotas did not figure in the manifesto or the NCMP, except that the latter mentioned the need 'to provide for full equality of opportunity, particularly in education and employment for Scheduled Castes, Scheduled Tribes, OBCs and religious minorities.' Despite huge opposition to the OBC reservation proposal from several different quarters, it was pursued swiftly. The Supreme Court's stay order delayed its immediate implementation, but the UPA government eventually succeeded in introducing reservations for OBCs in Central institutions of higher education from 2008.

The Supreme Court upheld reservations for OBCs in institutions of higher education in April 2008. In line with the Court's earlier ruling, it reiterated that the fundamental right to equality is compatible with special benefits for the disadvantaged, even if they are defined in caste terms. The near unanimous court verdict and, more importantly, the unanimous passage of both the constitutional amendment and the reservations bill in Parliament (as against the vacillation on the implementation of the recommendations of the SCR) vindicate the main argument of this book with regard to the primacy of caste identities in India's politics of inclusion.

The Congress party and the human resources development minister described the court verdict as 'historic', which reflected their perception that both the government and the ruling party had succeeded in providing reservations to the OBCs. Significantly, the anti-reservationists, including the media, also welcomed the verdict. Their positive reaction was clearly an attempt to salvage something from the refusal of the apex court to support their cause, especially as the critics were banking on the apex court to quash the law on OBC quotas. The positive reaction of both sides claiming victory has less to do with the verdict than the dilemmas and conflicts facing reservations in India in the context of the massive clout of backward castes in democratic politics, on the one hand, and the new assertiveness of the middle classes in the new economy, on the other.

One striking consequence of the excessive emphasis on reservations is that it has crowded out attention to broad-based policies that empower citizens and create genuine equality of opportunity: income generation, education, and access to public institutions. The reduction of the entire concept of social justice to reservations means that it has become a substitute for meaningful provisioning of social goods such as health, education, shelter, and employment.

On the whole, positive discrimination policies have worked more effectively than their critics are prepared to concede. But to appreciate this we must remember that reservation schemes are not intended to be a frontal assault on socio-economic inequalities but are primarily aimed at changing the social composition of public institutions and the elite who control them. They are essentially an effort to integrate disadvantaged sections of society by increasing their access to responsible positions. As a result of reservations, large numbers of SCs, STs, and OBCs have gained access to education and jobs despite escalating pressures on the job market. The fact that these three disadvantaged groups are now less under-represented in both education and government jobs than in the past is a measure of the success of reservation schemes and this has doubtless strengthened their relevance. In highlighting the positive fallout of affirmative action, we do not intend to obscure the continuing problems with existing reservation policies or to ignore the persistence of social discrimination against lower castes despite decades of affirmative action and anti-discriminations laws. Indeed, the point is that without some positive discrimination in their favour, these marginalized groups would have remained outside power structures.

At the same time, the Supreme Court verdict (2008) (as well as the recent debates) on reservations for socially and economically backward castes/classes has opened up the space for interrogating the prevailing positions and controversies surrounding the practice of reservation policies in India. One of these is the question of the relationship between caste and class, and the other is the relationship between caste and minority, which is the focus of analysis in this book. The principle of creamy layer is one way of dealing with these issues. The principle in this example is quite clear: when it comes to the nebulous category of OBCs, caste is not a sufficient criterion for identification of beneficiaries. In other words, it is important to recognize the multiple axes of disadvantage that characterize our society, and government policies must reflect this reality. This requires credible evidence connecting various axes of disadvantage to unequal access to education and employment, as well as fresh thinking on the changing face of social inequalities and forms of deprivation in India.

Although there are many spheres of society in which inclusion and representation matter, none concern representation and the exercise of power as centrally as the political sphere. In India, SCs have suffered greatly from being excluded from political power. Notable shifts have taken place in the sphere of political power owing to a substantial presence of SCs, STs, and OBCs in legislatures. Indeed, the significant increase in political representation has perhaps been the most important achievement of these policies because it has given considerable power and clout to the disadvantaged groups. The elected representatives of these groups have the opportunity to influence decisions concerning their groups and through that the social restructuring of society as a whole. Their representation has helped to promote the implementation of preferential treatment programmes even at a time when the economically powerful groups are opposed to extension of reservations and demands for greater resources.

This strategy has worked largely because of the strategic positioning of caste and caste inequalities within the rubric of social justice from the time of the Constituent Assembly debates, when Congress leaders took the lead in making the distinction between castes and minorities for the purpose of preferential treatment, making it clear that reservations were a matter of compensation or reparation reserved for caste groups. Even though the conception of social disabilities and disadvantage was effectively limited to the majority community, the beneficiary groups were constructed and perceived in terms of social justice and equity. The concerns of minorities, on the other hand, were anchored in the political framework of secularism–communalism and majority–minority syndrome, resulting in their exclusion from the substantive equality discourse and rendering them outside the development framework. The distinctive feature of the past decades in this regard is the translation of a collective caste identity into a more practical conception of political identity in relation to representation and governance to ensure a share in public institutions and power structure in the framework of social justice. This national recognition has given caste-based affirmative action and reservations a strong political grounding, which has in turn given a fillip to their political mobilization and leverage and weight to their demands. The flip side of this has been the reinforcement of caste through electoral mobilization politics.

The political representation of OBCs in Parliament has increased from 5 per cent in the first decades after Independence to 25 per cent in 2004. If we add the share of SCs and STs, the non-upper castes account for almost half the members of the Lok Sabha. The changes are even more dramatic in the states, where the backward castes constitute 50 per cent of the legislatures. By contrast Muslim representation has remained stationary in both Parliament and state legislatures. One of the main reasons for their under-representation is that under the FPTP system, political parties tend to under-nominate candidates from the minority communities owing to a misplaced fear of anti-minority consolidation by rival parties. In addition, the contrasting experience of the Muslims and OBCs suggests that the higher representation of OBCs has been spurred by reservations and the new collective identities it went on to create.

This underlines the main argument of this book that in India the politics of inclusion has to go beyond caste inequalities as deprivation and discrimination are widespread and not confined to a single community or group in India. For example, we have noted that vast majority of Muslims suffer from double discrimination by virtue of being Muslim and poor. This is partly the reason for their under-representation in the political, administrative, and security structures of the state. Their share of the resources of the state in terms of bank loans, educational facilities, employment, and so on, has been very limited. Yet, for over five decades, official discourse has privileged certain identities for positive discrimination, by implication leaving unaddressed the many other critical areas of deprivation and discrimination. The justification of caste-based reservation is that these groups have suffered injustice and discrimination in the past which requires remedial steps. Thus affirmative action primarily centres on efforts to provide opportunities denied to these groups to remedy the effects of historical injustice. It could be argued that disadvantage is so defined as to exclude non-Hindus, although theoretically the OBC category includes backward classes from all groups. Given this definitional bias it would be quite natural for the other groups to see themselves as objects of unfair treatment or structural discrimination. The benefits of this framework have been monopolized by the disadvantaged members of the majority community.

This book has tried to examine India's experience with the politics of inclusion from the standpoint of inter-group disparities, which are at least partly due to the differentiated approaches in dealing with disadvantaged groupings. The comparative dimension enabled us to look beyond the question of whether the reservation system is the best way of achieving fairness or whether it is meeting broader goals, and whether it is promoting the interests of the very groups it is designed to help. These are no doubt extremely important questions, but they are invariably limited to the caste paradigm of inclusion. We would do well to pause and reconsider this preoccupation with caste and caste alone. Owing to the widely shared assumptions about the relationship between caste and social justice, we often tend to ignore the religious underpinning of India's affirmative action policies even as we continuously restate the secular basis of such policies and the prohibition of affirmative action on the basis of religion. Reservations on the basis of religion are not permissible under the Constitution, yet from the beginning religious criteria have been inherent in the process of classification and designation of beneficiary groups and the definition of backwardness, since the government as well as the court have conceived caste as a constituent of Hinduism. This is obvious from the continuing exclusion of Dalit Muslims and Christians from the SC list, which has been discussed in Chapter 7.

A lot of evidence has become available since the last major judicial pronouncement on this question (*Soosai*) to justify the inclusion of Dalit Christians and Muslims in the SC category. Whether or not social discrimination suffered by these two groups can be proven in a court of law or not on the basis of official definitions of social disabilities, there is no compelling evidence to justify their exclusion from the SC category. Yet, the positive recommendation of the Ranganath Mishra Commission to amend the presidential order to include Dalits in the Muslim and Christian communities in the SC list has been put on ice. In fact the UPA government was so concerned about the political opposition that it did not release the Ranganath Mishra Commission report. As long as the religion bar remains in place, the SC category will include Dalits of certain religions and exclude others, regardless of their social disabilities. In the circumstances, it is hard to sustain the claim that the affirmative action framework is religion-neutral. Furthermore, such a conceptual grounding of the framework of affirmative action undercuts the secular potential of affirmative action programmes.

Membership of a minority religion is no bar to advancement in politics, employment, or business. Indeed, three presidents, three vice-presidents, and three Chief Justices have been Muslims. But their representation in arenas that matter is extremely low. For instance, the total number of Muslim candidates elected to the 14th Lok Sabha (2004) was thirty-five, slightly higher than in 1999, but in relation to their population share, only half as many or fewer Muslims get elected as legislators. In 2005 only eleven Muslim candidates could make the grade out of 422 selected for the IAS, IFS, IPS, and other Central services. Over sixty years after Independence the state's approach to the rights of minorities has proved inadequate in promoting inclusion, with the result that the country has not been able to ensure participation in governance for its largest minority group. Their empowerment is essential for their fuller participation in all fields of national activity.

It is in the context of the politics of inclusion and exclusion that this study has sought to question the foundations and basis of the policy approach towards minorities with its excessive stress on cultural rights and ensuing incapacity to promote inclusion.

For a long time the state avoided the subject of deprivation and disadvantage faced by religious minorities as this would provoke political disapproval and may end up emboldening the forces of disunity and division. However, there has been a discernible shift in this regard, reflected in the several initiatives of the UPA government after the submission of the SCR, which conclusively established that without affirmative action it would be impossible to harness India's social and economic potential and build an inclusive social order that respects diversity, plurality, and equity.

The UPA government's report card on the implementation of the SCR highlighted a number of measures, such as national-level scholarships for students in professional and technical institutions, corporations to promote entrepreneurship with increased credit flows, and, notably, provision of basic amenities in 90 minority-concentration districts (which would cover 30 per cent of the minority population), and the development of artisan clusters. But all these were small, piecemeal steps which did not add up to a concrete plan necessary to dent the structure of discrimination, deprivation, and exclusion. On the other hand, the Planning Commission in its full meeting in November 2007 rejected a proposal for a minority sub-plan to be integrated into the Eleventh Five Year Plan principally because of uneasiness over accusation of minority appeasement and questions that might be raised with regard to its constitutionality. This proposal, if implemented and monitored sincerely, could have made an impact on the uplift and empowerment of the largest religious minority. If the sub-plan was unacceptable, the UPA government, if it was serious about implementing the SCR, would have fleshed out the Prime Minister's 15-Point Programme and made it statutory; and defined a time-bound expenditure and physical achievement of targets for the 15 per cent budgetary allocation for the minorities. Even when decisions like scholarships, special coaching schemes, and infrastructure development plans for selected districts and towns have been taken, adequate funds have not been allocated and no implementation agency has been named or proper procedure prescribed for monitoring its expeditious implementation. The CPI (M) described these measures as 'tokenism'. Two years after it was submitted, the SCR has all but vanished from public debate and the critical questions pertaining to inclusion of minorities have been shelved.

If affirmative action or positive discrimination can be defined as the provision of some amount of preference, in processes of selection to desirable positions in a society, to members of groups that are under-represented in those positions, minorities have a justifiable claim over such preferences. The Constitution itself mandates affirmative action and state intervention to promote social justice and equality. Large sections of Muslims are in many ways disadvantaged and face systematic discrimination and exclusion. Yet, in India affirmative action for minorities remains the most misunderstood and controversial of strategies of affirmative action. Affirmative action need not take the form of reservations in jobs or college quotas. However, it is not mandatory quotas alone that are considered controversial; rather, all affirmative action measures for minorities are routinely condemned as appeasement and vote-bank politics. While there is definitely much greater recognition of injustices inherent in many policies that have adversely affected the economic and social progress of minorities, there is tremendous opposition to affirmative action on the grounds that it violates secular principles and would increase the salience of religious identity in the public domain.

The politics and practice of inclusion has become subject to political exigencies and political processes. While the Congress leadership, anxious to shore up its electoral support among Muslims, supported welfare measures, it lacked the political will to press ahead with measures for affirmative action. The unwillingness to introduce affirmative action for minorities despite evidence of deprivation and disadvantage remains strong owing to the communal polarization in the political and social climate vitiated by the sustained propaganda of right-wing parties. Some of the hesitation has to do with the debates within the UPA, especially within the Congress, about the target—should it be the Muslim community as a whole or Muslims who are really backward; and should it be limited to a caste basis or expanded on the basis of economic criteria. But it has mostly to do with the right-wing's opposition to any form of affirmative action for religious minorities, regardless of the level of their socio-economic development. Unarguably, this is the main stumbling block to introducing policies of inclusion based on notions of substantive equality so that minorities do not have to remain content with notions of formal equality. The basic problem is the lack of consensus on policies for the minorities, in contrast to a strong cross-party consensus for historically disadvantaged caste groups.

It is the implications of this differentiated approach in regard to inclusion and representation that this book has sought to emphasize. In the Indian context it should not be necessary to argue in support of affirmative action, as it is a constitutional mandate and a positive obligation of the state within the framework of Articles 14, 15 (4), and 15 (5) of the Constitution. There are several other constitutional provisions that direct the state to remove inequalities and provide opportunities not just for individuals but for groups as well. Evidently, in the context of minorities there can be two parts to an affirmative action programme: promoting empowerment and ending exclusion. Targeted intervention through the 15 per cent budgetary resource allocation for minorities in all government welfare schemes could help address empowerment issues. End of exclusion, on the other hand, would require much bolder initiatives, such as the recruitment of Muslims in government. In electoral democracies, important changes in public policy depend critically on the presence of legislators and decision makers from disadvantaged groups who can use legislative and policy arenas to bring about improvements. Greater representation of minorities in decision-making institutions would be necessary to make sure that their voice and interests are articulated and heard in the public domain. Although there is no direct relationship between minority proportionality in the administration and levels of social development and well-being, the presence of minorities in office and allocation of political positions provide opportunities to incorporate the concerns and interests of minority groups in the calculations of politicians belonging to a variety of groups. Such a two-pronged effort alone will be the true measure of the effectiveness of the paradigm shift and the political will to broad-base the reach of substantive equality so that India can retain its primacy as a democracy committed to justice and fairness.

The key issues in this regard are the criteria and the politics of determining beneficiary groups, and the extent to which the existing processes have resulted in denial of opportunities to a variety of disadvantaged groups. Strategies of inclusion should not be determined on the basis of caste identities alone, because intra-group and inter-group inequalities have enlarged over the decades and become greater than before. There can be no doubt that caste remains the prime source of discrimination in our society, and the historical burden of direct and indirect discrimination has to be recognized and remedial steps taken in this regard. Provision of equality of opportunity to historically disadvantaged groups is necessary in the light of historical and persisting inequalities, but this need not entail compromising the right to equality and equal access to public goods and resources of the state of other deprived groups.

The real question is how to open up opportunities for other excluded groups in education, employment, and other spheres. This brings us back to the point made in the preceding chapters that the focus on discrimination and disadvantage in official policy in India has been disproportionately on the past and not enough on the discrimination in relation to present disadvantage. The remedial goals that are required must include giving careful attention to current discrimination also. This is essential for removing barriers that systematically prevent the inclusion of various deprived groups. Clearly, the role of affirmative action for currently disadvantaged and under-represented groups to augment access to opportunities, whether in education or employment, cannot be overemphasized. It is time to address some of these strategic questions in implementing the social commitment to fairer distribution of advantage in our public institutions; higher education is a case in point. However, the real tasks are, first, to ensure that this important challenge of broad-basing affirmative action policies, so as to include in their ambit a focus on groups facing disadvantage and deprivation in the present context, becomes a compelling political issue; and, second, to initiate a reasoned debate on it.

The overall policy should be to balance the concept of social justice for society as a whole. The analysis in the previous chapters makes it clear that existing policies cannot fully address issues of exclusion emanating from the demands of non-Hindu groups, for instance, Dalits in the Muslim and Christian communities. An important test of democracy is the extent to which it succeeds in representing a diversity of groups and redressing discrimination of a variety of disadvantaged groups through equality of opportunity and access. While existing policies of inclusion have undoubtedly made a significant contribution towards enhancing the representation of disadvantaged castes, the goal of social justice in a plural and diverse society has to be adequate representation of all segments of the people, whatever their caste or religion.

Finally, affirmative action needs to expand in India, provided the whole system is revisited. The past two decades of unprecedented growth have been particularly dramatic in changing both the political and economic landscapes of the country in ways that reflect dynamic class configurations and social changes. The combination of high growth in the context of the liberalized economy and the partial rolling back of government from the social sector has resulted in widening the social divide between the privileged and the underprivileged. The polarization between rich and poor has given rise to the random explosions of discontent. While everyone would benefit from high growth rates, it is undeniable that those who have financial and intellectual capital, especially education, stand to benefit more as they are in a much better position to seize new opportunities in India's growth and expansion driven by information technology.

Also what matters in the changing scenario is relative deprivation, and not always absolute deprivation, as in the past. Relative deprivation in turn breeds greater aspirations and also greater resentments over exclusion. For this reason we need to shift the debate and reorient policies of affirmative action in order to extend its reach and benefits to the more deprived within beneficiary groups and to include categories outside its purview. Affirmative action needs to be sensitive to complex criteria such as income disparities, minority disadvantage, and gender. The existing policy can neither deal with issues of class inequalities (intra-group inequalities) nor inter-group inequalities. The silence on class in the reservation regime needs to be broken to promote new thinking on affirmative action. We cannot any longer afford to ignore the class criterion. In the *Indra Sawhney* judgment the court had dismissed the economic criteria in the definition of backwardness under Articles 15 and 16 of the Constitution. But rapid economic and social changes in the past fifteen years—with economic modernization and affirmative action programmes benefiting significant sections of the backward castes and adversely affecting many others—underline the need to take a fresh look at the economic criteria in framing affirmative action yardsticks. The stakes of the excluded are enormous, as they face marginalization from these policies. At the heart of the growing protests over exclusions is the larger question of the politics of inclusion into official categories, especially as economic growth has not trickled down. We need a new perspective that can grapple with increased economic inequalities, on the one hand, and entrenchment of social prejudices, on the other, and how both are implicated in a range of new social inequalities and hostility to bring change in areas where it matters most, namely, structural inequities and social exclusions. Up to now the single-minded emphasis on one dimension of group disadvantage has served to obscure these issues.

Appendix

TABLE 3.1
State-Wise Urban Poverty Incidence across Socio-Religious Communities (2004–05)

(in per cent)

States	*All*	*Hindus*				*Muslims*	*Other Minorities*
		All	*SCs/STs*	*OBCs*	*General*		
Total	22.8	20.4	36.4	25.1	8.3	38.4	12.2
West Bengal	12	10	22	13	6	27	1
Kerala	18	19	32	21	8	24	9
Uttar Pradesh	31	24	42	28	11	44	6
Bihar	36	34	65	39	8	45	4
Assam	3	3	4	5	1	5	0
Jammu & Kashmir	9	4	9	5	2	12	2
Jharkhand	18	16	37	15	5	32	27
Karnataka	30	27	52	30	13	45	9
Uttaranchal	15	14	29	20	8	24	0
Delhi	12	12	24	24	4	22	1
Maharashtra	26	20	33	25	12	49	27
Andhra Pradesh	26	25	41	27	11	35	16
Gujarat	11	10	17	18	3	24	0
Rajasthan	29	27	47	28	11	41	15
Madhya Pradesh	41	38	64	46	13	58	6
Haryana	5	5	16	5	1	6	0
Tamil Nadu	18	18	37	16	5	18	15

(Contd.)

(Table 3.1 contd.)

States	All	Hindus				Muslims	Other Minorities
		All	SCs/STs	OBCs	General		
Orissa	43	42	69	49	22	48	49
Himachal Pradesh	2	3	3	10	1	1	0
Chhattisgarh	38	38	48	47	13	61	10
Punjab	1	2	3	2	0	0	0
All Other States	5	6	14	6	3	9	1

Source: *SCR* (2006).

TABLE 3.2
State-Wise Rural Poverty Incidence across Socio-Religious Communities (2004–05)

(in per cent)

States	All	Hindus				Muslims	Other Minorities
		All	SCs/STs	OBCs	General		
Total	22.7	22.6	34.8	19.5	9.0	26.9	14.3
West Bengal	25	21	27	16	14	33	32
Kerala	9	9	19	7	4	11	4
Uttar Pradesh	28	28	39	26	10	33	40
Bihar	35	34	56	29	13	38	33
Assam	18	12	14	16	7	27	20
Jammu & Kashmir	3	3	4	0	2	4	0
Jharkhand	38	38	49	32	17	36	46
Karnataka	14	14	21	14	7	18	1
Uttaranchal	11	12	17	19	7	8	21
Delhi	–	–	–	–	–	–	–
Maharashtra	23	22	44	16	13	21	36
Andhra Pradesh	8	8	16	6	2	7	4
Gujarat	14	15	24	14	3	7	6
Rajasthan	16	16	28	9	6	11	15
Madhya Pradesh	30	31	45	22	6	25	2
Haryana	9	9	21	7	2	24	6
Tamil Nadu	17	17	23	14	14	10	18
Orissa	41	40	60	30	16	22	70

(Contd.)

(Table 3.2 contd.)

States	*All*	*Hindus*				*Muslims*	*Other Minorities*
		All	*SCs/STs*	*OBCs*	*General*		
Himachal Pradesh	8	8	16	7	4	4	6
Chhattisgarh	33	33	40	27	26	40	11
Punjab	6	4	4	7	3	4	6
All Other States	12	18	29	12	10	22	3

Source: *SCR* (2006).

TABLE 3.3
Graduates as Proportion of Population by Age Groups
(All India, 2004–05)

(in per cent)

Age Groups	*Hindus*			*Muslims*	*Others Minorities*
	General	*OBCs*	*SCs/STs*		
21–30 years	18.6	6.5	3.3	4.5	11.6
31–40 years	16.8	4.6	2.3	3.3	9.2
41–50 years	14.6	3.2	1.5	2.8	8.1
51 years & above	9.8	1.9	0.9	2.1	5.7
Total	15.3	4.4	2.2	3.4	8.9

Source: SCR (2006).

GRAPH 3.1
Worker Participation Rates by Socio-Religious Communities

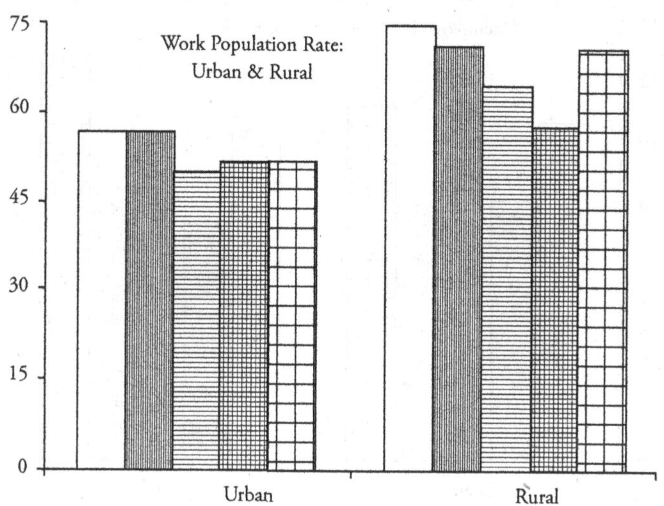

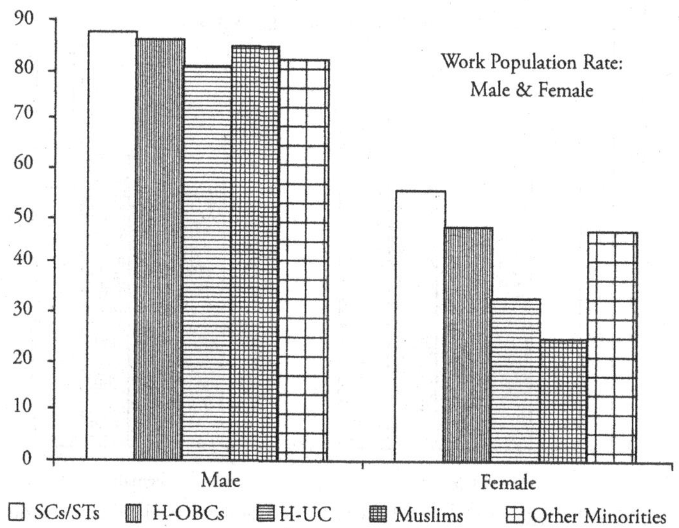

Notes: H: Hindu.
UC: Upper Caste.

Source: SCR (2006) (Data from NSSO 2004–05).

Graph 3.2
Unemployment Rate by Socio-Religious Communities

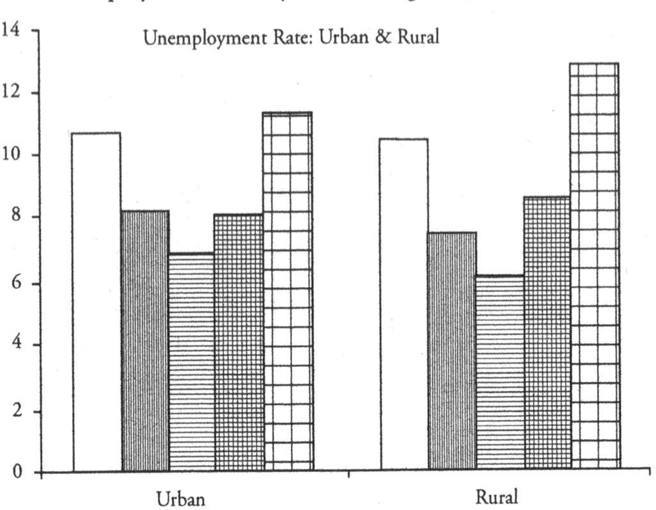

Notes: H: Hindu.
UC: Upper Caste.

Source: SCR (2006) (Data from NSSO 2004–05).

GRAPH 3.3
Activity Status of Male and Female Workers

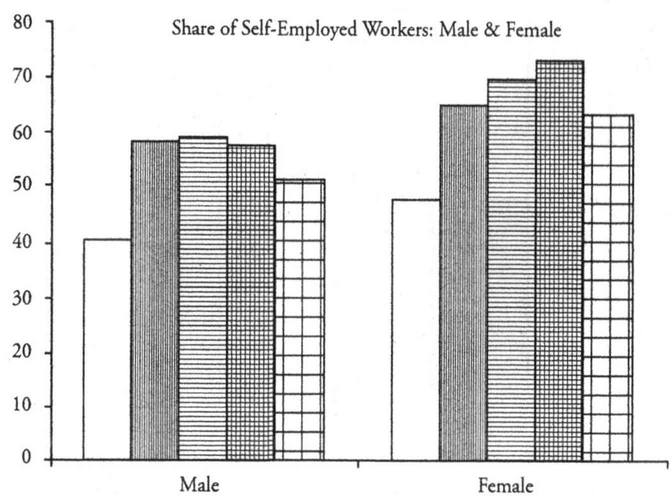

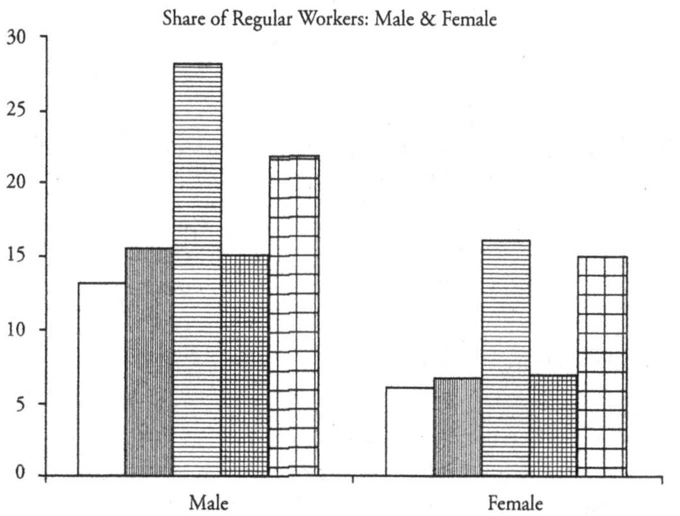

(Contd.)

(Graph 3.3 contd.)

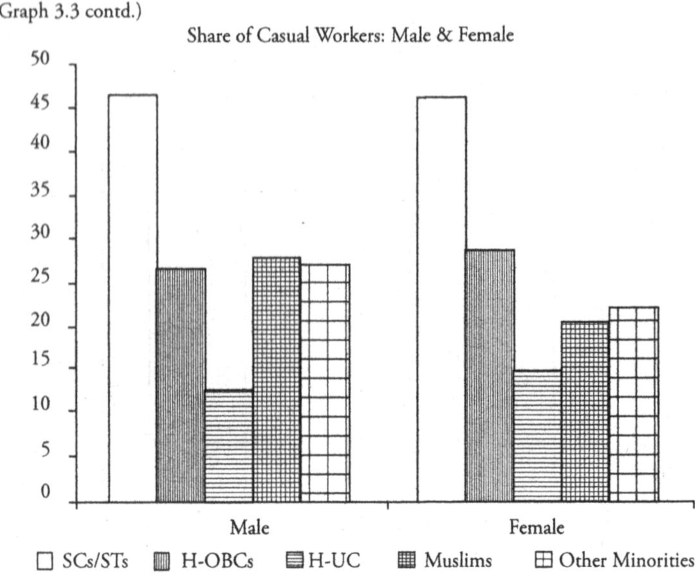

Notes: H: Hindu.
UC: Upper Caste.

Source: SCR (2006).

TABLE 3.4
Incidence of Violation of Civil Rights and Atrocities against the Scheduled Castes in India (1999–2001)

Sr. No.	*State*	*Incidence of Total Crime*				*Percentage of All-India figures*	*Rate per Lakh*	*Rank*
		1999	*2000*	*2001*	*Average*			
1	Andhra Pradesh	1749	1582	2933	2088	7.5	2.8	06
2	Assam	07	11	06	08	0.0	0.0	15
3	Bihar	820	741	1303	955	3.4	1.2	11
4	Gujarat	1781	1332	1242	1452	5.2	2.9	05
5	Haryana	121	117	229	156	0.6	0.7	12
6	Himachal Pradesh	54	52	110	72	0.3	1.2	10
7	Karnataka	1277	1329	1621	1409	5.0	2.7	07
8	Kerala	514	467	499	493	1.8	1.5	09
9	Madhya Pradesh	4667	4631	4212	4503	16.1	7.5	02

(Contd.)

(Table 3.4 contd.)

Sr. No.	State	Incidence of Total Crime				Percentage of All-India figures	Rate per Lakh	Rank
		1999	2000	2001	Average			
10	Maharashtra	605	489	625	573	2.0	0.6	13
11	Orissa	772	793	1734	1100	3.9	3.0	04
12	Punjab	39	34	134	69	0.2	0.3	14
13	Rajasthan	5623	5190	4892	5235	18.7	9.3	01
14	Tamil Nadu	883	1296	2336	1505	5.4	2.4	08
15	Uttar Pradesh	6122	7330	10732	8061	28.8	4.9	03
16	West Bengal	00	00	10	03	0.0	0.0	16
	India	25093	25455	33501	28016	100	2.7	

Note: All figures represent the number of cases registered under the PCR Act (1955) and SC/ST (POA) Act (1989).

Source: *Crime in India 1999–2001*, National Crime Records Bureau, Ministry of Home Affairs.

TABLE 3.5
Representation of Scheduled Castes and Scheduled Tribes in Central Government Services (1999)

Group	Total	SC	%age	ST	%age
A	93520	10558	11.29	3172	3.39
B	104963	13306	12.68	3512	3.35
C	2396426	378115	15.78	145482	6.07
D	949353	189761	19.99	66487	7.00
Excluding Sweepers					
Sweepers	66435	63233	65.57	5314	5.51
Total Excluding Sweepers	3544262	591740	16.7	218653	6.17
Total Including Sweepers	3640697	654973	17.99	223967	6.15

Source: National Commission for Scheduled Castes and Scheduled Tribes, Sixth Annual Report, 1999–2000 & 2000–01.

TABLE 3.6

Vacancies Reserved and Filled in Indian Administrative Service, Indian Foreign Service, and Indian Police Service on the basis of Civil Services Examination (2003)

			For SCs		*For STs*		*For OBCs*	
Services	*Vacancies Total*	*Vacancies Filled*	*Vacancies Total*	*Vacancies Filled*	*Vacancies Total*	*Vacancies Filled*	*Vacancies Total*	*Vacancies Filled*
IAS	89	89	12	12	5	5	26	26
IFS	18	18	4	4	–	–	5	5
IPS	88	88	12	12	7	7	26	26

Source: Ministry of Personnel, Public Grievances & Pensions, 2004.

TABLE 3.7

Representation of Scheduled Castes and Scheduled Tribes in Central Public Sector Enterprises (2000)

Group	*Total of emp*	*SCs*	*%age*	*STs*	*%age*
A	204127	21125	10.35	6057	2.97
B	175159	19355	11.05	7317	4.18
C	1013917	191931	18.93	85744	8.46
D Excluding Sweepers	407425	91729	22.51	46463	11.40
Total	1800628	324140	18.00	145581	8.09
Sweepers	27903	20412	73.15	878	3.15
Grand Total	1828531	344552	18.84	146459	8.01

Source: National Commission for Scheduled Castes and Scheduled Tribes, Sixth Annual Report, 1999–2000 & 2000–01.

TABLE 3.8
Access to Higher Education by Caste Groups (2000)

(in per cent)

Socio-Religious Groups	*All Categories*			*Scheduled Castes*		
			Total			
	Total Graduates			*Total Higher*		
	Male	*Female*	*Total*	*Male*	*Female*	*Total*
SC	5.08	2.62	3.88	6.63	3.48	5.09
General	14.22	11.09	12.71	19.20	14.11	16.74
Total	9.21	6.34	7.81	12.12	8.00	10.10
			Rural			
SC	3.85	1.27	2.57	5.07	1.70	3.40
General	8.82	5.01	6.93	11.79	6.19	9.01
Total	5.79	2.97	4.39	7.53	3.61	5.58
			Urban			
SC	9.48	8.16	8.87	12.19	10.75	11.53
General	22.44	21.65	22.07	30.50	27.87	29.28
Total	17.53	15.55	16.60	23.28	19.99	21.74

Source: Working Group on Empowerment of Scheduled Castes during the Eleventh Five Year Plan, 2007–12, Planning Commission, 2007.

Table 3.9
Representation of Scheduled Castes and Scheduled Tribes in Public Sector Banks and Financial Institutions

		As on 1 January 1998	*As on 1 January 1999*	*As on 1 January 2000*
Officers	Total	252072	254511	254692
	SC	29956	30857	31871
	%	11.80	12.12	12.51
	ST	10098	10412	10749
	%	4.00	4.09	4.22
Clerks	Total	465780	460909	456802
	SC	69902	70160	67975
	%	15.00	15.22	14.88
	ST	22416	22321	21755
	%	4.81	4.84	4.76
Sub-Staff	Total	183061	179606	178428
(Excluding Sweepers)				
	SC	42567	42766	43653
	%	23.25	23.81	24.46
	ST	11275	11138	11154
	%	6.15	6.20	6.25
Sweepers	Total	43509	43508	39406
	SC	22864	22707	20086
	%	52.55	52.18	50.97
	ST	2449	2386	2422
	%	5.62	5.48	6.14

Source: National Commission for Scheduled Castes and Scheduled Tribes, Sixth Annual Report, 1999–2000 & 2000–01.

TABLE 4.1
Mandal Commission: Caste Groups as a Percentage of India's Population

Caste Groups	*Percentage of India's Population*
Forward Hindu Castes and Communities	17.58
Backward Hindu Castes and Communities	43.70
Scheduled Castes	15.05
Scheduled Tribes	7.51
Non-Hindu Communities (including backwards)	16.16 (52% of these, or 8.40% of the total population, were identified as backwards among the non-Hindu communities)
Total	100

Source: Government of India, Report of the Backward Classes Commission (1980).

Table 4.2
Percentage Distribution of Postgraduate Enrolment by Course

Categories	*Total Enrolment*		*Hindus*				*Muslims*			*Others*
	Numbers	*Percentage to Total*	*All*	*SCs/STs*	*OBCs*	*General*	*All*	*OBCs*	*General*	
PG Arts	73,710	37.4	89.4	19.2	19.3	50.8	4.4	1.7	2.7	6.2
PG Commerce	33,228	16.9	87.8	10.8	17.9	59.0	7.3	5.3	2.0	5.0
PG Science	37,928	19.3	87.6	10.9	21.4	55.3	5.7	3.4	2.3	6.7
PG Engg	26,565	13.5	85.9	7.2	48.6	30.1	4.2	3.7	0.5	9.9
PG Medical	1,953	1.0	86.8	5.5	5.5	76.0	5.4	0.9	4.5	7.8
PG Professional	23,551	12.0	87.8	10.6	18.3	58.9	7.8	6.2	1.7	4.4
Total Postgraduate	196,935	100.0	88.1	13.4	23.2	51.5	5.5	3.4	2.1	6.4
Grand Total of Graduate & PG	1509,507		86.6	13.4	27.1	46.1	8.4	4.7	3.8	5.0

Source: SCR (2006).

TABLE 4.3
Inequalities in Higher Education (1999–2000)
(percentage of graduates in the population aged twenty years or above)

Castes/Communities	*Rural India*	*Urban India*
ST	1.1	10.9
SC	1.2	4.7
Muslim	1.3	6.1
Hindu OBC	2.1	8.6
Sikh	2.8	25.0
Christian	4.7	23.7
Hindu Upper Caste	5.3	25.3
Other Religions	5.4	31.5
All-India Average	2.6	15.5

Source: Satish Deshpande and Yogendra Yadav (2006).

TABLE 4.4
Graduates and Diploma Holders by Socio-Religious Communities

SRCs	*Number (in lakhs)*		*Percentage of 20 years + Population*		*Distribution across SRCs*	
	Graduates	*Diploma and Certificate*	*Graduates*	*Diploma and Certificate*	*Graduates*	*Diploma and Certificate*
Total	376.7	40.5	6.7	0.7	100	100
Muslims	23.9	2.7	3.6	0.4	6.3	6.8
SCs/STs	30.8	4.1	2.4	0.3	8.2	10.2
All Others	322	33.7	8.8	0.9	85.5	83.0

Source: SCR (2006).

TABLE 4.5
Over- and Under-Represented Groups (1999–2000)
(share of different caste and communities in the national pool of graduates as compared to their share of population)

Castes/Communities	*Rural India*	*Urban India*
ST	43	71
SC	47	30
Muslim	52	39
Hindu OBC	82	56
Sikh	107	164
Christian	200	154
Hindu Upper Caste	205	164
Other Religions	200	200

Source: Satish Deshpande and Yogendra Yadav (2006).

TABLE 4.6
Representation of Social Formations in Different Middle-Class Positions

Social Formation	*Number and percentage in sample*	*Education above high school*	*Occupation white collar*	*Brick and cement housing*	*Ownership of assets*	*Middle-class self-identification*
Upper Castes	2345 (24.8)	1057 (44.1)	873 (53.3)	1369 (45.2)	1112 (49.6)	1229 (43.8)
Backward Castes	3716 (39.3)	829 (34.6)	435 (26.6)	946 (31.3)	719 (32.0)	1001 (35.7)
Dalits	1863 (19.7)	281 (11.7)	151 (9.2)	373 (12.3)	196 (8.7)	254 (9.0)
Tribals	917 (9.7)	95 (4.0)	56 (3.4)	158 (5.2)	91 (4.1)	146 (5.2)
Muslims	616 (6.5)	134 (5.6)	123 (7.5)	181 (6.0)	126 (5.6)	177 (6.3)
Total	9457 (100.0)	2396 (100.0)	1638 (100.0)	3027 (100.0)	2244 (100.0)	2807 (100.0)

Source: D.L. Sheth (2000).

TABLE 5.1
Caste and Community of the MPs in Uttar Pradesh, Bihar, Madhya Pradesh, and Rajasthan (1952–2004) (percentages)

Caste & Communities	*1952*	*1957*	*1962*	*1967*	*1971*	*1977*	*1980*	*1984*	*1989*	*1991*	*1996*	*1998*	*1999*	*2004*
Upper Castes	64	58.6	54.9	55.5	53.9	48.2	40.88	46.9	38.2	37.11	35.3	34.7	35.4	33
Intermediate Castes	1	1.43	1.88	2.75	4.11	6.64	5.33	5.31	8	5.43	7.53	8.9	7.9	7.1
OBCs	4.45	5.24	7.98	9.64	10.1	13.3	13.74	11.1	20.87	22.6	24.8	23.6	24	25.3
SCs	15.76	18.1	19.72	18.35	18.26	17.7	17.78	17.26	17.78	18.1	18.14	18.2	18.6	17.8
STs	5.42	6.9	7.04	7.8	7.31	7.08	7.56	7.52	7.56	8.14	7.52	7.6	7.5	8.4
Muslims	5.42	4.76	4.23	3.67	4.57	5.75	11.56	9.73	5.78	4.52	3.54	5.3	5	7.1
TOTAL	96.06	95.03	95.75	97.71	98.25	98.67	96.85	97.82	98.19	95.9	96.83	98.3	98.4	98.7

Source: Christophe Jaffrelot and Sanjay Kumar (2009).

Table 5.2
Evolution of the Other Backward Class MLAs (state-wise)

States	*1952*	*1957*	*1962*	*1967*	*1969*	*1971–2*	*1977–8*	*1980–2*	*1985*	*1989–90*	*1991–3*	*1995–6*	*1998–2000*	*2001–5*
Type 1														
Tamil Nadu				66.2		61.6	59	57.7	56.9	61.5	62.4	62	–	–
Type 2														
UP	9	12	13	29.2	26.8	18.3	16.8	13.4	19.6	24.2	27.1	32.4	24.8	
MP		5.1	9.4	9.7		9.5	14.3	16.1	18.6	18.7		22.7	22	19.5
Bihar	20.6	19.4	24.4	26.6		25.7	28.3	30.4		34.9		46.8	40.3	42
Type 2'														
Rajasthan	3.7	2.5	4.4	2.2	5.5	2.5	7.4	8	12		5.2		6.6	8.9
Gujarat			8	11		16	15	24	24	26		21	21	29
Type 3														
Karnataka	7.3	13.1	14.1	11.2		12.6	13	13	10.1	13.9		12.8	12.1	
Maharashtra				22.3	21.4	23.3	19.8	19.8	24.7	26		23.3	23.6	23.9
Andhra Pradesh		8.7	13	14.3	19.5	19	20.7	20.1	20.1	11.9		12.9	11.9	18.3
Type 4														
West Bengal	0	0	0	0	0	0	0	0	0	0	0	0		
Himachal Pradesh				1.7		2.9	7.4	7.4	5.9	7.4	10.3		7.4	
Kerala		28.6	26.2	33.1	30.1		20	26.4	27.2	27.8	25	27.8		
Delhi														29.7

Source: Christophe Jaffrelot and Sanjay Kumar (2009).

TABLE 5.3
Muslim MPs Winning in Lok Sabha Elections (1952–2004)

Year	*Total Number of Seats*	*Seats Contested*	*Seats Won*	*Representation in the Lok Sabha*	*Success Rate*
1952	488	34	21	4.3%	61%
1957	494	45	24	4.8%	53%
1962	494	69	23	4.6%	33%
1967	520	70	29	5.5%	39%
1971	518	76	30	5.7%	39%
1977	542	83	34	6.2%	41%
1980	542	131	49	9%	37%
1984	452	123	46	8.4%	37%
1989	543	133	33	6%	25%
1991	543	149	28	5.1%	19%
1996	543	140	28	5.1%	20%
1998	543	146	28	5.1%	19%
1999	543	175	32	5.8%	18%
2004	543	168	35	6.4%	21%

Source: Statistical Reports published by the Election Commission of India and Ansari (2006).

TABLE 5.4
Constituencies according to the Percentage of Muslims

Year	*0–10%*	*11–20%*	*21–30%*	*31–40%*	*41–50%*	*Over 50%*	*NA*	*Total*
1952	3	5	3	3	1	2	4	21
1957	7	8	2	2	1	3	1	24
1962	4	6	2	3	2	4	2	23
1967	3	10	3	2	2	8	1	29
1971	3	7	4	2	2	9	3	30
1977	2	11	4	4	1	10	2	34
1980	6	17	9	5	1	10	1	49
1984	4	14	9	5	1	11	2	46
1989	5	5	6	5	2	9	1	33

(Contd.)

(Table 5.4 contd.)

Year	0–10%	11–20%	21–30%	31–40%	41–50%	Over 50%	NA	Total
1991	5	7	3	6	0	7	0	28
1996	4	5	3	6	1	10	0	29
1998	0	6	5	6	1	10	0	28
1999	1	8	5	6	2	10	0	32
2004								36
Total (escl. 2004)	47	109	58	55	17	103	17	406

Source: Ansari (2006).

TABLE 5.5
Muslim MLAs Winning in Vidhan Sabhas

State	*Year*	*Strength of the Legislature*	*Number of Muslim MLAs*	*Percentage of Muslim MLAs in the Legislature*
Assam	1951	94	15	16%
	1957	94	15	16%
	1962	105	15	14.2%
	1967	126	13	10.3%
	1972	126	21	16.7%
	1978	126	27	21.4%
	1983	126	31	24.6%
	1985	126	25	19.8%
	1991	126	19	15%
	1996	126	26	20.6%
	2001	126	24	19%
Bihar	1951	276	22	7.9%
	1957	264	26	9.8%
	1962	318	21	6.6%
	1967	318	20	6.3%
	1969	318	19	5.9%
	1972	318	24	7.5%

(Contd.)

(Table 5.5 contd.)

State	*Year*	*Strength of the Legislature*	*Number of Muslim MLAs*	*Percentage of Muslim MLAs in the Legislature*
	1977	324	26	8%
	1980	324	26	8%
	1985	324	31	9.6%
	1990	324	17	5.2%
	1995	324	23	7.1%
	2000	324	35	10.8%
	2005	236	24	10.1%
Kerala	1957	114	12	10.5%
	1960	114	17	14.9%
	1965	133	17	12.8%
	1967	133	16	12%
	1970	133	12	9%
	1977	140	24	17.1%
	1980	140	21	15%
	1982	140	24	17.1%
	1987	140	21	15%
	1991	140	26	18.6%
	1996	140	25	17.9%
	2001	140	22	15.7%
Uttar Pradesh	1951	347	43	12.4%
	1957	341	39	11.4%
	1962	430	29	6.7%
	1967	425	26	6.1%
	1969	425	28	6.6%
	1974	425	40	9.4%
	1977	425	45	10.6%
	1980	425	49	11.5%
	1985	425	52	12.2%
	1989	425	40	9.4%

(Contd.)

(Table 5.5 contd.)

State	*Year*	*Strength of the Legislature*	*Number of Muslim MLAs*	*Percentage of Muslim MLAs in the Legislature*
	1991	425	21	5%
	1993	425	27	6.4%
	1996	425	34	8%
	2002	403	45	11.2%
West Bengal	1951	187	25	13.4%
	1957	195	27	13.8%
	1962	252	28	11.1%
	1967	280	35	12.5%
	1969	280	39	13.9%
	1971	280	38	13.7%
	1972	294	39	13.9%
	1977	294	38	12.9%
	1982	294	45	15.3%
	1987	294	39	13.2%
	1991	294	43	14.6%
	1996	294	37	12.6%
	2001	294	38	12.9%

Source: Election Commission of India Statistical Reports.

TABLE 5.6
Constituencies according to the Percentage of Muslims and Number of Seats Won (1952–99)

Year	*0–10%*	*11–20%*	*21–30%*	*31–40%*	*41–50%*	*Over 50%*	*NA*	*Total*
1952	3	5	3	3	1	2	4	21
1957	7	8	2	2	1	3	1	24
1962	4	6	2	3	2	4	2	23
1967	3	10	3	2	2	8	1	29
1971	3	7	4	2	2	9	3	30
1977	2	11	4	4	1	10	2	34

(Contd.)

(Table 5.6 contd.)

Year	*0–10%*	*11–20%*	*21–30%*	*31–40%*	*41–50%*	*Over 50%*	*NA*	*Total*
1980	6	17	9	5	1	10	1	49
1984	4	14	9	5	1	11	2	46
1989	5	5	6	5	2	9	1	33
1991	5	7	3	6	0	7	0	28
1996	4	5	3	6	1	10	0	29
1998	0	6	5	6	1	10	0	28
1999	1	8	5	6	2	10	0	32
Total	47	109	58	55	17	103	17	406

Source: Ansari (2006).

TABLE 5.7

State Assembly Electoral Constituency/Tahsil Reserved for Scheduled Castes with Relative Share of Muslim Population

Tahsil	*Total Population*	*Muslim Population*	*SC Population*	*ST Population*	*SCs as Percentage of Total*	*Muslims as Percentage of Total Population*
Uttar Pradesh: Reserved Assembly Constituencies						
Hapur	773899	220996	181026	11	23.4	28.6
Najibabad	605199	297892	139227	418	23.0	49.2
Nagina	625366	264523	134807	2004	21.6	42.3
Koil	1373814	368210	283384	203	20.6	26.8
Khalilabad	605777	194538	123577	192	20.4	32.1
Mankapur	530697	95791	87701	9	16.5	18.1
Jansath	767827	280764	125816	0	16.4	36.6
Faridpur	383771	88280	61607	0	16.1	23.0
Uttar Pradesh: Unreserved Assembly Constituencies						
Marihan	189950	6167	93575	617	49.3	3.2
Ghorawal	225824	10198	100869	8	44.7	4.5
Lalganj	287983	17125	122031	189	42.4	5.9
Hardoi	975970	85110	391950	98	40.2	8.7

(Contd.)

(Table 5.7 contd.)

Tahsil	*Total Population*	*Muslim Population*	*SC Population*	*ST Population*	*SCs as Percentage of Total*	*Muslims as Percentage of Total Population*
Misrikh	764302	65750	289823	19	37.9	8.6
Sandila	828047	120541	309395	75	37.4	14.6
Haidergarh	507962	72085	182517	61	35.9	14.2
Bakshi Ka Talab	276134	33062	98476	93	35.7	12.0
Tahrauli	151202	4688	53302	57	35.3	3.1
			Bihar: Reserved Assembly Constituencies			
Raniganj	302261	86655	64383	13708	21.3	28.7
Phulwari	191005	41698	35844	212	18.8	21.8
Sakra	242815	50630	44809	26	18.5	20.9
Chhatapur	215493	39568	36445	2264	16.9	18.4
Bagaha	314874	53235	45190	947	14.4	16.9
Korha	210656	78482	29961	19209	14.2	37.3
Darbhanga	496486	131287	65236	280	13.1	26.4
Mairwa	93497	11713	10310	1617	11.0	12.5
Dhuraiya	186270	55960	18899	1474	10.1	30.0
			Bihar: Unreserved Assembly Constituencies			
Dumaria	100411	13420	39474	29	39.3	13.4
Banke Bazar	100354	11903	39220	263	39.1	11.9
Dobhi	117763	9620	43803	129	37.2	8.2
Manpur	108516	9368	40169	3	37.0	8.6
Amas	81640	12190	29668	164	36.3	14.9
Tan Kuppa	93175	3721	33606	4	36.1	4.0
Mohanpur	161817	15796	58185	214	36.0	9.8
Gurua	142853	19924	49980	2	35.0	13.9
Sirdala	136369	10431	46468	61	34.1	7.6

Source: SCR (2006).

TABLE 5.8
State Assembly Electoral Constituency/Tahsil Reserved for Scheduled Castes with Relative Share of Muslim Population

Tahsil	*Total Population*	*Muslim Population*	*SC Population*	*ST Population*	*SCs as Percentage of Total*	*Muslims as Percentage of Total Population*
	West Bengal: Reserved Assembly Constituencies					
Basanti	278592	114736	107602	17462	38.6	41.2
Rajarhat	145381	60108	52233	938	35.9	41.3
Nanoor	193775	64827	61803	3834	31.9	33.5
Kulpi	242752	88230	77380	141	31.9	36.3
Ketugram-I	145859	64975	39011	582	26.7	44.5
Sankrail	290924	92942	73191	1761	25.2	31.9
Keshpur	288489	76866	72536	17012	25.1	26.6
Khargram	234780	120557	55320	1918	23.6	51.3
Sagardighi	252293	156870	44992	16882	17.8	62.2
Kaliganj	290957	161705	49349	1447	17.0	55.6
	West Bengal: Unreserved Assembly Constituencies					
Sitai	96347	26491	64869	8	67.3	27.5
Haldibari	93867	30036	58070	254	61.9	32.0
Jalpaiguri	280927	40519	170394	16774	60.7	14.4
Kaliaganj	190019	39334	114922	8656	60.5	20.7
Khejuri – II	117438	8306	66658	819	56.8	7.1
Kharibari	88230	4128	44863	17099	50.8	4.7
Tufanganj- II	167455	22083	84790	3176	50.6	13.2
Bamangola	127252	11287	63459	25083	49.9	8.9
Gaighata	300588	18841	144293	4401	48.0	6.3
Bongaon	344044	69777	161918	10245	47.1	20.3

Source: SCR (2006).

TABLE 6.1
Percentages of Religious Minorities in the Civil Services (as of 1 January 1980)

Name of Service	*Muslims*	*Christians*	*Sikhs*
Indian Administrative Service	3.22	2.74	4.15
Indian Police Service	2.64	2.26	5.41
Indian Foreign Service	3.14	1.60	3.07

Source: Report of the High Power Panel on Minorities, SCs, STs and Weaker Sections (1983).

TABLE 6.2
Share of Muslims in All-India Civil Services (2006)

Service	*All Officers*	*No. of Muslim Officers*	*Muslims as Percentage of Total*	*Unconfirmed Names*
Civil Service Officers *(IAS, IFS and IPS)*	8827	285	3.2	10
Direct Recruitment through competitive examination	6460	155	2.4	4
Promoted from State Service	2367	130	5.5	6
Indian Administrative Service	4790	142	3.0	4
Direct Recruitment through competitive examination	3542	80	2.3	0
Promoted from State Service	1248	62	5.0	4
Indian Foreign Service	828	15	1.8	0
Direct Recruitment	621	12	1.9	0
Grade I of IFS (B) Personnel	207	3	1.4	0
Indian Police Service	3209	128	4.0	6
Direct Recruitment through competitive examination	2297	63	2.7	4
Promoted from State Service	912	65	7.1	2

Source: *SCR* (2006).

TABLE 6.3
Muslim Employees in Government Employment

Departments (Institutions Reporting)	*Reported Number of Employees*	*Reported Number of Muslim Employees*	*Muslims as Percentage of Reported Employees*
State-Level Departments	4452851	278385	6.3
Railways	1418747	64066	4.5
Banks and RBI	680833	15030	2.2
Security Agencies*	1879134	60517	3.2
Postal Service	275841	13759	5.0
Universities**	137263	6416	4.7
All Reported Government Employment (Excludes PSUs)	8844669	438173	4.9
Central PSUs***	687512	22387	3.3
State PSUs	745271	80661	10.8
AII PSUs	1432783	103048	7.2

Notes: *CRPF, CISF, BSF, SSB, and other agencies
**129 Universities (Central and State) and 84 Colleges
*** Data from 154 PSUs
Source: *SCR* (2006) (Data was supplied on the request of the SCR by respective departments and ministries, and information was received during 2005).

TABLE 6.4
Percentage Share of Muslim Employees in Selected Central Government Departments and Institutions

Category/ Level of Employment	*Total Number of Employees*	*Civil Service*	*Railways*	*Posts & Telegraph Services*	*Security*	*Banks*	*University*	*PSU*
Group 'A'	231619	4.8	2.5	3.8	3.1	1.7	3.7	2.3
		(35.8)	(18.7)	(28.4)	(23.1)	(12.7)	(27.6)	(17.2)
Group 'B'	122551	–	3.4	4.4	3.9			
			(25.4)	(32.8)	(29.1)			
Group 'C'	1486637	–	4.9	4.8	4.6	2.5	5.4	3.9
			(36.6)	(35.8)	(34.3)	(18.7)	(40.3)	(29.1)
Group 'D'	659113	–	5.0	5.3	4.3			
			(37.3)	(39.6)	(32.1)			

Source: SCR (2006) (Data was supplied on the request of the SCR by respective departments and ministries, and information was received during 2005).

Table 6.5

Share of Muslim Employees in Selected State Governments

States	*Total Number of Employees*	*Muslims as Percentage of Population*	*Higher Positions*	*Lower Positions*	*Group A*	*Group B*	*Group C*	*Group D*	*Others*
			Percentages						
West Bengal	134972	25.2	4.7	1.8	6.7	3.9	2.1	2.5	1.4
Kerala	268733	24.7	10.3	10.4	11.8	10.1	11.1	9.1	10.5
Uttar Pradesh	134053	18.5	7.5	4.9	4.6	8.0	4.3	5.4	6.7
Bihar	78114	16.5	7.2	7.6	7.9	7.0	7.3	8.4	5.2
Assam	81261	30.9	10.2	11.4	9.2	10.7	11.5	9.9	10.5
Jharkhand	15374	13.8	3.8	7.2	4.0	3.7	9.0	4.5	–
Karnataka	528401	12.2	4.9	8.9	4.7	5.1	9.3	6.0	–
Delhi	135877	11.7	2.1	3.3	3.5	1.4	3.9	1.1	1.6
Maharashtra	915645	10.6	3.1	4.5	2.3	3.4	4.4	4.6	–
Gujarat	754533	9.1	3.4	5.5	–	–	–	–	–
Tamil Nadu	529597	5.6	4.2	2.9	4.0	4.2	3.1	2.5	–
Total of States*	4452851	16.0	5.7	5.6	5.8	6.1	5.9	5.1	3.3

Notes: Higher Positions: Aggregate of Group A and Group B.

Lower Positions: Aggregate of Group C, Group D, and Others

*876291 employees from Andhra Pradesh are included in the Sum of States. Further break-up of these data is not available.

Source: SCR (2006) (Data was supplied on the request of the SCR by respective departments and ministries, and information was received during 2005).

Table 6.6
Percentage Share of Muslim Employees in Selected State Government Departments

States	*Muslims as percentage of total Population*	*Education Dept.*		*Home Dept.*		*Health Dept.*		*Transport Dept.*		*Others Depts*	
		Higher Positions	*Lower Positions*	*Higher Positions*	*Lower Positions*	*Higher Positions*	*Lower Positions*	*Higher Positions*	*Lower Positions*	*Higher Positions*	*Lower Positions*
West Bengal	25.2	–	–	14.1	5.1	1.3	0.9	–	–	4.3	2.2
Kerala	24.7	13.0	11.7	10.8	10.7	11.2	10.2	9.4	9.2	8.9	10.5
Uttar Pradesh	18.5	–	–	8.1	9.9	4.3	5.6	1.9	4.9	7.6	4.8
Bihar	16.5	14.8	11.8	5.9	7.1	–	2.6	8.3	10.9	7.5	7.6
Assam	30.9	–	–	9.3	11.5	8.0	11.1	13.9	11.5	12.2	11.4
Jharkhand	13.8	–	–	5.7	7.6	6.0	3.2	–	–	3.7	7.8
Karnataka	12.2	5.0	12.4	3.6	4.2	4.7	5.1	16.8	7.0	5.1	7.3
Delhi	11.7	5.9	7.2	1.5	2.3	1.0	1.8	1.4	1.1	0.3	0.9
Maharashtra	10.6	2.9	4.7	4.2	4.2	2.6	3.3	–	–	2.2	3.9
Gujarat	9.1	1.7	4.5	5.6	5.6	2.2	1.5	9.4	16.3	–	–
Tamil Nadu	5.6	5.8	5.3	0.0	2.6	4.6	3.3	1.0	2.6	2.9	2.1
Sum of States	16.0	5.7	6.2	8.7	5.6	4.4	3.5	1.6	6.9	5.5	5.1

Notes: Higher Positions: Aggregate of Group A and Group B.
Lower Positions: Aggregate of Group C, Group D, and Others.
Source: SCR (2006) (Data was supplied on the request of the SCR by respective departments and ministries, and information was received during 2005).

TABLE 7.1
Estimated Class Composition of Dalits by Religion, Rural India (2004–05)

Religious Community	*Monthly Per Capita Consumption Expenditure Classes*					*All Classes*
	Below Poverty Line	*Rs 357–450*	*Rs 451–650*	*Rs 651–1200*	*Rs 1200+*	
Hindu	37.7	23.6	25.0	11.7	2.0	100.0
Muslim	39.6	15.8	37.1	4.9	2.6	100.0
Christian	30.1	33.5	14.0	16.4	6.1	100.0
Sikh	7.6	19.1	41.2	28.5	3.6	100.0
Buddhist	45.9	21.4	23.7	6.6	2.5	100.0
All Dalits	36.8	23.5	25.4	12.2	2.1	100.0

Source: NCM Report on the Dalits in the Muslim and Christian Communities (2008).

TABLE 7.2
Estimated Class Composition of Dalits by Religion, Urban India (2004–05)

Religious Community	*Monthly Per Capita Consumption Expenditure Classes*					*All Classes*
	Below Poverty Line	*Rs 539–800*	*Rs 801–1251*	*Rs 1251–2500*	*Rs 2500+*	
Hindu	40.9	28.3	21.2	8.1	1.6	100.0
Muslim	46.8	33.1	9.8	10.3	0.0	100.0
Christian	32.3	30.9	22.0	12.7	2.1	100.0
Sikh	24.8	39.6	20.1	12.3	3.2	100.0
Buddhist	28.9	28.1	28.4	13.1	1.6	100.0
All Dalits	39.8	28.5	21.5	8.6	1.6	100.0

Source: NCM Report on the Dalits in the Muslim and Christian Communities (2008).

TABLE 7.3
Occupational Structure of Dalit Households by Religion, Rural India (2004–05)

Religious Community	*Self-Employment in Non-Agriculture*	*Agricultural Labour*	*Other Labour*	*Self-Employment in Agriculture*	*Others*	*Total*
Hindu	14.1	40.1	15.4	20.9	9.5	100.0
Muslim	25.1	24.8	12.4	26.6	11.1	100.0
Christian	17.1	34.7	16.5	7.4	24.3	100.0
Sikh	13.0	45.2	25.3	4.6	12.0	100.0
Buddhist	9.4	56.7	6.8	15.8	11.4	100.0
All	*14.1*	*40.5*	*15.4*	*20.2*	*9.8*	*100.0*

Source: NCM Report on the Dalits in the Muslim and Christian Communities (2008).

TABLE 7.4
Occupational Structure of Dalit Households by Religion, Urban India (2004–05)

Socio-Reigious Community	*Self-Employed*	*Regular Wage/Salary*	*Casual Labour*	*Other Labour*	*Total*
Hindu	30.6	40.6	21.0	7.8	100.0
Muslim	31.9	15.1	38.2	14.8	100.0
Christian	13.9	51.9	24.9	9.3	100.0
Sikh	22.9	51.1	20.9	5.1	100.0
Buddhist	16.6	44.6	31.7	7.2	100.0
All	*29.4*	*41.1*	*21.8*	*7.8*	*100.0*

Source: NCM Report on the Dalits in the Muslim and Christian Communities (2008).

TABLE 7.5
Comparative Educational Profile of Castes among Muslims, Rural India (2004–05)

Religion	*Not Literate*	*Up to Primary*	*Up to Secondary*	*Higher Secondary*	*Diploma/ Graduate and above*	Total
SC	48.08	32.85	15.39	2.14	1.53	100.0
OBC	47.36	33.61	15.97	1.74	1.32	100.0
UC	43.37	39.63	14.24	1.66	1.1	100.0
All	44.91	37.22	14.96	1.7	1.22	*100.0*

Source: NCM Report on the Dalits in the Muslim and Christian Communities (2008).

TABLE 7.6
Comparative Educational Profile of Castes among Muslims, Urban India (2004–05)

Religion	*Not Literate*	*Up to Primary*	*Up to Secondary*	*Higher Secondary*	*Diploma/ Graduate and above*	Total
SC	31.79	36.95	25.14	1.88	4.24	100.0
OBC	35.21	36.89	21.53	3.23	3.15	100.0
UC	27.49	34.59	26.44	5	6.48	100.0
All	30.3	35.34	24.56	4.5	5.3	*100.0*

Source: NCM Report on the Dalits in the Muslim and Christian Communities (2008).

Table 7.7
Comparative Educational Profile of Castes among Christians, Rural India (2004–05)

Religion	*Not Literate*	*Up to Primary*	*Up to Secondary*	*Higher Secondary*	*Diploma/ Graduate and above*	Total
SC	38.42	30.67	23.1	6.29	1.52	100.0
OBC	21.19	36.52	31.54	4.26	6.5	100.0
UC	12.88	30.45	39.26	6.26	11.14	100.0
All	24.39	36.44	29.16	4.31	5.69	*100.0*

Source: NCM Report on the Dalits in the Muslim and Christian Communities (2008).

Table 7.8
Comparative Educational Profile of Castes among Christians, Urban India (2004–05)

Religion	*Not Literate*	*Up to Primary*	*Up to Secondary*	*Higher Secondary*	*Diploma/ Graduate and above*	Total
SC	15.69	33.47	30.95	8.45	11.45	100.0
OBC	8.72	30.44	35.59	9.36	15.89	100.0
UC	6.49	23.3	36.84	10.34	23.03	100.0
All	8.34	27.74	35.76	10.12	18.03	*100.0*

Source: NCM Report on the Dalits in the Muslim and Christian Communities (2008).

Bibliography

Ahmad, Imtiaz (1967), 'The Ashraf and Ajlaf categories in Indo-Muslim Society', *Economic and Political Weekly*, Vol. II, No. 19.

Ahmad, Imtiaz (1978), 'Introduction', in Imtiaz Ahmad (ed.), *Caste and Social Stratification among Muslims in India,* Manohar Publishers and Distributors, New Delhi.

Ahmad, Imtiaz (2007), 'Recognition and Entitlement: Muslim Castes Eligible for Inclusion. Category "Scheduled Castes"', in Ashfaq Husain Ansari (ed.), *Basic Problems of Dalit and OBC Muslims,* Serials Publisher, New Delhi.

Ahmad, Irfan (2003), 'A Different Jihad: Dalit Muslims Challenge to *Ashraf* Hegemony', *Economic and Political Weekly,* Vol. XXXVIII, No. 46.

Akbar, M.J. (2006), 'A Job to Do', *The Asian Age,* 17 December.

Alam, Aniket (2004), 'Quota for Muslims', *Frontline,* Vol. 21, Issue 17.

Alam, Anwar (2003), 'Democratisation of Indian Muslims: Some Reflections', *Economic and Political Weekly,* Vol. XXXVIII, No. 46.

Alam, Javeed (2004), *Who Wants Democracy,* Orient Longman, New Delhi.

Alam, Javeed (2008),'The Contemporary Situation of Muslims in India', *Economic and Political Weekly,* Vol. XLIII, No. 2.

Alexander, K.C. (1977), 'The Problem of Caste in the Christian Chruches of Kerala', in Harjinder Singh (ed.), *Caste among Non-Hindus in India,* National Publishing House, New Delhi.

Ali, Imran and Yoginder Sikand (2006), 'Survey of Socio-economic Conditions of Muslims in India', *Countercurrents.org,* 9 February, www.countercurrents.org.

Ansari, Ghaus (1959), *Muslim Castes in Uttar Pradesh*, Ethnographic and Folk Culture Society, Lucknow.

Ansari, Iqbal A. (2006), *Political Representation of Muslims in India: 1952–2004*, Manak Publications, New Delhi.

Ansari, Shabbir (1996), Memorandum from President of the All India Muslim OBC Organization to Welfare Minister B.S. Ramoowalia, 16 September.

Anwar, Ali (2001), *Masavat ki Jung: Pasmanda Bihar ke Pasmanda Musalman* (in Hindi), Vani Prakashan, New Delhi.

Austin, Granville (1986), *The Indian Constitution: The Cornerstone of a New Nation*, Oxford University Press, New Delhi.

Austin, Granville (1999), *Working a Democratic Constitution: The Indian Experience*, Oxford University Press, New Delhi.

Bajpai, Rochna (2006), 'Redefining Equality: Social Justice in the Mandal Debate', in V.R. Mehta and Thomas Pantham (eds), *Political Ideas in Modern India: Thematic Explorations, Vol. X Part 7, History of Science, Philosophy and Culture in Indian Civilization,* Sage Publications, New Delhi.

Bajpai, Rochna (2008), 'Minority Representation and the Making of the Indian Constitution', in Rajeev Bhargava (ed.), *Politics and Ethics of the Indian Constitution*, Oxford University Press, New Delhi.

Banducci, Susan A., Todd Donovan, and Jeffrey A. Karp (2004), 'Minority Representation, Empowerment and Participation', *Journal of Politics*, Vol. 66, No. 2, May.

Barooah, Vani, Amaresh Dubey, and Sriya Iyer (2007), 'The Effectiness of Job Reservation: Caste, Religion and Economic Status in India', *Development and Change*, Vol. 38, No. 3, May.

Barth, Frederic (1969), *Ethnic Groups and Boundaries*, George Allen Unwin, London.

Basant, Rakesh (2007a), 'Diversity among Indian Muslims', *Seminar*, No. 569, January.

Basant, Rakesh (2007b), 'Social, Economic and Educational Conditions of Indian Muslims', *Economic and Political Weekly*, Vol. XLII, No. 10.

Bayly, Susan (1999), *The New Cambridge History of India (IV–3): Caste, Society and Politics in India from the Eighteenth Century to the Modern Age*, Cambridge University Press, Cambridge.

Béteille, André (1996), 'Caste in Contemporary India', in C.J. Fuller (ed.), *Caste Today*, Oxford University Press, New Delhi.

Bhargava, Rajeev (ed.) (2000), *Secularism and its Critics*, Oxford University Press, New Delhi.

Bhargava, Rajeev (2002), 'India's Secular Constitution', in Zoya Hasan, E. Sridharan, and R. Sudarshan (eds), *India's Living Constitution: Ideas, Practices and Controversies*, Permanent Black, New Delhi.

Bhargava, Rajeev (2007), 'On the Persistent Underrepresentation of Muslims in India', *Law & Ethics and Human Rights*, Vol. 1, Issue 1.

Bhargava, Rajeev (ed.) (2008), *Politics and Ethics of the Indian Constitution*, Oxford University Press, Oxford.

Bidwai, Praful (2006a), 'The Anti-quota Stir is Misguided', rediff News, 30 May, www.rediff.com.

Bidwai, Praful (2006b), 'Bringing Caste-aways on Board', *South Asia*, 2 June, http://www.atimes.com.

Bidwai, Praful (2006c), 'The "Merit" Fallacy', *Frontline*, Vol. 23, No. 11, 3–16 June.

Bidwai, Praful (2006d), 'Combating Muslim Exclusion', *Frontline*, Vol. 23, No. 23, 18 November–1 December.

Bidwai, Praful (2007), 'Not by Haj Subsidies Alone', *Frontline* , Vol. 24, No. 24, 8–21 December.

Brennan, Geoffrey, and Alan Hamlin (1999), 'On Political Representation', *British Journal of Political Science*, Vol. 29.

Canon, David (1999), 'Electoral Systems and the Representation of Minority Interests in Legislatures', *Legislative Studies Quarterly*, Vol. 24, No. 3, August.

Centre for Dalit Studies (2001), *Equal Rights to Dalit Christians*, Centre for Dalit Studies, New Delhi.

Chakrabarty, Dipesh (1998), 'Modernity and Ethnicity in India', in David Benett (ed.), *Multicultural States: Rethinking Difference and Identity*, Routledge, London.

Chandhoke, Neera (1999), *Beyond Secularism: The Rights of Religious Minorities*, Oxford University Press, New Delhi.

Chandra, Kanchan (2000), 'The Transformation of Ethnic Politics in India: The Decline of Congress and the Rise of Bahujan Samaj Party in Hoshiarpur', *Journal of Asian Studies*, Vol. 59, No. 1, February.

Childs, S., J. Lovenduski, and R. Campbell (2006), *Women at the Top: Changing Politics*, The Hansard Report (London), Vol. 26, Issue 1.

Constituent Assembly Debates (1989), Official Report, 12 vols, Lok Sabha Secretariat, 1946–50, New Delhi.

Cunningham, Clark and N.R. Madhav Menon (1999), 'Race, Class, Caste? Rethinking Affirmative Action', *Michigan Law Review*, Vol. 97, No. 5, March.

D'Souza, Rohan (2006), 'The OBC Quota and the New Economy', *Seminar*, No. 569, July.

Desai, I.P. (1984), 'Should "Caste" be the Basis for Recognising Backwardness?', *Economic and Political Weekly*, Vol. 19, No. 28.

Desai, Radhika (1999), 'The Last Satrap Revolt?', *Economic and Political Weekly*, 19 June.

Deshpande, Ashwini (2007), 'Where the Path leads: The Role of Caste in Post-University Employment Expectations', *Economic and Political Weekly*, Vol. XLI, No. 41.

Deshpande, Satish, and Yogendra Yadav (2006), 'Redesigning Affirmative Action: Castes and Benefits in Higher Education', *Economic and Political Weekly*, Vol. XLI, No. 24.

Deshpande, Satish (2006), 'Exclusive Inequalities: Merit, Caste and Discrimination in Indian Higher Education Today', *Economic and Political Weekly*, Vol. XLI, No. 24.

Deshpande, Satish (2008), 'Quota Sans Creamy Layer in Education?', *Economic Times*, 16 April.

Dhavan, Rajeev (1987), 'Religious Freedom in India', *The American Journal of Comparative Law*, Vol. 35, No. 1, Winter.

Dhavan, Rajeev (2003), 'Reservation for All?' *The Hindu*, 13 June.

Dhavan, Rajeev (2007), 'Parliament versus Courts: Episode Three', *The Indian Express*, 27 April.

Dirks, Nicholas B. (2001), *Castes of Mind: Colonialism and the Making of Modern India*, Permanent Black, New Delhi.

Dushkin, Lelah (1967), 'Scheduled Caste Policy in India: History, Problems and Prospects', *Asian Survey*, Vol. 7, No. 9, September.

'Editorial: Caste, Courts and Reservations' (2007), *Economic and Political Weekly*, Vol. XLII, No. 14.

Forrester, Duncan B. (1980), *Caste and Christianity: Attitudes and Politics on Caste of Anglo-Saxon Protestant Missions in India*, Curzon Press, London.

Frankel, Francine, Zoya Hasan, Rajeev Bhargava, and Balveer Arora (eds) (2000), *Transforming India: The Social and Dynamics of Democracy*, Oxford University Press, New Delhi.

Galanter, Marc (1978), 'Who Are the Other Backward Classes? An Introduction to a Constitutional Puzzle', *Economic and Political Weekly*, Vol. 43–44, No. 13.

Galanter, Marc (1979), 'Compensatory Discrimination in Political Representation: A Preliminary Assessment of India's Thirty-Year Experience with Reserved Seats in Legislatives', *Economic and Political Weekly*, Vol. 14, Nos 7&8.

Galanter, Marc (1984). *Competing Equalities: Law and the Backward Classes in India*, Oxford University Press, New Delhi.

Galanter, Marc (1998), 'The Indian Constitution and Provisions for Special Treatment', in Gurpreet Mahajan (ed.), *Democracy, Difference and Social Justice*, Oxford University Press, New Delhi.

Gandhi, Rajiv (2006), Speech on Reservation Issue in Lok Sabha on 6 September 1990, reproduced in *The Indian Express*, 9 June.

Ghildiyal, Subodh (2006), 'Quota for Dalit Christians/Muslims?', *The Times of India*, 27 May.

Ghosh, Jayati (2004), 'Income Inequality in India', www.countercurrents.org, 17 February.

Ghosh, Jayati (2006), 'Case for Caste-based Quotas in Higher Education', *Economic and Political Weekly*, Vol. XLI, No. 24.

Ghosh, Partha (1997), 'Positive Discrimination in India: A Political Analysis', *Ethnic Studies Report*, Vol. XV, No. 2.

Gould, Harold (1993), 'Mandal, Mandir, and Dalits: Melding Class with Ethno-religious Conflict in India's Tenth General Election.', in Harold Gould and Sumit Ganguly (eds), *India Votes: Alliance Politics and Minority Governments in the Ninth and Tenth General Elections* , Westview Press, Boulder, Colorado.

Gould, Harold (1999), 'The 12th General Election in Karnataka', in Ramashray Roy and Paul Wallace (eds), *Indian Politics and the 1998 Election: Regionalism, Hindutva and State Politics*, Sage Publications, New Delhi.

Government of Andhra Pradesh (2004), Report of the Ex-officio Commissionerate of Minorities Welfare, Backward Classes Welfare Department, No. 33 (G.O. 33) 12 July.

Government of India (1955), *Report of the Backward Classes Commission, Vol. I* (Chairman Kaka Kalelkar), New Delhi.

Government of India (1980), *Report of the Backward Classes Commission, Vol. I* (Chairman B.P. Mandal), New Delhi.

Government of India (1983), Report of the High Power Panel on Minorities Scheduled Castes, Scheduled Tribes and Other Weaker Sections, Ministry of Home Affairs, New Delhi.

Government of India, Planning Commission (2001), *Report of the Working Group on Empowering the Minorities, The Tenth Five Year Plan (2002–2007)*, New Delhi.

Government of India (2004), Report of the Standing Committee on Social Justice and Empowerment (2005–2006), Fourteenth Lok Sabha, Ministry of Social Justice and Empowerment, the Constitution One Hundred and Third (Amendment) Bill, 2004 and National Commission for Minorities (Repeal) Bill, 2004 Fourteenth Report, Lok Sabha Secretariat, New Delhi.

Government of India (2004), Report of Union Public Service Commission, *54th Report, 2003–04*, New Delhi.

Government of India (2005), *Annual Report, 2004–05*, Ministry of Personnel, Public Grievances and Pensions, New Delhi .

Government of India (2005), Report of the Union Public Service Commission, *55th Report, 2004–05*, New Delhi.

Government of India (2006), Prime Minister's High Level Committee, *Social, Economic and Educational Status of the Muslim Community of India, Prime Minister's High Level Committee*, Cabinet Secretariat, New Delhi .

Government of India (2006), Report of Standing Committee on Social Justice and Empowerment (2006–2007), Fourteenth Lok Sabha, *Twentieth Report*, Lok Sabha Secretariat, New Delhi.

Government of India (2006), Report of the Union Public Service Commission, *56th Report, 2005–06*, New Delhi.

Government of India (2007), *Report of the Committee to Enquire into the Allegations of Differential Treatment of Scheduled Castes/Scheduled Tribes in All India Institute of Medical Sciences*, Ministry of Health and Family Welfare, New Delhi.

Government of India, Planning Commission (2007a), *Report of the Working Group on Empowering the Minorities, Eleventh Five Year Plan (2007–2012)*, New Delhi.

Government of India, Planning Commission (2007b), *Report of the Working Group on the Empowerment of Scheduled Castes, Eleventh Five Year Plan (2007–2012*), New Delhi.

Government of India, Planning Commission (2007c), 'Status of Minorities and Prime Minister's New 15-Point Programme', Chapter on Minorities, in *Eleventh Five Year Plan (2007–2012)*, New Delhi.

Government of Madhya Pradesh (2002), *The Bhopal Document: Charting A New Course for the 21st Century*, Government of Madhya Pradesh, Bhopal.

Goyal, Santosh (1989), 'Social Background of Officers in the Indian Administrative Service', in Francine Frankel and M.S.A. Rao (eds), *Dominance and State Power in Modern India: Decline of a Social Order*, Vol. 1, Oxford University Press, New Delhi.

Goyal, Santosh (1990), 'Social Background of Indian Corporate Executives', in Francine Frankel and M.S.A. Rao (eds), *Dominance and State Power in Modern India: Decline of a Social Order*, Vol. 2, Oxford University Press, New Delhi.

Groffman, Bernard, and Arend Lijphart (eds), (1986), *Electoral Laws and Their Political Consequences*, Agathon, New York.

Guhan, S. (2001), 'Comprehending Equalities', in Sanjay Subramanian (ed.), *India's Development Experience*, Oxford University Press, New Delhi.

Gupta, Dipankar (2005), 'Caste and Politics: Identity over System', *Annual Review of Anthropology*, Vol. 34, No. 21, October.

Gupta, Dipankar (2007), 'Caste-Based Identification of OBCs and Consequent Vote Bank Politics', *Muslim India*, Vol. XXIV, No. 276, June.

Gutman, Amy (2003), *Identity in Democracy*, Princeton University Press, Princeton.

Habib, Irfan (2006), 'Muslims in India: Some Issues for State Action', *Social Scientist*, Vol. 34, Nos 3–4, March–April.

Harriss-White, Barbara (2002), 'India's Religious Pluralism and its Implications for the Economy', Working Paper Number 82, QEH Working Paper Series, Queen Elizabeth House, University of Oxford.

Hasan, Mushirul (1998), *Legacy of a Divided Nation: India's Muslims since Independence*, Oxford University Press, New Delhi.

Hasan, Mushirul (ed.) (2001), *India's Partition: Process, Strategy and Mobilization*, Oxford University Press, New Delhi.

Hasan, Mushirul (ed.) (2006), *Selected Works of Jawaharlal Nehru*, Vol. 37, Oxford University Press, New Delhi.

Hasan, Rana and Aashish Mehta (2008), 'Underrepresentation in Colleges: What Do The Data Tell Us?', in S.K. Thorat and Narender Kumar (eds), *In Search of Inclusive Policy: Addressing Graded Inequality*, Rawat Publications, New Delhi.

Hasan, Zoya (2000), 'More Equal, But Still Not Equal? State and Inter-Group Equality in Contemporary India', in Imtiaz Ahmad, Partha Ghosh, and Helmut Reifeld (eds), *Pluralism and Equality: Values in Indian Society and Politics*, Sage Publications, New Delhi.

Hasan, Zoya (2005), 'Reservations for Muslims', *Seminar*, No. 549, May.

Hasan, Zoya (2006), 'Constitutional Equality and the Politics of Representation in India', *Diogenes*, No. 56.

Hasan, Zoya and Ritu Menon (2004), *Unequal Citizens: Socio-economic Status of Muslim Women in India*, Oxford University Press, New Delhi.

Heuze, Gerard (1991), 'Troubled Anthropologists: The Controversy over Quotas in India', *Anthropology Today*, Vol. 7, No. 6, December.

Htun, Mala (2003), 'Why Identity Groups Get Represented in Politics', mimeo.

Council for Social Development (2006), *India: Social Development Report*, Oxford University Press, New Delhi.

Indian Social Institute (1980), *Scheduled Caste Converts and Social Disabilities: A Survey of Tamil Nadu*, Indian Social Institute, New Delhi.

International Institute for Democracy and Electoral Assistance (2005), *Women in Parliament: Beyond Numbers*, International Institute for Democracy and Electoral Assistance, Stockholm.

Jaffrelot, Christophe (2000), 'The Rise of the Other Backward Classes in the Hindi Belt', *The Journal of Asian Studies*, Vol. 59, No. 1, February.

Jaffrelot, Christophe (2003), *India's Silent Revolution: The Rise of the Lower Castes in North Indian Politics*, Permanent Black, New Delhi.

Jaffrelot, Christophe (2004), 'Composite Culture is not Multiculturalism: A Study of the Indian Constituent Assembly Debates', in Ashutosh Varshney (ed.), *India and the Politics of Developing Countries: Essays in Memory of Myron Weiner*, Sage Publications, New Delhi.

Jaffrelot, Christophe (2005), 'Politics of OBCs', *Seminar*, No. 549, May.

Jaffrelot, Christophe (2008), 'Why Should We Vote: The Indian Middle Class and the Functioning of the World's Largest Democracy', in Christophe Jaffrelot and Peter van der Veer (eds), *Patterns of Middle Class Consumption in India and China*, Sage Publications, New Delhi.

Jaffrelot, Christophe, and Sanjay Kumar (eds) (2009), *Rise of Plebians: The Changing Face of Indian Legislative Assembly*, Routledge, New Delhi.

Jaitley, Jaya (2007), 'Counting Heads, Missing the Picture', *The Indian Express*, 2 June.

Jayal, Niraja Gopal (2001), *Democracy in India*, Oxford University Press, New Delhi.

Jayal, Niraja Gopal (2004), 'A Malevolent Embrace: The BJP and Muslims in the Parliamentary Elections of 2004', *India Review*, Vol. 3, No. 3, August.

Jayal, Niraja Gopal (2006), *Representing India: Ethnic Diversity and Governance of Public Institutions*, Palgrave, London.

Jayal, Niraja Gopal (2006), 'Democratic Dogmas and Disquiets', *Seminar*, No. 557, January.

Jayal, Niraja Gopal (2007), 'So Many Social Inequalities', *The Indian Express*, 14 April.

Jenkins, Laura Dudley (2001), 'Becoming Backward: Preferential Policies and Religious Minorities in India', *Commonwealth and Comparative Politics*, Vol. 39, No. 1, July.

Jenkins, Laura Dudley (2003), *Identity and Identification in India: Defining the Disadvantaged*, Routledge Curzon, London.

Jha, Shefali (2008), 'Rights versus Representation: Defending Minority Interests in the Constituent Assembly', in Rajeev Bhargava (ed.), *Politics and Ethics of the Indian Constitution*, Oxford University Press, New Delhi.

Jodhka, Surinder (2005), 'Debates on Reservations', *Economic and Political Weekly*, Vol. 40, Nos 44 and 45, 29 October–4 November.

Joshi, Barbara (1982), *Democracy in Search of Equality: Untouchable Politics and Indian Social Change*, Hindustan, New Delhi.

Kananaikil, Jose (1983), *Christians of Scheduled Caste Origin*, Indian Social Institute, New Delhi.

Kapur, Ratna and Brenda Cossman (1996a), *Subversive Sites: Feminist Engagements with Law in India*, Sage Publications, New Delhi.

Kapur, Ratna and Brenda Cossman (1996b), 'Women, Familial Ideology and the Constitution', in Ratna Kapur and Brenda Crossman (eds), *Feminist Terrains in Legal Domains: Interdisciplinary Essays on Women and Law in India*, Kali for Women, New Delhi.

Karlekar, Karin Deutsch (2004), 'Muslim Women in Indian Politics 1947–2002', in Zoya Hasan and Ritu Menon (eds), *In A Minority: Essays on Muslim Women in India*, Oxford University Press, New Delhi.

Kesavan, Mukul (2007), 'Keeping Them in the Fold', *The Telegraph*, 13 January.

Khare, Harish (2002), 'The Business of Separatism', *The Hindu*, 15 May.

Khilnani, Sunil (2002), 'The Indian Constitution and Democracy', in Zoya Hasan, E. Sridharan and R. Sudarshan (eds), *India's Living Constitution: Ideas, Practices, Controversies*, Permanent Black, New Delhi.

Khalidi, Omar (2005), *Muslims in the Indian Economy*, Three Essays, New Delhi.

Klass, Morton (1998), *Caste: The Emergence of South Asian Social Systems*, Manohar, New Delhi.

Kohli, Atul (ed.) (2001), *The Success of India's Democracy*, Cambridge University Press, Cambridge.

Kumar Bhaumik, Sumon and Manisha Chakrabarty (2006), 'Earnings Inequality in India: Has the Rise of Caste and Religion Based Politics in India Had an Impact?', IZA Discussion Papers No. 2008, Institute for the Study of Labour, IZA, http://www.iza.org.

Lama-Rewal, Stephanie Tawa (ed.) (2005), *Electoral Reservation, Political Representation and Social Change in India: A Comparative Perspective*, Manohar Publishers, New Delhi.

Lijphart, Arend (1996), 'The Puzzle of Indian Democracy: A Consociational Interpretation', *American Political Science Review*, Vol. 90, No. 2, June.

Louis, Prakash (2003), *The Political Sociology of Dalit Assertion*, Gyan Publications, Delhi.

Mahajan, Gurpreet (1998a), *Identities and Rights: Aspects of Liberal Democracy in India*, Oxford University Press, New Delhi.

Mahajan, Gurpreet (1998b), 'Introduction', in Gurpreet Mahajan (ed.), *Democracy, Difference and Social Justice*, Oxford University Press, New Delhi.

Mahmood, Tahir (2001), *National Commission for Minorities: Minor Role in Major Affairs*, Pharos Publications, New Delhi.

Mansbridge, Jane (2003), 'Rethinking Representation', *American Political Science Review*, Vol. 97, No. 4.

McMillan, Alistair (2005), *Standing at the Margins: Representation and Electoral Reservation in India*, Oxford University Press, New Delhi.

Mehta, Mona (2007), 'Missing the True Picture?', *The Indian Express*, 16 June.

Mehta, Pratap Bhanu (2006a), 'Democracy, Disagreement and Merit', *Economic and Political Weekly*, Vol. 41, No. 24.

Mehta, Pratap Bhanu (2006b), 'Unthinking Political Use of Reservation is Destroying Higher Education', *The Indian Express*, 7 April.

Mehta, Pratap Bhanu (2007), 'Let Them Have Scholarships', *The Indian Express*, 3 April.

Mendelsohn, Oliver, and Marika Vicziani (2000), *The Untouchables: Subordination, Poverty, the State in Modern India*, Cambridge University Press, Cambridge.

Metcalf, Barbara (1995), 'Presidential Address: Too Little and Too Much—Reflections of the Muslims in the History of India', *Journal of Asian Studies*, Vol. 54, No. 4, November.

Mitta, Manoj (2003), 'The First Anti-Mandal Amendment', *The Indian Express*, 29 May.

Mohanty, Amarnath (2007), 'Affirmative Action in India: An Alternative Perspective', *Economic and Political Weekly*, Vol. 42, No. 30.

Mohapatra, Bishnu (2002), 'Democratic Citizenship and Minority Rights', in Catarina and Kristina Jonsson (eds), *Globalization and Democratizations in Asia: The Construction of Identity*, Routledge, London and New York.

Mohapatra, Bishnu and Niraja Gopal Jayal (2004), 'The National Commission for Scheduled Castes and Scheduled Tribes: A Report', in Nanda P. Wanasundera (ed.), *Protection of Minority Rights and Diversity*, International Centre for Ethnic Studies, Colombo.

Momin, A.R. (2004), *The Empowerment of Muslims in India: Perspective, Context and Prerequisites*, Institute of Objective Studies, New Delhi.

Murlidharan, Sukumar (1999), 'Politics of Reservations', *Frontline*, Vol. 16, No. 24, 13–26 November.

Naqvi, Farah (2006), 'Open a Window', *Hindustan Times*, 2 November.

National Commission for Minorities (1983), *First Annual Report of the National Commission for Minorities for the year ending 31 December 1978, 1979 and Report on Minorities*, Vol. 2, Ministry of Home Affairs, New Delhi.

National Commission for Minorities (2006), *Annual Report 2005–06*, National Commission for Minorities, New Delhi.

National Commission for Minorities (2008a), *Dalits in the Muslim and Christian Communities: A Status Report on Current Social Scientific Knowledge*, National Commission for Minorities, New Delhi, http://www.ncm.nic.in/pdf/report%20dalit%20%20reservation.pdf.

National Commission for Minorities (2008b), Socio-economic Status of the Notified Minority Communities (other than Muslims), http://ncm.nic.in/pdf/IHD/%20Report%20Final.pdf.

National Commission for Scheduled Castes and Scheduled Tribes (2001), *Sixth Report, 1999–2000 & 2000–2001*, New Delhi.

National Human Rights Commission (2004), *Report on Prevention of Atrocities against Scheduled Castes*, NHRC, New Delhi.

National Sample Survey Organisation, Government of India, 50th Round (July 1993–June 1994 and 55th Round July 1000–June 2000), *Reports on differences in level of consumption among socio-economic groups*, Ministry of Statistics and Programme Implementation, New Delhi.

Nehru, Jawaharlal (2006), *Letters to Chief Ministers, III, 1947–1964*, G. Parthasarathy (ed.) Oxford University Press, New Delhi.

Nesiah, D. (1999), *Discrimination and Reason? The Role of Reservations in US, India, and Malaysia*, Oxford University Press, New Delhi.

Nigam, Aditya (1996), 'India after the 1996 Elections: Nation, Locality, and Representation', *Asian Survey*, Vol. 36, No. 12.

Nigam, Aditya (2004), 'Caste and Politics', *South Asian Journal*, April–June.

Oommen, T.K. (1994), 'Inconsistency in Denial of Reservation to Dalits, Muslims and Christians', *Muslim India*, No. 137, May.

Osborne, Eva (2001), 'Culture, Development and Government: Reservations in India', *Economic Development and Cultural Change*, Vol. 49, No. 3, April.

Panandiker, V.A. (1997), *The Politics of Backwardness: Reservation Policy in India*, Konark Publishers, New Delhi.

Pande, Rohini (2003), 'Can Mandated Political Representation Increase Policy Influence for Disadvantaged Minorities? Theory and Evidence from India, *The American Economic Review*, Vol. 93, No. 4, November.

Pandey, Gyanendra (1993), 'Which of Us are Hindus?' in Gyanendra Pandey (ed.), *Hindus and Others: The Question of Identity in India Today*, Viking, New Delhi.

Pandey, Gyanendra (1999), 'Can a Muslim be an Indian?', *Comparative Studies in Society and History*, Vol. 41, No. 4, November.

Pandey, Gyanendra (2006), 'The Time of the Dalit Conversion', *Economic and Political Weekly*, Vol. XLI, No. 18.

Parekh, Bhiku (1999), 'Balancing Unity and Diversity in Multicultural Societies', in D. Avon and A. De-Shalit (eds), *Liberalism and Its Practice*, Routledge, London.

Parekh, Bhiku (2006), 'Limits of the Indian Political Imagination', in V.R. Mehta and Thomas Pantham (eds), *Political Ideas in Modern India: Thematic Explorations*, Sage Publications, New Delhi.

Parikh, Sunita (1997), *The Politics of Preference: Democratic Institutions and Affirmative Action in the United States and India*, Michigan University Press, Ann Arbor.

Parikh, Sunita (2001), 'Caste, Party Politics in Contemporary India', in John Sketrny (ed.), *Colour Lines: Affirmative Action, Immigration, and Civil Rights Options for America*, University of Chicago Press, Chicago.

Parthasarathy, Malini (2008), 'Return to the Spirit of 2004', *The Hindu*, 29 January.

Phillips, Anne (1995), *The Politics of Presence*, Clarendon Press, Oxford.

Phillips, Anne (1999), *Which Equality Matters?* Polity Press, Cambridge.

Pitkin, Hanna (1967), *Concept of Representation*, University of California Press, Berkeley.

Puri, Anjali (2007), 'Meet Your New DM', *Outlook,* 7 August.

Prakash Louis (2007), 'Caste-based Discrimination and Atrocities on Dalit Christians and the Need for Reservations', Indian Institute of Dalit Studies, Working Paper Series, Vol. II, No. 4.

Prasad, A. (1997), *Reservation and Justice to Other Backward Classes*, Deep and Deep, New Delhi.

Prasad, K.V. (2006), '27 Percent Quota for OBCs from 2007', *The Hindu*, 24 May.

Radhakrishnan, P. (1997), 'Mandal Commission Report: A Sociological Critique', in M.N. Srinivas (ed.), *Caste: Its Twentieth Century Avatar*, Penguin Books, New Delhi.

Radhakrishnan, P. (2006), *Religion, Caste and State*, Rawat Publications, Jaipur.

Raman, Anuradha (2007), 'Keep it Skimmed', *Outlook*, 16 April.

Rao, Shiva (1967), *The Framing of India's Constitution: Select Documents*, Vols I and II, Indian Institute of Public Administration, New Delhi.

Rau, B.N. (1960), *India's Constitution in the Making*, Allied Publishers, Bombay.

Reddy, C. Rammanohar (2002a), 'Deprivation Affects Muslims More', *The Hindu*, 12 September.

Reddy, C. Rammanohar (2002b), 'The Gap Widened During the 1990s', *The Hindu*, 13 September.

Reddy, C. Rammanohar (2002c), 'Facts on Appeasement', *The Hindu*, 14 September.

Robinson, Rowena (2005), *Tremors of Violence: Muslim Survivors of Ethnic Strife in Western India*, Sage Publications, New Delhi.

Robinson, Rowena, and S. Clarke (2003), *Religious Conversion in India: Modes, Motivations and Meaning,* Oxford University Press, New Delhi.

Rodrigues, Valerian (ed.) (2002), *Essential Writings of B.R. Ambedkar*, Oxford University Press, New Delhi.

Rudolph, I. Lloyd, and Susanne Hoeber Rudolph (1987), *In Pursuit of Lakshmi: The Political Economy of the Indian State*, Princeton University Press, Chicago.

Rudolph, Susanne Hoeber, and Lloyd I. Rudolph (2001), 'Living With Difference in India: Legal Pluralism and and Legal Universalism in Historical Context', in James Larson (ed.), *Religion and Personal Law in Secular India: A Call to Judgment*, Social Science Press, New Delhi.

Sainath, P. (2008), 'Discrimination for Dummies: V.2008', *The Hindu*, 18 January.

Sankaran, S.R. (2000), 'Welfare of Scheduled Castes and Scheduled Tribes in Independent India – An Overview of State Policies and Programmes', *Journal of Rural Development*, Vol. 19, No. 4.

Sarkar, Sumit (2001), 'Indian Democracy: The Historical Inheritance', in Atul Kohli (ed.), *The Success of India's Democracy*, Cambridge University Press, Cambridge.

Schneider, Anne, and Helen Ingram (1993), 'Social Construction of Target Populations: Implications for Politics and Policy', *American Political Science Review*, Vol. 87, No. 2, June.

Shah, Ghanshyam (1985), 'Caste, Class and Reservations', *Economic and Political Weekly*, Vol. XX, No. 3, 19 January.

Shahabuddin, Syed (2004), 'Reservations of Muslims: Constitutionally and Socially Necessary', *Alpjan Quarterly: A Chronicle of Minorities*, Vol. IV, No. 4, July–September.

Shani, Ornit (2007), *Communalism, Caste and Hindu Nationalism: The Violence in Gujarat*, Cambridge University Press, Cambridge.

Sharif, Abusaleh (1995), 'Socio-Economic and Demographic Differentials between Hindus and Muslims in India', *Economic and Political Weekly*, Vol. 30, No. 46.

Sharif, Abusaleh and Azra Razzack (2006), *Communal Relations and Social Integration*, in *India: Social Development Report*, Indian Council of Social Development, New Delhi.

Sharma, B.A.V., and K. Madhusudan Reddy (eds) (1982), *Reservation Policy in India*, Light and Life Publications, New Delhi.

Sheikh, Farzana (1993), 'Muslims and Political Representation in Colonial India: The Making of Pakistan', in Mushirul Hasan (ed.), *India's Partition: Process, Strategy and Mobilization*, Oxford University Press, New Delhi.

Sheth, D.L. (2000), 'Caste and Secularization Process', in Peter Ronald deSouza (ed.), *Contemporary India: Transitions*, Sage Publications, New Delhi.

Sheth, D.L. (2002), 'Caste and Class: Social Reality and Political Representations', in Ghanshyam Shah (ed.), *Caste and Democratic Politics in India*, Permanent Black, New Delhi.

Sheth, D.L. (2004a), 'Reservations Policy Revisited', in Manoranjan Mohanty (ed.), *Class, Caste, Gender*, Sage Publications, New Delhi.

Sheth, D.L. (2004b), 'Reservations: No Provisions for Communal Quotas', *Alpjan Quarterly: A Chronicle of Minorities*, Vol. IV, No. 3, April–June.

Shri, Godwin (1997), *The Plight of Dalit Christians – A South Indian Case Study*, Asian Trading Corporation, Bangalore.

Sikand, Yoginder (2004), *Muslims in India Since 1947: Islamic Perspectives on Inter-faith Relations*, Routledge Curzon, London.

Sivaramakrishnan, K.C. (2001), 'Constituencies Delimitation: Deep Freeze Again', *Economic and Political Weekly*, Vol. XXXVI, No. 51.

Sridharan, E. (2002), 'The Origins of the Electoral System: Rules, Representation, and Power-Sharing in India's Democracy ', in Zoya Hasan, E. Sridharan, and R. Sudarshan (eds), *India's Living Constitution: Ideas, Practices and Controversies*, Permanent Black, New Delhi.

Sridharan, E. (2006), 'Elections and Muslim Representation in India', in Sustainable Development Policy Institute (SDPI) (eds), *Troubled Times: Sustainable Development and Governance in the Age of Extremes*, Sustainable Development Policy Institute, Islamabad.

Sridharan, E. (forthcoming), 'Does India Need to Switch to Proportional Representation', in Paul Flather (ed.), *Recasting Indian Politics: Essays on a Working Democracy*, Palgrave, London.

Srivastava, B.N. (2000), 'Working of the Constitutional Safeguards and Protective Measures for the Scheduled Castes and Scheduled Tribes', *Journal of Rural Development*, Vol. 19, No. 4.

Stuligross, David, and Ashutosh Varshney (2002), 'Ethnic Diversities, Constitutional Designs, and Public Policies in India', in Andrew Reynolds (ed.), *The Architecture of Democracy: Constitutional Design, Conflict Management, and Democracy*, Oxford University Press, Oxford.

Suri, K.C. (1995), 'Competing Interests, Social Conflict and the Politics of Caste Reservations in India', *Nationalism and Ethnic Politics*, Vol. 1, No. 2, Summer.

Symposium on Sachar Committee Report (2007), *Economic and Political Weekly*, Vol. XLII, No. 10.

Taneja, Nalini (2001), 'Politics of Census', *People's Democracy*, Vol. XXX, No. 1, 1 April.

Thorat, S.K. (2002), 'Oppression and Denial: Dalit Discrimination in 1990s', *Economic and Political Weekly*, Vol. 37, No. 6.

Thorat, S.K., and Katherine S. Newman (2007), 'Caste and Economic Discrimination: Causes, Consequences and Remedies', *Economic and Political Weekly*, Vol. XLII, No. 41.

Thorat, S.K., and Paul Attewell (2007), 'The Legacy of Social Exclusion: A Correspondence Study of Job Discrimination in India', *Economic and Political Weekly*, Vol. XLII, No. 41.

Thorat, S.K., M. Mahamallik, and S. Venkateshan (2007), 'Human Poverty and Socially Disadvantaged Groups in India', Human Development Resource Centre, UNDP, Discussion Paper Series, No. 18, New Delhi.

Thummala, Krishna (1995), 'Politics of Preference in Public Service: The Case of Mandal', *Indian Journal of Political Science*, Vol. 55, No. 4, October–December.

Varadarajan, Siddharth (2006), 'Coming to Terms with India's Missing Muslims', *The Hindu*, 4 November.

Varshney, Ashutosh (2000), 'Is India Becoming More Democratic?', *Journal of Asian Studies*, Vol. 59, No.1, February.

Varshney, Ashutosh (2005), *Ethnic Conflict and Civic Life: Hindus and Muslims in India*, Oxford University Press, New Delhi.

Venkatesan, V. (2006), 'Legal Backing', *Frontline*, Vol. 23, No. 8, 22 April–5 May.

Venkatesan, V. (2008), 'Equity in Education', *Frontline*, Vol. 25, No. 9, 26 April–9 May.

Vishwanathan, S. (2004), 'The Dalit Cause, A New Perspective', *Frontline*, 19 November.

Weiner, Myron, Mary Katzenstein, and Barbara Joshi (1982), *Democracy in Search of Equality*, Hindustan Publishing Corporation, New Delhi.

Weiner, Myron (1983), 'The Political Consequences of Preferential Policies: A Comparative Perspective', *Comparative Politics*, Vol. 16, No. 1, October.

Weiner, Myron (1997), 'India's Minorities: Who Are They? What Do They Want', in Partha Chatterjee (ed.) *State and Politics in India*, Oxford University Press, New Delhi.

Weiner, Myron (2001), 'The Struggle for Equality: Caste in Indian Politics', in Atul Kohli (ed.), *The Success of Indian Democracy*, Cambridge University Press, Cambridge.

Weisskopf, Thomas (2004), 'The Impact of Reservation on Admissions to Higher Education in India', *Economic and Political Weekly*, Vol. 39, No. 39.

Wilkinson, Steven (2005), *Votes and Violence: Electoral Competition and Ethnic Riots in India*, Oxford University Press, New Delhi.

Williams, Melissa (1998), *Voice, Trust and Memory: Marginalised Groups and the Failings of Liberal Representation*, Princeton University Press, Princeton.

Wright, Theodore P. (1997), 'A New Demand for Muslim Reservations in India', *Asian Survey*, September.

Wyatt, Andrew (1998), 'Dalit Christians and Identity Politics in India', *Bulletin of Concerned Asian Scholars*, Vol. 30, No. 4.

Yadav, Yogendra (2000), 'Understanding the Second Democratic Upsurge: Trends of Bahujan Participation in Electoral Politics in the 1990s', in Francine R. Frankel, Zoya Hasan, Rajeev Bhargava, and Balveer Arora (eds), *Transforming India: Social and Political Dynamics of Democracy*, Oxford University Press, New Delhi.

Yadav, Yogendra (2001), 'A Radical Agenda for Political Reforms', *Seminar*, 506, October, p. 20.

Yadav, Yogendra (2006), 'The A to Z of OBCs', *Sunday Express*, 4 June.

Young, Iris Marion (1990), *Justice and the Politics of Difference*, Princeton University Press, Princeton.

Young, Iris Marion (2002), *Inclusion and Democracy*, Oxford University Press, New York.

Zakaria, Rafiq (2004), *Indian Muslims: Where Have They Gone Wrong*, Popular Prakashan and Bhartiya Vidya Bhawan, Mumbai.

Zelliot, Eleanor (1992), 'The Leadership of Babasaheb Ambedkar', in Eleanor Zelliot (ed.), *From Untouchable to Dalit: Essays on the Ambedkar Movement*, Manohar, New Delhi.

Zwart, Frank De (2000), 'The Logic of Affirmative Action: Caste, Class and Quotas in India', *Acta Sociologica*, Vol. 43, No. 3.

Index

Advani, L.K. 188
Advisory Committee on
 Fundamental Rights 22, 23–4
affirmative action 7, 14, 16, 18,
 65, 229, 231, 237–8
 for disadvantaged castes 12, 43
 for minority 1925 236
  rights of, and 36–9, 171
 and Muslim backwardness
  159–91
 Muslim under-representation
  and 179–82
 opponents of 184
 policy of 37, 118, 119, 161
 Sangh Parivar on 188, 189
 for Scheduled Castes (SCs)
  32
ajlaf category, of Muslims 176
Akbar, M.J. 184
Alam, Javeed 72
Ali, Ejaz 203
All India Backward Classes
 Federation (AIBCF) 86
All India Backward Muslim
 Morcha (AIBMM) 203
All India Christian Council 202,
 205
All India Civil Services,
 minorities in 264
All India Institute of Medical
 Sciences, protests over
 reservations 102–3
All India Muslim Backward
 Classes Organization 173
All India Muslim Majlis-e-
 Mushawarat (AIMMM) 173,
 174, 182, 204
All India United Christian
 Movement for Equal Rights
 222
Ambedkar, B.R. 30, 31, 33, 37
Andhra Pradesh, Congress
 government on reservation for
 Muslims 179
 Kammas and Reddys in
  politics of 138
 Muslims in government
  employment 164
 quota for SCs/STs and OBCs
  180
Ansari, Ghaus 176
Ansari, Iqbal 145
anti-Brahmin movement 132–3
arzal category, of Muslims 176

Ashoka Thakur v. *Union of India* 11
ashraf category, of Muslims 176
Assam, Muslims in government employment 164
Attewell, Paul 169
Austin, Granville 19
Ayodhya controversy 141
    and violence 144
Azad, Abul Kalam 22, 28, 39n9, 146

Babri mosque, demolition of 71, 141, 151
    excavation at the site of 168
backward-caste(s), ascendancy of 138–46
    definition of 89, 197
    identity 133
    mobilization 136
    movements in Tamil Nadu and Karnataka 131
    politics 85, 151
    representation in legislatures 126–55
'backward classes' 29, 33, 81
    category 30–1
    preferential treatment to 101
    in South India 30
    see also Other Backward Classes (OBCs)
Backward Classes Commission 86, 179, 193n30
    in 1960s 84
    Report of 92, 83, 171
'backward community', definition of 31
'backwardness' 11, 18, 79, 80, 81
    concept of 161, 220
    definition of 32, 84, 86, 90
    and disadvantage 7
    inclusion and issue of 161
    politics of 127
    social 29
Bahujan Samaj Party (BSP) 109, 143, 216
    Muslim candidates from 150
Balaji v. *The State of Mysore* 86, 120n32, 124n87
    decision on 92
Balakrishnan, Chief Justice K.G. 112
banks, representation of SCs and STs in public sector 250
Bhandari, Justice Dalveer 112
Bharatiya Janata Party (BJP) 106, 136, 138, 143, 186, 187
    on Hindu SCs 208, 209
    led-NDA government 227
    on minorities 55–7, 100, 189
    and the Muslims 152–3
    opposition, to include Christians and Muslims as SCs 208
        to reservations 110
    and politics of polarization 56, 152
    rise in power 144
    SC/ ST Morcha 208
Bharatiya Lok Dal 130
Bhardwaj, H.R. 183
Bhargava, Rajeev 153
Bihar, backward-caste MLAs in 137
    Muslims in government employment 164
biradari 176, 177
Brahmanical order, of caste hierarchy 131
Buddhism 210, 213, 214
Buddhists, benefits to 221

caste, and backward classes 82, 85
-based occupation 61–2
-based parties 133, 140
and class 90–5
and concept of disadvantage 160
and deprivation 112–19
group rights based on 5
identities 83
inequality 73, 216–20, 230
and politics 38, 128, 130
and reservation policy 114, 231
and social justice 220–4, 231
system, in India 2, 3, 6, 31, 36, 61, 132, 140, 176, 212
reform of 33
Catholic Bishops Conference of India 202, 205
Central Educational Institutions (Reservation) Bill 2006 102
controversies and protests over 102–4
Centre for Public Interest Litigation 202, 209
Chidambaram, P. 102
Christian(s), educational profile of, in urban and rural India 273
employment of 50
status recognizing as OBCs 217
see also Dalit Christians
civil rights 20
violation of 248–9
civil services, OBC representation in 95
SCs and STs in 62
see also government jobs
class, and caste 91–5
Commissioner for Scheduled Castes and Scheduled Tribes 58
communal politics 57
Communist Party of India 138
Communist Party of India (M) 138, 151
Communist Parties, and class politics 83
Congress party 20, 84, 130, 139, 173
on Backward Classes Commission's recommendations 82
breakaway factions of 130
on converts from Islam and Christianity in SC list 208
dominance of 129, 140, 144
Karachi Resolution of 1931 28–29
in Karnataka 138
leadership 129
and the lower castes 131
on minorities 57, 58
on Ranganath Mishra Commission recommendation 215
and Muslims 141, 151, 180, 188
opposition to reservations to OBCs 85
on OBCs 81, 90
and patronage system 129, 130
on reservations to SCs 31
support to reservations 92, 108–10
Working Committee, Muslim members in 150
see also UPA government

Constituent Assembly 18
debates 13, 118, 220, 230
on reservation for lower castes 19
Constitution of India, 4, 80, 236
on backward classes 35
making of 18–39
on SCs 200
on social disabilities of 43
(SC) order 199
Constitution of India, Amendments to, 73rd 139
77th 94
81st 94
85th 94
91st (2001) 149
(103rd) Bill 2004 69
Constitution of India, Article(s)
15 of 4, 239
16 of 37, 239
340 of 82
Constitutional Amendment Act, First (1951) 99
93rd (2005) 98, 112
conversion/ converts, from Hinduism, and demand for SC status 201
in India 207–8
legislation on anti- 224n31
creamy layer, exclusion from reservation 95, 111–14
Supreme Court on 110
culture(al), autonomy, to minorities 141
diversity 13, 18, 32
rights, of minorities 5, 43
and affirmative action 36–9

Dalit Hindus, class component of 269
conditions of 45
conversion to Buddhism and Sikhism 208, 220
and deprivation 222
discrimination against 60
emancipation of 59
identity 202
leaders 47
movement 202
'occupations' 122n61, 270
representation in Parliament 139
rights 66
special status to 220
Dalit Christians, concentration of 216
demand for SC status 162, 197–224
opposition, to reservations for 206–7
to SC status for 206–10
State response to 210–17
in OBC list 201, 210
position of 220
Dalit Muslims, demand for SC status 197–22
opposition, to reservations for 207–10
to SC status for 206–10
State response to 210–17
in OBS list 201, 210
poverty among 221
Dalit Sikhs, living below-poverty line 220–1
Das, Asha 213
Delimitation Act of 1972 147
Delimitation Commission (2007) 149
'delimitation policy' 148
depressed classes, preferential treatment of 34

deprivation 3, 13, 15, 18, 184, 230, 238
Deshpande, Satish 106
Dhavan, Rajeev 117
Directive Principles of State Policy 4
'disadvantage(d)' 4, 9, 11, 15, 18, 236
  approach to 7
  castes/ groups 8, 117
    in legislatures 126
  definition of 6
  empowerment of 74
  Muslims 169–71
  policies and protection to 13, 41–74
  discrimination 15, 18, 37, 218, 220, 231
  and exclusion 13, 234
Dravida Munntera Kazhgam (DMK) 114, 143

economic liberalization 118
economic reforms, of early 1990s 89
Economic Survey, on economic disparities 104
'economically backward section', reservations for 91–2
education(al), among OBCs 80
empowerment of SCs and STs 45
  profile, of Christians in rural and urban India 273
    of Muslims in rural and urban India 272
  reservations in 81, 86, 110
  electoral system, in India 27, 147
  electorate, characteristics of 126

Eleventh Plan, Working Group on Empowerment of Minorities 53–5
Eleventh Plan Working Group for Empowerment of the Scheduled Castes 46–7
Emergency of 1975 130
empowerment 4, 53–5, 92
  inclusion and 5
  and participation of
    backward castes in public institutions 90
equality 3, 4, 20, 81, 236
  of treatment 191n1
ethnic identity 146
ethnic minorities, in public institutions 169
ethnic politics 131
exclusion, active and passive 2
  imbalance and 104
  of minorities 185

federalism 20
freedom, of conscience 214
  of religion 19, 36
Fundamental Rights 4, 28

Galanter, Marc 80
Gandhi, Indira 50, 55–6, 87
  Hindu votes under 141
  on minorities 163
  victory in 1980 elections 130
Gandhi, Mahatma, anti-untouchability campaign of 33
Gandhi, Rajiv 56, 87, 107, 116, 141
  on OBC 108
  victory in 1984 elections 130
Gandhi, Sonia 52, 109

Gangadharan, Rudhra 121n43
general elections (1952–71), Muslim candidates in 151
Gopal Singh Committee Report, 1983 8, 50
Government of India Act 42
government jobs, Muslims in 267
  reservations in 81, 86, 88, 95
  see also Muslims, reservations
graduates, among religious groups 243
  by socio-religious communities 252
group rights, individual rights v. and minority rights 6, 21–9
Gujarat, Muslims in government employment 165

Habib, Irfan 71
higher education, access to, by caste groups 250
  inequalities in 254
  reservations in 14, 96–98
  upper caste monopoly in 106–7
  see also education
Hindu caste system *see* caste system
Hindu–Muslim relations 30, 33
Hindu social structure 7, 82
Hindu society 4, 30
Hindu upper castes, in professional and higher education 100, 106–7
Hinduism 179
  converts from 203–4
Hindutva, ideology 204, 235
  politics 151
human development indicators 65–6

identity, and affirmative actions 162
  politics 129, 176
Imperial (SC) Order 1935 199
Inamdar case, Supreme Court judgment on 98, 100
inclusion/ inclusive, democracy 3
  and empowerment 5
  strategies of 1
Indian Institute of Management (IIMs), quota in 111
  protests over reservations 102
Indian Institute of Technology (IITs), quota in 112
  protests over reservations 102
Indian Medical Association 103
Indian Railways, Muslims employed in 165
Indra Sawhney v. *Union of India* 91, 239
individual rights, v. group rights 6
inequalities, economic 90
  minorities and 13, 161–2
  in status and power 89
institutional framework 58–66
Integrated Child Development Programme 51
Islam 174, 202
  on equality 184
Islamic Academy of Education +1 v. *State of Karnataka & Others* 98, 121n50
Ismail, Mohammed 30
Izhava community, in Kerala 138

Jaffrelot, Christophe 138
Jain, Ajit Prasad 24
Jaitley, Jaya 194n67
Jamiat Ulema-I-Hind (JUH) 182
Janata Dal 136
  government in Karnataka 138

-led National Front
government 79, 80
Janata Party, government of 86
victory in 1977 elections 130
jatis 80, 177, 219
Jethmalani, Ram 222
Joshi, Barbara 65
judicial perspectives 202–3
judiciary, intervention by
111–13
justice 4, 20

Kalelkar, Kaka 82, 116
Kalelkar Commission 86, 171
Kalelkar Report *see* Backward
Classes Report
Karnataka, Lingayats and
Vokkaligas in state politics
137–39
Muslims in government
employment 165
reservations in 85, 139
for Muslims 173, 187
Kerala, backward caste
representations in legislatures
in 139
Muslims in public sector
undertakings 165
quota for Muslims in 172,
187
Kesavan, Mukul 222
Khan, Arif Mohammed 188
Khurshid, Salman 158n53, 187
Krishnamachari, T.T. 31
Krishnan, P.S. 178
Kumar, Meira 123n68
Kunzru, H.N. 29

land reforms 129
Law Commission's Report (1999)
153

legislature(s), backward castes'
representation in 126–57
caste-composition in 135–39
reservation of seats in 20, 35
under-representation of
minorities in 126–56
liberal democracy 1, 6
Lok Sabha, backward caste
members in 138
debate on reservation bill 110
reservation for SCs and STs
in 35
Lokur, B.N. 210
Lokur Committee 211
lower castes, of Hindu society
31
disparate experience of 11
empowerment of 42–7
status and deprivation of 3
upward mobility of 132
see also Scheduled Castes

Madras Presidency, 'backward
classes' in 81
Mandal, Bindeshwari Prasad 87
Mandal Commission 78, 86, 87,
88, 90, 162, 171, 193n30
on caste and class 114
Congress initiation of 111
protest and unrest over 94,
111
recommendations 14, 173–5
backlash at 87
Report 62, 87, 92, 203
on reservation, in higher
education 96–98
to OBCs 131, 135, 190
marginalized groups, exclusion
of 1
in higher education 98
market reforms 104, 105

Maulana Azad Educational Foundation 51, 75n23
medical students, and doctors, strike over reservation 103
Members of Legislative Assemblies, Muslims among 260–2
Mendelsohn, Oliver 33
middle class 104
 in managerial and executive jobs 105
Ministry of Minority Affairs 52, 67
Ministry of Social Justice and Empowerment 67, 211, 213
minorities, affirmative actions for 115, 160, 190–2
 backwardness among 115
 benefits to 20
 Constitution on 29, 36, 67
 cultural rights of 5, 28
 debated on rights of 8
 development programmes 71
 exclusion of 113, 184
 protection of 42, 47–58
 in public institutions 8
 quotas, argument against 183
  multiple identities and 172–9
 and religious freedom 5
 representation in Lok Sabha 139
 rights 5, 8, 18–39, 156
  and group rights 21–9
 socio-economic and cultural rights of 28
 under-representation in legislatures 126–57
 see also religious minorities
minority institutions, rights of 98
mobilization, caste-based 128, 132
Moily, Veerappa 172, 186
Mukherjee, H.C. 26
Mungekar, Bhalchandra 55, 75n34
Munshi, K.M. 19
Muslim League 138
Muslim majority constituencies 157n40
Muslim population/minority, in India 41, 48
 access to higher education 99, 100, 116
 affirmative action for 179–84
 backward-caste 174–6
  quota for 182
 backwardness 11, 167, 169
  and affirmative action 159–92
 and Congress 142, 143
 constituencies 257–8, 260–1
 converts to 176
 discrimination and exclusion of 14, 49, 169, 170
 economic deprivation of 49
 educational status of 49, 167
 elites, and Congress 175
 in employment/ jobs 49–50, 192n27
 in government/ public employment 160–70, 192n19, 195n76, 265–7
 -Hindu relations 30, 33
 identity 142
 in Indian Administrative Service 163, 233
 members of Parliament 144–6, 231, 233, 256
 middle class 166

minority status of, in India 177
OBCs 182
employment status of 181
in formal sector 180–1
organizations of 174, 183
reservation for 179, 181
states recognizing 216
orthodox organizations 177
and regional political parties 143
reservations, dilemmas of 185–9
opposition to 184
in self-employment 163
and social inequality 3
socio-economic status of 178, 179
states with significant 145
stratification pattern among 175
territorial distribution of 147
underprivileged sections of 71
under-representation of 9, 14, 49, 127, 147–57, 186
in government jobs 68
unskilled labour category among 178
in Vidhan Sabha 144–5
voters 141, 152
women in Central and state legislatures 144
Muslim Women's Act 141

National Commission of Backward Classes (NCBC) 80, 114, 182
recommendations 93, 94
National Commission for Backward Classes Act 93
National Commission for Minorities (NCM) 5, 58, 65–73, 219
on Dalit Muslims and Dalit Christians in SC list 214, 221
and National Commission on Scheduled Castes and 70
Reports of 69
National Commission of Minorities Act 1992 66
National Commission for Minority Educational Institutions 52–3
National Commission for Religious and Linguistic Minorities (NCRM) 53, 173, 189
recommendations 214
on Scheduled Caste converts 212, 213
National Commission to Review the Working of the Constitution 153–4
National Commission on Scheduled Castes (NCSC) 13, 58–66, 70
on Dalit Muslims and Dalit Christians in SC list 214
National Commission on Scheduled Castes/ Scheduled Tribes (NCSC/ST) 58–60, 67
Report of 59, 61, 212
on Scheduled Caste status 215
National Commission for Scheduled Tribes (2002) 59
National Commission for Women (NCW) 58
National Council of Dalit Christians (NCDC), memorandum of 204–5

National Development Council (NDC) 56
National Democratic Alliance government 227
National Human Rights Commission (NHRC) 58
  on atrocities against Scheduled Castes 212
  Report of 61, 64, 76n46
National Knowledge Commission, opposition to OBC reservation 103
National Minority Finance and Development Corporation (NMFDC) 51–2
National Rural Employment Guarantee Scheme 227
NSSO data, on deprived groups 161
  on higher education 99
nationalism 20
nationalization policy 129
Nehru, Jawaharlal 19, 108, 128, 140, 163, 200
  on minority rights 33
  mixed economy of 79
  on reservation 25, 33, 83
  and secular-nationalism 129
Nehru Report of 1928, on proportional representation 28
Nehruvian consensus, on mixed economy 104
neo-Buddhists, demand for SC status 199, 200
non-Brahmin movement 33

Oommen, T.K. 148
Orissa, anti-Christians violence in 224n32
Other Backward Castes (OBCs) 4, 80–8, 114
  access, education 229
    to public jobs 171, 229
  caste identifying of 92
  Congress on 81, 90
  employment status of 181
  in government service 95
  lobby, of members of Parliament 114
  Members of Legislative Assemblies 256
  Members of Parliament 231
  political empowerment of 152
  political representation of 127, 152
  politicization and mobilization of 134
  preferential treatment to 97
  quota, in higher education 98–102
    law of 2006 113
  reservation for 14, 78–81, 88, 95, 115, 228
    opposition to 6
  Scheduled Castes and 216
  see also Muslims

Pai Foundation case 98
Pakistan, formation of 21, 24
Palshikar, Suhas 195n69
Panikkar, K.M. 31
Pant, Govind Ballabh 19, 82
Parliament, reservation for SCs and STs in 35
  SC and ST members of 135
  under-representation of Muslims in 143–4
Parliamentary Standing Committee 116
  on Social Justice and Empowerment 68, 69

Partition 16, 18, 21, 24, 36, 170, 185
 legacy of 159
Pasayat, Justice Arijit 112
Pasmanda Mahaz, Muslim group 173
Patel, Sardar Vallabhbhai 19, 23, 24, 25, 199
Patil, Shivraj 189
Pattali Makkal Katachi (PMK) 114
peasants, low status of 80
Phillips, Anne 2
Planning Commission 45, 54–55, 234
 Report on Empowering the Scheduled Castes 63
political consequence, of preference 98
political discourse 2, 19–21, 128, 129
political mobilization 134–5, 202–5
political power, monopoly of 1
 and social transformation 89
political process 2, 12, 14, 70, 107
political safeguards, opposition to 24–5, 26
post-graduate enrolment, distribution of 252
Prasad, Lalu 183
Prasad, Rajendra 200
preferential policies 2, 20, 33, 133
Prevention of Atrocities Act (1989) 45, 60, 61
Prime Minister, 15-Point programme on Minorities 53, 55–6, 57, 75n27, 227
promotions, reservations and, for SCs and STs 94
proportional representation, in electoral system 153–4, 158n56
 Nehru Report on 28
 rejection of 26, 27
Protection of Civil Rights Act (1955) 60, 61
public debate, shift in 104–8
public institutions/sector, access to OBCs to 80
 employment of SCs in 62
 Muslims employment in 162–70

Rajasthan, Muslim OBCs in employment 181
Ramakrishna Singh v. *State of Mysore* 120n32
Ranga, N.G. 19
Ranganath Mishra Commission, report of 191, 215, 233
Rao, P.V. Narasimha 90
Rashtriya Janata Dal (RJD) 143, 173
Rau, B.N. 27
Raveendran, Justice R.V. 112
Reddy, Justice Jeevan 91
religion, separation of State from 24–5
religious freedom 28–9, 213
religious minorities 31
 on civil service 265
 exclusion of 116
 political representation of 127
 rights of 5
 see also minorities
representation, politics of 6, 128–35
reservation 7, 18–39, 183, 190
 impact on political system 127, 134, 152

issue 5–6
for minorities 28
notification of 148
policy 15, 80, 96, 131, 132
for OBCs 14, 81, 96
opposition to 85, 100, 105–6
for SCs and STs 20, 29–35, 81, 149, 165–6
support to 105–6
ritual status, in caste system 32–3, 37
rural poverty, state-wise 241–2

Sachar, Justice Rajinder 40
Sachar Committee Report (SCR) 10, 151, 163, 179, 180, 227
appointment of 185, 189
on bifurcation of OBC category 216
Report 9, 48–9, 50, 51, 57, 70, 71, 74n15, 151, 163, 164, 169, 171, 176, 185–6, 189, 191, 194n67, 220, 228, 234, 236
Saksena, Shiban Lal 31
Samajwadi Party 109, 143, 172
Muslim candidates from 150
Sangh Parivar 177, 179
on minorities 188, 189
Sanskritization 133
Scheduled Castes (SCs) 3, 4, 41, 80, 230
access to education and jobs 229
admission to schools and colleges 61
affirmative action for 19
atrocities against 246–7
as backward 210, 211
classification of 199–202
difference between OBCs and 107
discrimination against 13
employment, in banks 250
in government 247
in public sector enterprise 248
empowerment of 42–7, 72
enrolment in higher education 63–4
as Hinduism-specific 206
Members in Parliament 135
middle class 63–4
and OBCs 216
political mobilization of 65
in public institutions 65, 248
reservations for 5, 29–35, 45, 60, 78, 81, 166, 211
for state assemblies 261–3
rights and welfare of 44
social uplift of 70
social welfare schemes for 59
Scheduled Castes Sub-Plan (SCSP) 45–7, 55
Scheduled Castes/ Scheduled Tribes (Prevention of Atrocities) Act 60
Scheduled Tribes (STs) 3, 4, 80
access to education and jobs 229
affirmative action for 19
employment, in banks 248
in government 247
in public sector enterprise 250
Members in Parliament 136
reservations for 5, 29–35, 45, 78, 81
rights and welfare of 44
social uplift of 71
secularism 20, 24, 141

Muslims on 143
Sen, Amartya 2
Shah, K.T. 19
Shah Bano case, verdict in 141
Sheth, D.L. 63
Sikhs, benefits to 221
demand for SC status 199
untouchables among 199
Sikhism 208, 213
Singh, Arjun 88, 108, 110
on reservations to OBCs in educational institutions 96
Singh, Manmohan 52, 185
Singh, V.P. 88, 106, 107, 110, 136
implementation of Mandal Commission recommendations 78–80, 87
quota policy of 116, 133
single member constituency 135
social backwardness 78, 80, 90–1
social disability 202, 230
and caste inequality 216–20
social discrimination 4, 60
social equality 36, 70, 72
social exclusion 2, 161
social justice 18, 24, 88, 89, 92, 93, 118, 231, 238
caste and 220–3
and equality 235
social reform movements 4
Socialist Party 130
socially and educationally backward classes (SEBC) 113
Soosai & Others v. *Union of India & Others* judgment 201
southern states, reservation quotas in 84
Sree Narayana Dharma Paripalana (SNDP) Yogam, Kerala 138
Sridharan, E. 155
Srivastava, R.K. 122n57
State Commission for Minorities, Conference of (2008) 186, 189
Standing Committee of Parliament on Social Justice and Empowerment 59
Sub-Committee on Minority Rights 22, 23, 28
on reservations 24
Subramanian, Gopal 124n82
Supreme Court, judgement in *Inamdar* case 98
on reservation 91, 98, 190, 215
verdict on reservation 229
verdict on *Sawhney* case 92, 93, 94

Tamil Nadu, backward caste MLAs in 137
Muslims in government employment 165
reservation quotas in 84
Telugu Desam 143
Thakur case 114
Thommen, Justice T.K. 93, 120n37
Thorat, S.K. 102, 169, 122n57
two-nation theory 188

ulema 166
unemployment rates, by socio-religious groups 245
Union Public Service Commission (UPSC), report of 62

United Progressive Alliance government 56, 116, 204, 227
appointment, of NCRLM 189, 213
of Sachar Committee 185, 189
Central Educational Institutions (Reservation in Admission) Bill 2006 of 102
Constitution amendment in 2005 100
implementation of Sachar Committee Report 234, 235
on minorities 52
on non-exclusion of creamy layer 111
on reservations to OBCs 78, 79, 97, 100, 108, 190, 228
on Sachar Committee Report 189
support to inclusion of Dalit Muslims and Dalit Christians in SC list 216
University Grants Commission (UGC) 102
untouchability/ untouchables 29, 33, 37, 38, 171, 199, 211–13, 219
abolition of 72
conversion by 38
upper caste(s) 16n9
advantage of 3
hegemony in politics 131
in managerial and executive jobs 105
Members of Parliament 136
monopoly in government jobs 88
urban poverty, state-wise incidence of 240–1
Urs, Devraj 137
U.S.V. Balaram v. *State of Andhra Pradesh* 120n32
Uttar Pradesh, Muslims in government employment 165
Muslim MLAs in 153–4
rise of lower castes in 138–9
upper caste MLAs in 137

varna 218
Vahanvati, G.E. 121n39
Venkatachalliah Commission 179–80
Venkataraman v. *State of Madras* 124n87
Venugopal, K. 124n90
Vicziani, Marika 33
vote bank politics 102, 151

West Bengal, Muslims in government employment 164
women, political representation of 127
reservation for 140, 154
Women's Reservation Bill 140
worker–participation rates, by socio-religious groups 243
Wright, Theodore 25

Youth for Equality 102

Zakaria, Rafiq 50